T0375707

In This Man's Army

In This Man's Army

✦

Stan Sutherland

iUniverse, Inc.
New York   Bloomington

In This Man's Army

The views expressed in this work are solely those of the author and do not
necessarily reflect the views of the publisher, and the publisher hereby disclaims
any responsibility for them.

iUniverse books may be ordered through booksellers or by contacting:

iUniverse
1663 Liberty Drive
Bloomington, IN 47403
www.iuniverse.com
1-800-Authors (1-800-288-4677)

Because of the dynamic nature of the Internet, any Web addresses or links
contained in this book may have changed since publication and may no longer
be valid.

ISBN: 978-1-4401-9861-8 (sc)
ISBN: 978-1-4401-9862-5 (ebk)

Printed in the United States of America

iUniverse rev. date: 3/1/2010

Foreword

By General Peter Cosgrove (Retired)

One of the great joys of being a soldier are the great men and women with whom you are privileged to serve, especially when that service is at war. I served at war with Stan Sutherland and I count that as one of the great privileges of a long career. As you will see when you read this most fascinating and inspiring account of ordinary diggers living an extraordinary life, we were together as officer and NCO for part of one of his two meritorious tours of duty in South Vietnam during that war of jungles, paddi-fields, of ambush and endless patrolling. Stan saw it all and emerged with his honour, dignity and humanity intact – and indeed strengthened – as a fundamentally decent man under the stresses of war found himself admired and loved by his comrades in arms.

The Army of the sixties and seventies was a potpourri of experiences and backgrounds with many wonderful, hugely experienced warriors of World War II and Korea and the counter-guerrilla conflicts of Malaya and Confrontation salted in senior positions throughout the ranks, together with 'baby-boomer' recruits such as Stan and me. To this mix was added that tremendously energising mix of 'nashos' – national servicemen – those many thousands of conscripts who, having been drafted, became magnificent soldiers in their own right and kept every regular army soldier striving to be the most professional man or woman they could be. This was the military world that Corporal Stan Sutherland of the Royal

Australian Infantry Corps inhabited. His two tours of duty in that dangerous war zone meant that, when I met him in 1969, I was that most fortunate of junior commanders, a man with wise, experienced, helpful and courageous subordinates like Stan to guide me along. For a considerable period on combat operations, Stan was my acting Platoon Sergeant – he was a natural, brave, patient (especially with me!), firm but friendly with the diggers (including with his fellow corporals, who deeply respected him). It was with considerable anguish when I evacuated him by helicopter out of the field with raging malaria, which I thought might kill him, late in our time together in 1970 – I was not only losing my right hand man but my friend. I have never underestimated the influence of the likes of Stan on my long and lucky career.

"*In This Man's Army*" is a frank and insightful story of men on operations and in training for war. From its hilarity and its drama, its irreverence and its tragedy, you will be reminded that Australians, an unwarlike people, nonetheless when needed make the best warriors in the world.

Stan Sutherland was one of them, and this is his story.

General Peter Cosgrove, pictured here, served in Vietnam 1969-70 as a lieutenant, initially as Platoon Commander of 5 Platoon B Coy 9RAR – during which time he was awarded the Military Cross – and subsequently as Platoon Commander of Defence and Employment Platoon, a long-range reconnaissance infantry platoon, First Australian Task Force. He eventually became Australia's best known soldier, retiring in July 2005 as Chief of the Australian Defence Force. Last year he published his own autobiography,

"*My Story*".

Introduction

My objective in writing this book is to give the reader an insight into the normal tasks and experiences of the Australian Infantry Soldier's day-to-day life during an active tour of duty to South Vietnam in the mid sixties through to the early 1970s. *In This Man's Army* takes you on a journey and gives you an appreciation, not only of the fine qualities of the Australian fighting soldier, but also of what they did and how they did it.

To all who wore the Australian uniform, whether you be Army Regulars, National Servicemen, Australian Navy, or RAAF, it was indeed an honour and pleasure to serve with, and alongside you.

The source of material that makes up this book has been extracted from the contemporaneous notes made by me on a day-to-day basis during my service in Vietnam, 1968-1970, as well as material and anecdotes from my ex-service mates. Memory of first hand experiences and anecdotal knowledge plays a big part. Getting shot at and blown up sticks in your memory quite well, and some of the accounts related in this book are as clear as if they happened only yesterday.

My early childhood was spent in the North Eastern Victorian township of Yackandandah. I had a typical Australian country upbringing, in that my early years were spent ferreting and trapping for rabbits, fishing in the Yackandandah creek as well as shooting game. I commenced work at 16 for the National Bank of Australasia Ltd. A month after my seventeenth birthday, my job took me to different towns where my accommodation was either a boarding house or the local pub. This background provided an easy transition into army life when I signed on in 1967 at the age of 22.

Acknowledgements

The writing of this book has only been made possible by the continued friendship over the years of all my ex-service mates.

I have endeavoured to capture the humour and the mischief that has always been characteristic of Australians at war. This book has primarily been written for the diggers themselves as a strong reminder of the times, the smells, jungle operations, the weather and the discomforts of the Infantryman's life as well as their great sense of humour under adverse conditions.

A special thanks to General Peter Cosgrove, John (Jack) English and Robert (Bob) Hannah. Also, I acknowledge the assistance afforded by reference to 3 RAR Tour of Duty 1967- 1968 and 9 RAR Vietnam Tour of Duty 1968 where my memory was left wanting and my notes were deficient. I'm so grateful, too, to all the old diggers who submitted a photograph of themselves in their prime for inclusion. The photographs enhance the book quite substantially.

Thanks too to all the brave men with whom I served in B Company 3 RAR, B Company 9 RAR, as well as the independent group of great diggers in Defence and Employment Platoon, Headquarter Company, 1 ATF. The stories contained herein are your stories and I hope you enjoy revisiting them as much as what I have had in recording them here. *In This Man's Army* is dedicated to you all. The fact that we are very much in touch with each other after forty years is testimony to the bonds of friendship that were forged in South Vietnam all those years ago.

Glossary and abbreviations

Agent Orange: A chemical defoliant

ALSG: Australian Logistic Support Group

AO: Area of operations

APC: Armoured Personnel Carrier

AK47: Soviet made assault rifle most commonly used by the enemy

Armalite M16: American made automatic rifle

ARVN: Army of the Republic of Vietnam (South Vietnamese Army)

Chopper: Helicopter

Clacker: Hand held electrical device for detonating Claymore Mines

The Dat: Commonly used expression for Nui Dat, the headquarters of the Australian Task force

CO: Commanding Officer

CSM: Company Sergeant-Major

Fd Bty: Field Battery

Goffa: can of soft drink

Gunship: A helicopter fitted with rockets and machine guns

Harbour up: To go into a defensive position, more often, a temporary position for the night

Hoi Chanh: An enemy soldier who has surrendered

M60: An American made general purpose machine gun

Mama–san: An older Vietnamese woman

Medevac: Medical evacuation

MO: Medical Officer

NCO: Non Commissioned Officer

Nog: An enemy soldier but considered derogatory by the Vietnamese

OC: Officer Commanding

Pl: Platoon

Pte: Private soldier

Pogo: Personnel on garrison operations

RAR: The Royal Australian Regiment

R & C: Rest and convalescent leave

RAP: Regimental Aid Post

R & R: Rest and recreation leave

Reg: A volunteer enlisted man.

RF: South Vietnamese Regional Forces

RPG: Rocket propelled grenade

RSM: Regimental Sergeant-Major

Silk: A lightweight sleeping bag liner

TAOR: Tactical area of responsibility

Track: Commonly used slang expression for Armoured Personnel Carrier

VC: Viet Cong

Vungers: Short name for the town of Vung Tau

White Mice: A term applied in reference to the South Vietnamese Police. They wore white gloves, white trousers and white helmets.

Contents

The author, Stan Sutherland, pictured in Vietnam while with 6 platoon, B Company, 3 Btn Royal Australian Regiment.

Chapter 1

Induction and training

✦

I signed on to join the Australian Army in May, 1967. At that time, the Vietnam War was well under way. Australia's commitment was bolstered in 1965 when the Government decided to send 1RAR (Royal Australian Regiment) together with the 105mm Battery of the R.A.A. (Royal Australian Artillery) as an integral Infantry Battalion and Artillery Battery within the United States of America 173d Airborne Brigade. The New Zealand Government also sent the 161st Field Battery of the RNZA as part of this Brigade. In May 1965 the Brigade became the first US Army Combat Unit committed to the war in South Vietnam.

Recruit training. I received a letter from the Army telling me to report to the Army Recruiting Centre, St. Kilda, at 9.00am on 29/05/1967. By the time nine o'clock came around, there were about twenty of us waiting for the proceedings to begin. A sergeant appeared and organized us into a semi circle. Bibles were handed out and we were all asked to raise our right hand and repeat after him something like, *"I"* (our names) *"swear that I will well and truly serve our Sovereign Lady, the Queen, in the Military Forces of the Commonwealth of Australia for the duration of the period of my enlistment or until sooner*

1

lawfully discharged, dismissed, or removed, and that I will resist Her Majesty's enemies and cause Her Majesty's peace to be kept and maintained, and that I will in all matters appertaining to my service faithfully discharge my duty according to law. So Help Me God." We then signed our Oath of Enlistment before a captain who applied his signature in witness thereof. We were in the Army now and there was no turning back.

After being sworn in at St. Kilda, we were directed by a corporal to board a waiting bus, which took us out to the barracks at Watsonia, primarily an army signals base. Everyone on the bus was quiet and they only made themselves known to the person sitting alongside, each in thought as to how his life had just changed and probably quite drastically. It was the most quiet bus ride I'd ever been on. After processing at Watsonia, which took only one day, we were allocated sleeping quarters for the night. At this stage of our career we were not placed under duress by any corporals or the like, so we felt we weren't really in the Army, even though, deep down, we knew we were. With the recruits who joined with me, I was posted to Kapooka (2RTB) Recruit Training Battalion. Kapooka is a few kilometres out of Wagga Wagga, NSW.

The following morning we were bussed into Spencer Street railway station to board a train for Wagga Wagga. The train pulled in to Wagga Wagga early that afternoon and an army bus was waiting for us to get off the train. The bus driver, well turned out in uniform, was a gorgeous looking blond and my immediate thought was that army life is going to be OK, especially if there are more honeys like this wandering around the camp. I can't recall seeing another female for the duration of basic training, which was a ten-week course. Instead, the lovely blond was never to be seen again and this delightful introduction to the army gave way to Regimental Drill Instructors prone to snapping, snarling and frothing at the mouth.

Our first encounter was with a corporal from the Armoured Corps. He was immaculately dressed as if his uniform had been poured over him. His trousers had creases so sharp that if you touched them you would cut your finger. His black beret, adorned with a silver gleaming badge, sat firmly perched on his head. But it was his boots that really caught the eye . . . they gleamed like a black mirror, not a mark on them. I wondered how much spit and polish it took to get them looking like that.

On our first day we were trained, firstly, to pull our finger out, and get a move on. We were then issued with kit and given a haircut to about two millimetres. Once the general administration was out of the way, we were allocated into a Platoon, broken down into teams and sent to barracks known as Silver City, a couple of kilometres by road from the rest of the camp. The main camp was of modern construction while the Silver City barracks were pre- Second World War vintage comprised of corrugated iron Nissan huts.

On our first day of training we were called on parade and the NCO in charge introduced himself like this:

"My name is Corporal Tom Cross and I'm not your mate – I'm your worst nightmare. Behind me, you will see a cage containing a selection of parrots, cockatoos etc. These birds have been in the army longer than any of you and therefore they outrank you. If you keep your mouth shut when it should be shut, your brain switched on when it should be switched on and your ears tuned in when they should be tuned in, there might be a slight chance, just a slight chance, of us getting on. If we don't get on, you'll spend most of your evenings and early mornings cleaning the latrines and bird barracks." Then he yelled: "Do you understand!"

The response from the recruits was rather mediocre and fell well short of the required army response.

"Come on girls don't we have any balls. Prove to me you have balls, even if they're only the size of a pea. DO YOU UNDERSTAND!" he yelled again, many times louder.

"YES CORPORAL" came the reply . . . audibly a hundred fold louder than the previous effort. "AGAIN!" he barked.

"YES CORPORAL."

"Not good, but at least better. We've got a right bunch of girls and pansies here, haven't we Corporal Dayton."

"Most decidedly, Corporal Cross, most decidedly. If they've got any balls, which I doubt, we'll make them grow."

The latrines and ablution blocks were old concrete and corrugated iron buildings. The brass tap fittings and copper pipes were highly polished and kept so by a good source of recruits who couldn't keep their senses tuned in as per Corporal Cross's introduction. The birdcage, which was about seven metres long, two metres high and three metres wide, was maintained in a like manner.

Fortunately, after a couple of weeks, a platoon completed their recruit training and left the camp for Corp training. This enabled us to move into their vacated barracks in the main camp. The quarters were modern and we were able to march to all facilities. Walking was forbidden . . . we never walked but marched, with purpose in our stride.

Basic training was a ten week course in which heavy emphasis was put on physical exercise, drill, weapons training and field craft. The training was engineered to take a group of about forty men from all walks of life, Regulars and National Servicemen alike, divide them into teams and, at the end of the training, have them moving as one, irrespective of the task. For example, a five-mile run at the start of training saw quite a number of stragglers unable to run the distance. At the end of basic training, they could all run as one, and in step. For some, the initial introduction into Army life was hard. Many were away from home for the first time and had never been shouted at before. Others found it easy. They'd been knocking around in the university of life and had no problem coming to grips with it all. The roll was called each morning at 6.00 am and everyone was required to be on parade with a sheet from their bed over their left shoulder. This was to ensure you made your bed properly every morning.

The barracks and personal living quarters were inspected daily by the platoon sergeant or corporals at 7.30 am. Your bed had to be made to regulation, clothes folded to regulation size and stored in your locker to regulation, boots spit polished and everything about you spic and span. The floor coverings and barrack passages were washed and polished every morning. Each team had their areas of responsibility. Any shortcomings would see you polishing brass and copper pipes in the latrines as well as spit polishing the NCOs' boots. You soon learnt the easiest way to get through the day was to listen, do as you're told, and keep your mouth shut.

The idea behind splitting the training platoon into teams was seen as pitting teams against teams. The slower and worst performing teams copped extra duties, like polishing brass taps and copper piping, cleaning the bird-cage or some other obnoxious task. The poor performers in the team that led to this situation had it heaped upon them. If you didn't up your game you could expect a miserable life handed out by your fellow team members. The instructors were from various Corps within the Army; for example, the physical education instructors were artillery men, drill instructors were from the armoured corps and weapons instructors came from infantry.

NCOs, otherwise known as RDIs (Regimental Drill Instructors), had unbridled power, knew how to use it to advantage and could make life tough for you. At recruit training battalions they had absolute control over your life. For example, if you had a poor shave or neglected to shave that morning, the whole platoon would be assembled on the parade ground in front of you. You would then give a demonstration of a dry shave. This was guaranteed to cure your bad shaving habits.

A mate of mine, John English, who served with me later in Vietnam with 9RAR (Royal Australian Regiment), tells this story from his recruit training:

This bloke, George Tucker, was brought up as a strict Methodist. (now Uniting Church in Australia) He'd been involved in his local church at home. George was older than most, having deferred his National Service to finish his mechanic's apprenticeship. He never swore and read the bible and prayed most nights. None of us gave him shit about this. We just respected his beliefs. George could not believe the language the RDIs used, such as when a recruit did not keep his eyes straight ahead while on parade. "What are you looking at me for you fuckin' prick, perhaps you love me! You know what love leads to. It leads to fucking. Do you want to fuck me, you poofter?" All this yelled at the recruit fifteen centimetres from his face. Or, "What are you smiling at boy? Get that smile off your face or I'll hit you over the bridge of your nose with a sock full of diarrhoea. Where does this country find such a bunch of ball-less, weak bastards? Most of you will be dead within a year. The fuckin' VC will have a fuckin' picnic with you dickheads!"

George said to me "Why do the RDIs have to use such foul language? It's totally unnecessary to speak to us in such a way, totally unnecessary!" He was genuinely upset by it and took this berating to heart.

One Sunday afternoon, George and I had to scrub a concrete path, one metre by twenty metres, with our toothbrushes. I can't remember what this extra duty was for. After a couple of hours we'd almost completed the task when a corporal came along and asked us if we thought the path was clean.

We shouted, "Yes Corporal!" Recruits always had to shout the reply to a question. The corporal then purposely walked through a patch of mud under a leaking tap then walked back down the path. Looking back at his muddy tracks he said, "Oh no, it's not, look at that mud you missed. Now get to and clean it properly!" George went red in the face, he stood up and said "You b-b-b-bastard!"

I burst out laughing. It sounded so funny. No one had ever heard George swear. I don't think he had ever said "bastard" in his life. Of course we got extra duties, George for swearing at an NCO and me for laughing. From then on George referred to the NCOs as "those bastards".

The work-day started at 0730hrs. Everything was done at quick time. Changing from P.E. gear – singlet, runners and shorts – to full battle gear, complete with packs and webbing, required you to be back and all assembled in three minutes. Failure to do so meant twenty push-ups or worse. As the days and weeks went by a marked improvement in all aspects of time management was evident. Those who continually dragged the chain to the detriment of all copped a bucket of shit to sponsor quicker movement

We were allowed a weekend off at about the six-week mark; by then the army had knocked you out of your slack civilian life and thinking and you were well on your way to becoming a soldier. No more slouching around, no more standing with your hands in your pockets, no more standing with arms folded in front. To use a common army expression, we stood braced up.

At the end of basic training our platoon was chosen to be part of a full ceremonial Guard of Honour for Sir Roden Cutler VC, Governor of NSW. There we were, dressed to our best in battle dress, along with a contingent from the Air Force, marching with rifles at the shoulder along the main street of

Wagga Wagga, to "Beat the Retreat". Everyone felt so proud and understood what their training was all about. This event was followed a few days later by a formal march out parade by our platoon. On the parade ground we performed a number of marching drills such as changing direction but not formation and changing formation but not direction etc. It was indeed a superb performance to which parents and friends were invited to attend. There was no doubt about the high level of pride within the recruits in knowledge of their personal development since day one when we all presented as a shower of shit, to what was, on march out, a body of well trained well disciplined, responsive fit young men.

The only thing left now was for us to individually go before an allocation board to determine which unit within the army we would be posted to for corps training. We were permitted to write our first, second and third preferences for submission to the board. Notwithstanding one's preference, we were made aware that the infantry would be soaking up a lot of us.

At this time, the Army had two infantry battalions in Vietnam with a third battalion in training to bolster the task force to three battalions. With this in mind, it should have come as no surprise to anyone who was suited for the Infantry to end up at the School of Infantry at Ingleburn, NSW.

I volunteered for the Infantry as a first preference – albeit, I had spent the last four years as a signalman in a Citizens Military Force unit (3 Div Sig Regt) based at Albert Park, South Melbourne. In effect, I transferred from the CMF to the Regular Army, taking my CMF serial number with me. I kept my CMF training close to my chest, telling no one about it. I did not want to invite any undue attention from the NCOs who were quite adept at bringing you down to size. The allocation board had my documents in front of them and asked me why I did not choose the Signals Corp. I made up some yarn about always having had trouble tuning a radio in.

Knowing I was having them on, they gave a small grin and allocated me to the Infantry.

Corps Training. Once posted to Battle Wing at Ingleburn, we were now known as Privates . . . a considerable step up in rank from 'recruit'. Due to the expansion of the army, there were insufficient barracks for the numbers of men being trained. There were just as many men accommodated in large marquees – which provided for twenty men in each – as what were accommodated in barracks. My platoon was in barracks, which was good in winter. Marquee accommodation, however, was better in summer. Infantry training, on completion, was designed to enable posting to a battalion within the Royal Australian Regiment.

The training was heavily orientated towards proficient use and handling of the 7.62 mm Self Loading Rifle, 7.62 mm General Purpose Machine Gun, 5.56mm M16 Armalite, 9mm F1 Sub Machine Gun, 40 mm M79 Grenade Launcher, Anti Personnel Claymore Mines, M26 Fragmentation Grenade and the 66 mm Anti Tank Rocket as well as Flares and Smoke Grenades etc.

Weapon training was structured to train the soldier first in safe handling, and then the use of the weapon. We stripped and re-assembled weapons until such time as we could pull them down and re-assemble them in the dark.

We carried our rifles all day every day. To be caught separated from your rifle by one of the instructors was to invite a punishment as well as a measure of embarrassment and humiliation upon oneself. All the instructors I'd come across in the Army thus far were highly skilled at dishing out this effective medicine.

We were regularly trucked off to the rifle range for target shooting at distances from fifty metres to six hundred metres. On our first rifle shoot we zeroed our rifle in to personally suit. After our rifles were zeroed in, the positions adopted at each distance were standing, sitting, kneeling and lying prone on the ground.

We were required to qualify at shooting and if the visit to the range coincided with a cold and frosty morning, then standing unsupported and shivering at the same time didn't help. However, I was a pretty good shot and always looked forward to range practice. In these sessions we alternated between manning the rifle butts where we held up the targets for our shooter, patched them after each shoot, and yelled out the scores to the NCO in charge at the butts.

The poor shooting from some of the blokes never failed to prompt good humour. The targets were of human shape stuck to a cardboard backing. The men in the butts pasted a black sticker on the bullet hole to indicate where you hit the target. The idea was to fire three shots in a position such as standing or kneeling. The shooter was required to have his shots hit the target in a tight-knit triangle. This was known as a group. If you sprayed your shots all over the place, well, this just wasn't good enough.

One day, while having a go with the M72 rocket launcher, I commented to the instructor that I felt the downward pressure on the trigger mechanism in order to fire the rocket tended to make the rocket launcher move upwards and downwards and therefore was not conducive to accuracy.

"In the jungle, you'll be so close to the enemy you'll be able to stick it up his arse before firing," he said. Of course, everybody burst out laughing.

Something else was also good for a laugh, although the instructors failed to see the funny side of it. This was at grenade throwing practice. The grenade throwing range consisted of two holding bunkers with a concrete wall about two metres long and waist high between each bunker. The first bunker held the men waiting to be called out for their turn at throwing the grenade. The second bunker held the men who had already thrown.

Jack English tells this story:

On marching up to the live throwing area, I noticed the instructors looking nervous. We were instructed once more on grenade handling. A grenade explodes five to seven seconds after the lever is released. The Instructors were making sure everyone knew exactly what to do, and we were to do only exactly what we were told. This grenade-throwing seemed to be a serious business. A group ahead of ours moved to the throwing area. The first grenade exploded. None of us had heard a live grenade explode before. It was a lot louder and more powerful than any of us had expected. We felt the shock wave in our shelter.

Now, when us twenty year olds were growing up there was a T.V. series called *Combat*. It was about a group of American infantry fighting the Germans in World War Two. When the heroes, the Americans, threw a grenade, they always threw it with a stiff-arm motion, as you would in bowling a cricket ball.

We moved up to the bunker in section groups to take our turn. Each of us was to throw two grenades as far as we could over the blast wall.

The first bloke in our group moved out of the bunker to the throwing area. We heard the instructor tell him, "Before you throw the grenade, you will shout "GRENADE". You will throw the grenade at the target. You will watch the grenade land, and only when the grenade lands, will you duck below the wall. Do you understand."

" Yes Corporal," he shouted.

"Take the grenade in your right hand. Place the index finger of your left hand through the pin ring. Pull the pin. Now throw the grenade." The instructor shouted.

This was in the last days of recruit training. We were obeying orders without question and spoke to an instructor only when invited by them to do so.

We heard the bloke shout, "Grenade!"

A couple of seconds later we heard the instructor shout, "Take Cover!"

Next thing he comes tearing into the bunker, dragging this bloke by the shirt. A loud explosion followed as the grenade went off alongside the bunker.

The bloke had thrown with a stiff-arm motion, letting go the grenade too early, sending it flying straight up into the air. When it began to descend, the instructor couldn't tell whether it was going to land outside the blast wall or inside where they were. The instructor is calling this bloke everything he can think of. He's calling his parents idiots for not drowning him at birth. The bloke then pipes up and says, "But Corporal, I'm left handed."

The corporal made sure he asked every trainee after that whether he was right or left handed.

Without exception, there were always one or two blokes who couldn't get it right. They'd throw the grenade straight up in the air so that it came back down on them, the grenade bouncing off the ledge of the waist high safety wall and sometimes rolling off on their side. However, you couldn't help but grin to yourself, our life in the army up until now, only had the trainees under stress and it was refreshing to see an NCO under stress, even if it meant a live grenade coming down on him.

There was one thing about the army I liked. You had to cop everything sweet. Take it on the chin and rock and roll with the punches. There was always the funny side of things no matter how serious the moment. The NCOs might be putting shit on someone but it was invariably funny to everybody else in the group. If you took too seriously what the NCOs were capable of dishing out you were buggered. Every day was good for a laugh – I really liked that. Sometimes, though, you had to pick the times when you burst out laughing, otherwise the bucket of shit came your way.

Field Craft Training was in the form of map reading with compass and protractor, night operations, target identification by distance using a clock face as a reference for direction and night patrolling etc.

You couldn't place the training in any sort of priority because it all came together in an integrated fashion in order for the soldier to do his job. That, put simply, is "kill the enemy", put politely, it is to "close with to destroy or capture him". Contact drills were practised over and over again until such time as we could act spontaneously to good effect.

Contact drills were practised using blank cartridges and normally there were no mishaps with the use of blanks. One day, whilst practising a contract drill, one of the blokes who was running, tripped and fell forward. The muzzle of his rifle dug into the soft ground to a depth beyond the flash suppressor. Unfortunately, he had his finger on the trigger, the fall causing him to fire the rifle. The charge went down the barrel and, unable to escape due to the muzzle being firmly embedded into the ground, came back up the barrel into the breach and magazine, blowing up all the blank cartridges in the magazine. The whole lot was blown to the shithouse. The rifle was a total wreck. The slide cover of the rifle was found all bent and twisted about twenty metres away. The magazine was blown apart and the muzzle on the rifle expanded. Luckily, he escaped injury but it was a good lesson for all of us.

Contact drills were practised over and over. On contact with the enemy the speedy reaction by the soldier is necessary to surprise the enemy, obviating any advantage he might have, irrespective of who initiated the contact.

Every now and again we were trucked to French's Forest to bivouac for a few days and taught how to dig fox holes, shell scrapes, bunkers etc. as well as other forms of infantry training such as moving in arrowhead and lineal formation, setting up ambushes, contact drills and the like.

On one of these bivouacs I had a touch of diarrhoea. Just after our Section set up an ambush, I felt the desperate need to go.

"I need to withdraw for a crap," I said to the NCO in charge.

"Jeez bloody Christ! I've heard it all now. We've got to stop the war because of a bloody crap," he yelled so all could hear. The NCO though, being a reasonable bloke and seeing the stress I was in, allowed me the indulgence to leave the ambush site and make myself comfortable. On my return a few minutes later he yelled, "Now can we get on with the War!"

The leeches at French's Forest were not the type that gorge themselves and simply drop off. These ones were black in colour, very large and latched onto you at night. Latching onto your neck as you lay asleep, they remained all night sucking away and disgorging blood at the same time. In the morning, when you woke up, the amount of blood around your neck made it appear as though your throat had been slit during the night. There was no escaping. The best way to get them off you was to place a burning cigarette on them.

During our training at Battle Wing, each platoon had to do a week of duties. This meant helping out in the mess halls and kitchens, guard duty, orderly room runner and other activities. My assignment was on guard duty. Guard duty at Ingleburn is a full ceremonial affair, complete with a band. Mounting the guard required twelve of us to be turned out as spic and span as one could get. We formed up outside the barracks to be met by the Sergeant of the Guard, who marched us to the parade ground. On one occasion, we had a sergeant who was fondly nicknamed "The Frog." He was about five foot two inches tall, quite rotund, a full round face with spectacles, and all in all, looked like a bull frog.

At the parade ground, "The Frog", standing out in front, commenced proceedings by calling, "Guard, Aaa-tten-shun!!"

Now, it didn't matter how good the drill was carried out, the Frog always said, "Shithouse" and called, "Guard, Stand at Ease," followed by "Guard Aaa-tten-shun!!"

This time, the twelve sets of boots lifted the full six inches and slammed to the asphalt in one crisp bang. The Frog, closing his eyes and groaning as if in sexual ecstasy, then said. "Ejaculation."

We all had wide grins on our faces as he turned around and saluted the Officer of the Guard, who was just out of hearing and who then inspected the men on guard duty. Once the Guard was inspected, the band struck up, and we marched to the Guardhouse situated at the entrance to the camp. There we carried out the Changing of the Guard.

In winter it was freezing, and guard duty was two hours on and four hours off. On entering the Guard House we were issued with a helmet and pick handle. Someone at night was going around and hitting the guards doing their rounds over the head with a baseball bat. He then retreated over the obstacle course or assault course and made good his escape. No one had a clue who it was, but by his ability to thread his way through the obstacle and assault courses, it was suspected that he was from within the camp itself. Apart from looking behind me regularly, I made sure I gave the corners of my round a wide berth so as to get the chance to wield my pick handle if necessary.

Jungle Training Centre, Canungra, Queensland. On completion of our infantry training at Ingleburn, we were bussed to Canungra in Queensland for further training at the Jungle Training Centre.

This training, characterized by a very physical three weeks, was the finishing school for an infantry soldier. The training, known as a Battle Efficiency Course, was particularly orientated towards infantry and jungle warfare, as we would expect to find it in South Vietnam. We were introduced to a typical Viet Cong hamlet set up with hidden tunnels, booby-traps, command detonated devices such as claymore mines, zig-zag fighting trenches, bunker fighting positions, underground chambers, escape tunnels and all sorts of nasty things. Although the training was aimed at the infantry, other corps were represented. Some non-infantry personnel did it tough . . . they were not physically fit enough to handle the course. One day an artillery corporal in the middle of an early morning five kilometre run peeled away from the squad and sat on the bank at the edge of the road. He was totally done in. There was no more run left in him. No threat in the world was capable of moving him. The instructor could have threatened to shoot him but it wouldn't have made any difference.

Even for the infantry, the course was quite demanding. We had the advantage of being fit enough to handle a twenty-mile Route march, complete with rifle and pack. It was obvious the artillery corporal wasn't bludging. He was the personification of the word 'buggered".

At Canungra everything was done at double time. Movement from one place to the next was at the double. Even going to meals was at the double.

One of the strangest nights in all my life was spent at Canungra. Our task was to put in a night ambush on a track and, after springing the ambush, to then withdraw to a harbour position about two hundred metres to the rear. It was raining heavily and we were to ambush the CSM as he walked down the road. There were about 25 of us in the ambush, and each of us was to fire three or four blank rounds. Having shot the shit out of the CSM, our withdrawal was the most unimaginable experience of all time.

The rain, coupled with the complete darkness due to the thick canopy of the rain forest, the like of which I had never seen before, had us groping around not knowing which way was up. All you could do was hang onto the bloke in front of you, hoping he was hanging onto the fellow in front of him, and so on. We literally could not see a thing. When we stopped to harbour up, it was raining cats and dogs and, being so dark, the best I could do was put my back against a tree and place my poncho over my shoulders for the night. We were all cold and as wet as shags. From time to time I lit a hexamine cooking tablet to get a little warmth. I was to experience more nights in the jungle where there was total darkness, and I mean *total*.

At Canungra the training was notched up to battle-like conditions. The assault course was wired up with command detonated explosive devices that went off as you ran past, while all the time a fixed positioned Vickers machine gun fired live rounds over our heads.

On the obstacle course, a hidden staff member fired a few rounds from a Vickers machine gun just as you put your feet on a thin wooden plank across a muddy ditch. If the purpose was to startle the hell out of you, then it worked. There were a few who lost their balance and ended arse up in the ditch.

Towards the end of the obstacle course, there was a man made cesspool of stinking putrid water. This was known as the bear pit. One of the diggers said, "You know, I bet the NCOs and staff pee in this pit at every opportunity". A lot of the blokes agreed. You had to jump into the pit, and when your feet hit the bottom, the water was over your head. You clambered out stinking like a polecat, then ran to the next obstacle.

The bear pit was the topic of a lot of conversation amongst the diggers, particularly as to what might have gone into it to make it so putrid. The peeing theory was the most widely supported.

The last thing to negotiate on the obstacle course was the tower on the bank of the river. We climbed the ladder to the platform about ten metres in height and jumped into the river. If you didn't mind heights, it was quite refreshing and washed away the stinking smell of the bear pit.

Reinforcement Wing – Ingleburn. With Canungra completed, we were bussed back to Ingleburn, stopping at Surfers Paradise for lunch and a stroll. We could now look forward to a posting, either to a battalion or Reinforcement Wing. Reinforcement Wing was immediately adjacent to Battle Wing and shared the same mess hall and other amenities in the camp. After a few days, I was, along with a lot of others from my platoon, posted to Reinforcement Wing. All the men including myself were looking forward to going to Vietnam and applying our training against the enemy.

Time spent in Reinforcement Wing was considered as time wasted, in that we had no meaningful work to do. Our days were spent getting our kit ready for Vietnam and filling in time by raking leaves that continually fell from the gum trees. There was quite a movement of troops through Reinforcement Wing, the three battalions in Vietnam – 2, 3 and 7 RAR – required a continuous supply of reinforcements for all sorts of reasons. There were National Servicemen in the country whose two years service was up, others had been killed or wounded, and a further number repatriated due to ill health etc.

My number eventually came up and I was sent on pre-embarkation leave prior to flying out on a Qantas charter from Sydney to South Vietnam on the evening of March the 10th 1968.

Chapter 2

To Vietnam

✦

. . . and beyond the wire

The aircraft touched down at Darwin for a couple of hours, the stopover being sufficient to allow us get off the plane and stretch our legs. The next stop was at Singapore about mid morning, and again we got off the plane for another stretch. I'd never been in the tropics before. The thick, smelly, hot atmosphere at Singapore hit me full on in the face.

Arrangements between the Australian Government and Singapore Government provided for us to pass through Singapore wearing civilian clothing. It looked a little odd to see a whole plane load of young men, all about the same age, sporting the same military style short back and sides haircut. Notwithstanding the obvious reason why we were there, as we entered the airport the Singaporean official examining our travel documents looked at us individually as if he was taking a mental photograph. Our travel documents did not carry a photograph.

The flight to Tan Son Nhut airport in Saigon was arranged so that we landed in daylight hours. As the plane descended on the approach to Saigon, flying at only a couple of hundred metres altitude, looking out the window, I thought a surface to air missile could easily put paid to us before we even set foot on the country.

Despite these thoughts, the plane landed safely and we disembarked immediately. Our weapons, tagged with our names, were taken from the cargo hold and issued to us, along with 20 rounds of live ammunition to fill the magazine on our rifles.

We had to wait at the edge of the tarmac for a couple of hours pending the arrival of the aircraft that was to take us on to Nui Dat, in Phuoc Tuy Province.

While we waited, three C 130 aircraft landed and disgorged a battalion of South Vietnamese soldiers, all with weapons and dressed in battle kit. It was obvious they'd just returned from combat somewhere. There were a large number of them with dressed wounds, a lot on crutches and a further number being carried on stretches. Seeing this sight drove home for the first time that, from here on in, it was the real thing. Up until now, the fact that we were heading for a combat zone and would be engaged as infantry soldiers lacked a certain measure of impact. The scene unfolding before us, along with the issue of rifle and live rounds, drove the message home.

Our aircraft to transport us to Nui Dat eventually arrived and we filed in one by one and sat on the floor of the craft in rows across the fuselage. The flight to Nui Dat took about twenty minutes or so and everybody on board seemed lost in their thoughts, saying very little.

The skill of the American pilot was made obvious by the perfect landing. There was not even the slightest hint of a bump as the plane landed and rolled to a halt at Luscombe Airfield, Nui Dat.

Vehicles from 1 ARU (Australian Reinforcement Unit) were there to truck us to the south-eastern area of Nui Dat, which was to be our home for the immediate future. Army vehicles are invariably the same throughout and unit vehicles are identified by the colour patch and number painted on the vehicle.

The first thing at 1ARU was to hand in to the Orderly Room our AB 83. This document details all our personal data. The next thing was to get our digs squared away.

The arrival of 3 RAR, only a few months earlier to build 1ATF (Australian Task Force) to three battalions had a corresponding flow on to all other units who had to increase in size accordingly. This meant there was still a lot of work to be done in consolidating the task force. The Royal Australian Engineers were flat out building a whole raft of administrative buildings etc. The Infantry, apart from their normal operational duties, were flat out putting up and sandbagging tents, as well as providing work parties to assist the engineers.

Nui Dat was consistent with a large country town found anywhere in Australia. Once the Task Force had built to three Battalions, it meant there were about 8500 Australians in Vietnam involved in the conflict. Obviously, not all were at Nui Dat. There was a large number at 1ALSG (Australian Logistic Support Group) at Vung Tau, others at Command Headquarters in Saigon and others elsewhere. Even if there were around six thousand at Nui Dat, it still represents a fair sized town. If one walked the perimeter wire it would have probably been about eleven kilometres around. This is only a guess on my part.

1 ARU was situated at a little bend in the fence at the south western part of Nui Dat. Further along, to the east, was 3 RAR. All the fighting corps units – Infantry, Armour etc. – were camped on the perimeter and each was responsible for defending the length of perimeter they occupied. Machine gun bunkers were located about every seventy metres or so around the whole perimeter. Weapon pits, each capable of holding at least three riflemen were located in between. Also, there were more pits in depth.

In the event of a full-scale frontal attack, each soldier knew where his pit was. The OC at 1 ARU had us standing to at first light and at dusk each day. This meant all the combatants in the unit were in their allocated pit for the duration of the "Stand To". Every soldier carried his rifle loaded with twenty rounds in the magazine at all times.

Infantry Platoon Profile. As 1 ARU is an infantry unit, the men are allocated to Platoons, which are then broken down to Sections. A full strength Infantry Platoon consists of thirty-three men inclusive of NCOs plus one officer. It is doubtful whether a full strength platoon actually exists. I never came across any.

Text book conditions provides for a Lieutenant in command, a Platoon Sergeant as 2IC and three Sections, each with ten. Each Section has a Corporal as Section Commander and a Lance Corporal as Section 2 IC. Platoon Headquarters consists of the Platoon Commander, Platoon Sergeant, Radio Operator and Medic.

At operational level outside the Task Force fence, the average platoon strength including platoon headquarters is round twenty-four to twenty-six men, dependent on a number of factors. When leaving the wire on an operation, it is always incumbent upon the platoon to leave behind about six men on what is known as rear detail. Their task is to assist with the ongoing function of the Company.

The Platoon's machine gun position overlooking the wire has to be manned around the clock. Also, there are other support functions. Diggers out on operations have to be re-supplied every three days. During the dry season, water sometimes has to be dropped in, dependant upon where the operation maybe taking place.

The men left behind on rear detail are, more often than not, reporting to the Company Sergeant Major or, when the CSM is out on operations as part of Company Headquarters, some other ranking officer or NCO is in charge. Apart from that, men are absent on R & R (Rest & Recreation) or simply not operational, due to ill health – for example, some fair skinned fellows might have severe heat rash. The men in the platoon's sections soon worked out the pecking order as to who amongst their number was less suited to the field and invariably, the same blokes were left behind to look after the fort. For example, there are those that are prone to wandering along through the jungle, unable to concentrate, tripping over every stick underfoot and getting themselves entangled in every jungle vine. No proficient digger wants to be out in the scrub relying on these blokes. Somehow they end up in the infantry but they're more suited to other Corps. Notwithstanding their deficiencies as combat soldiers, they are still able to carry out a worthwhile function on rear detail and, better still, are happy to do it.

The typical section on patrol comprises a forward scout, followed by the section commander, then the machine gunner and his number two on the gun. Behind them are three to four riflemen. This generally is our best-case scenario.

Weapons and ammunition. The weaponry carried in a typical section, starting with the forward scout, sees him carrying a 5.56mm M16 Automatic Armalite Rifle, plus about 200 rounds of ammunition; he also carries at least one or two M26 fragmentation grenades on his belt.

The same also applies to the section commander following the scout. The Section Commander quite often is the one carrying the claymore mines. Later in my career I carried six as Section Commander and a rifleman the other two.

Next in line is the machine gunner carrying an M60 general purpose machine gun. This gun is capable of firing about eight hundred rounds per minute. The gun is carried with a lead load of about thirty or forty rounds clipped together by metal links. Across his shoulders he carries two linked ammunition belts, each of one hundred rounds. His number two on the gun follows behind and carries the spare barrel to the machine gun as well as four hundred rounds of ammunition for the gun. He also carries his personal weapon, a 7.62 millimetre SLR (Self Loading Rifle) together with two hundred rounds for his rifle. The three or four riflemen following the No. 2 on the gun carry SLRs and two hundred rounds. Each of them carries another hundred rounds for the machine gun. The M72 rocket is carried by one of the riflemen and the M79 grenade launcher by another. There are variations to this profile, but this is generally the scenario.

Going back up front to the forward scout, patrolling through jungle or thick scrub sees him cutting his way through with a good pair of secateurs in his left hand, and his rifle in the right hand. He always carries his rifle at the ready and with the safety catch off while in the lead. The Section Commander holds his rifle in his right hand and, at times, a prism compass in his left hand. Anyone who is a natural left hand shot was converted during the training process to become a right-handed shot. This is necessary due to SLR cartridges ejecting from the right of the rifle. Shooting right-handed obviates getting hit in the eye with spent shells as they're ejected. At regular intervals, the scout turns his head to the section commander, who directs him right or left, or straight ahead as the case may be.

The forward scout's job is stressful. It requires him to use stealth, all his senses and concentration as he knows he's most likely to be the first one shot dead.

The section commander's job is no less stressful – he's also up there in the firing line, immediately behind the scout. He is responsible for navigation and tactical movement forward by his section. He keeps alert to the topography, vegetation and lie of the land to keep the body of troops unexposed to ambushes. At all times he observes the conditions for a contact in the event the section encounters the enemy. As a battle commander, he has a fair share of things to think about.

The machine gunner is a real workhorse due to the weight of the gun. He keeps his eyes open, surveying the ground to right and left in the event a contact occurs. He needs to know where to position the gun for maximum effect. Likewise, his number two, whose job it is to assist the machine gunner by ensuring the linked rounds feed in straight and joining more linked rounds before the belt runs out. He needs to really be on the ball because the first thirty or forty rounds have to be linked with more ammunition, preferably before they're all fired. While it takes only a few seconds to load the gun with another belt in a contact, these are unaffordable seconds. He also has to be ready to change the barrel when it gets hot.

The riflemen keep their eyes open to right and left. The rear rifleman is known as tail-end-charlie. He's required to regularly keep his eye on the rear so that the section is not followed or shot up the arse. The tail-end-charlie also counts the number of steps taken between points A and B. He's assisted by the man in front of him, who also counts the steps. Notes are compared from time to time to facilitate a good fix on the distance travelled. The norm is that 120 steps is equivalent to one hundred metres. The jungle does not afford you the luxury of being able to see where you are and therefore the compass map and protractor assume great importance.

Platoon Commander. Behind the first section comes the Platoon Commander. He's generally a first lieutenant in rank or quite often a second lieutenant. The platoon commander is responsible for the big picture. His role is to command the platoon strategically and tactically. He's responsible for plotting the course and overall navigation and does this by keeping an eye on his own compass, checking to ensure the lead section remains on course. He's responsible for morale and the overall well being of the troops under his command. His job is to ensure the objectives of the mission are carried out. Coming behind him is the rest of platoon headquarters, radio operator, platoon sergeant and medic.

Platoon Sergeant. The Platoon Sergeant, apart from being platoon 2IC, is responsible for the administration aspects of the platoon. Normally, the Sergeant is an experienced soldier and handy to have around.

Following him, are the next two sections. If you extend movement by single file out to a company of three platoons, plus company headquarters, the footprint of the company at any given time covers a fair distance, anything up to a kilometre. More often than not, however, platoons move forward independently of one another, tactically spaced apart, but heading in the same direction. Platoons on their own are able to move faster than a company as a whole, and, at the same time, check out more area for signs of the enemy.

An Infantry Section carries a number of ancillary items spread across the men. Each Section has four or five different coloured smoke grenades a flare or two and about eight anti-personnel claymore mines, detonators, detonating cord and a couple of clackers. Clackers, as they're colloquially called, are hand-held self-contained electrical devices for the purpose of detonating the claymore mines.

Around his waist, mounted on his webbing belt, the digger carries a number of items. Moving clockwise around the belt, commencing at the front buckle, is an M26 hand grenade which, apart from the pin, is additionally secured by insulation tape around the lever and grenade. This is precautionary to minimize the risk of accidental explosion in the event the pin gets hooked on something and inadvertently pulled from the grenade.

The NCOs carry their compass in a small pouch held on the web belt. Pouches holding ammunition magazines came next, the most favoured pouches for magazines are Second World War webbing pouches. During the Second World War, these pouches were on the belt as well but further supported by straps buckled to the rear of the pouch and running over the shoulders under the epaulets. To use them effectively, we cut two vertical slits in the back of the pouch, about seven centimetres apart, to the width of our belt. We simply thread our belt through the slits. They're a good size, about 15 cm wide and 21cm deep, and sufficiently wide enough to comfortably slip in about five magazines for an SLR and eight or nine for the M16 Armalite. Next is your machete and bayonet. The diggers soon discovered that, by taking out the machete sharpening stone from its pocket on front of the machete holder and cutting a slit in the bottom of the sharpening stone pocket, you could push your bayonet scabbard down through the pocket. The tight fit holds it firmly in place. Next, you have a water bottle situated more or less on the right hip.

On the other side of your belt, you have another pouch with loaded magazines, a smoke grenade, toggle rope, a pouch containing a few personal items, a camera for example, then, another water bottle. It was not uncommon to see three or even four water bottles around the waste. I also carry a grenade launching attachment for an SLR. The diggers alter the scheme of things to personally suit, but nevertheless this is what they generally carry hanging off their belts. My belt, fully laden, weighed 6½ kilos or more.

On preparing for an operation, all the aforementioned weaponry takes priority over and above any creature comforts. Once you've packed these away, you can fill available space with personal items and rations.

The normal extras carried, amongst other things, are, firstly, your ground sheet. In Australia, your ground sheet is your poncho. Ponchos were not suitable for Vietnam so we left them in Australia. Instead, we rely on a light-weight item made of synthetic material, which is divided into three compartments. Into each compartment we slide a pneumatic section. They're, in effect, blow up mattresses. The trouble is, if you blow air into them, they squelch in the quiet of the night when you roll over. Infantry soldiers, unlike other corps, are not fond of noise. The last thing they want is the night air being punctuated by squelching caused by diggers rolling over in their sleep. This is overcome by not blowing them up. Apart from that, once they're punctured, that's the end of them.

It is not unusual to doss down at night sometimes wondering if the enemy is going to creep up and slit your throat. The more quiet you are the better your chances.

The overall thickness of the pneumatic sections and holder gives you a four-ply waterproof ground sheet, which mitigates the effect of small stones and sticks poking into you when you're sleeping.

Each man carries a "hootchie." This is a two metre square, waterproof synthetic material item with press studs that allows two men to clip their respective parts together to end up with an open ended A-shaped tent standing about chest high. Or, if alone, you can pitch a tent, but it only allows you enough height to crawl in and sleep under. The circumstances determine whether you pair up or remain alone. In a static position such as in protection of a fire support base, you may see the troops paired up. Out on patrol and harboured up for the night the troops are in single defensive positions. Personally, I find pitching a hootchie undesirable. Firstly, it tends to reflect light and therefore your position can be more easily identified. Secondly, when it rains, the sound of the raindrops on the plastic is amplified, knocking out your sense of hearing. Thirdly, in the wet season, it rains every day towards late afternoon, making you wet anyway. Nevertheless, in the wet season we still put them up because it quite often rains all night and they're handy to catch rainwater to fill our water bottles.

In my back-pack I carried six claymore mines and one sandbag. This bag is used along with the sandbags other soldiers carry for the re-supply of water. The platoon places their empty water bottles in sandbags and then we swap them over for full ones bagged up when the re-supply chopper comes in. At other times a small patrol leaves the platoon harbour with the platoon's empty water bottles in the sandbags and they locate a nearby stream shown on the map and refill the bottles.

When the gun is on the ground, the machine gunner and his number two lay their ammunition on the sandbags they carry. The ammunition is laid out in such a fashion to facilitate good feed into the gun. When the gun is firing, the sandbag prevents debris from the jungle floor being picked up by the linked belt and fed into the breach, jamming the gun.

We also carry an entrenching tool – a fold out shovel-come-pick. We use these to dig defensive shell scrapes etc. and, from time to time, bury the enemy dead. Entrenching tools are handy for all sorts of things. Another item in our pack is the all-important silk which is a one-ply silk sleeping bag liner. You can roll it up in size to about two clenched fists. It's a very important part of your kit, however more on the silk later.

Once you have all this in your pack, you can then put in your rations. It's necessary to carry three days rations on an operation. Standard operational procedures provides for re-supply choppers to fly in every third day.

Australians were fortunate because we were able to mix our combat ration packs with the American ration packs. Each country's pack is deficient on its own. The Americans stack plenty of food into their packs and they have a number of delicacies like canned peaches, canned fruit salad, canned apricots, canned pound cake, fruit-cake and cinnamon rolls. They also have canned meat dishes, such as ham and lima beans, meat-balls in spaghetti and tomato sauce, chicken as well as ham slices and apple sauce. There is also a can of frankfurts – about a dozen – each around 40mms long. The diggers call them "little doggies dicks." You won't go hungry on American rations but the downside is, no tea bags, poor quality instant coffee and something they call milk substitute which is a heap of chemicals mixed together into a white powder bagged up into little sachets.

The American rations come in individual boxes marked with the contents. They don't distinguish well between breakfast, lunch and evening meal. Each box also contains a plastic spoon, matches, can opener, toilet paper and a pack of four cigarettes along with salt, pepper, coffee and sugar.

The Australian rations come in five menus marked A,B,C, D and E. Each pack weighs a little over a kilogram. They are very nutritional and will certainly keep you alive. But they're short on niceties. Apart from the fruit tingles and the high energy chocolate, there are no other frills, like cake and canned fruit as in the American packs. There is one aspect, however, in which they're good, and that is the sachets of tea and sugar. The Australian way of life still holds tea as a more favoured brew than coffee, therefore there is adequate amounts of tea to get you through the day. The packs also contain coffee, which is better than the Americans. Our coffee is not ground to as fine a powder as is the Americans. Furthermore, there is no comparison between American milk substitute and a good tube of Australian condensed milk. Every now and again we open our rations to find a little note from the girl who packed it. The note gives her name and address and invites us to drop her a line. We always like to receive these notes and we respond accordingly.

The Australian ration packs keep you going and get you down to your best fighting weight but they leave you still hungry at the end of the day.

Having access to both American and Australian rations gives us the best of both worlds. Most times the Australian rations are available only in A & B or B & C. Apart from this, we can pick through both lots taking what we please, provided we're able to carry it on our backs. If restricted to Australian rations, then three packs for the three days can quite easily be accommodated in your pack. On the other hand, without a donkey, you have no hope of carrying the full three days of American rations. You take as much as you can carry and leave the rest behind – at least a third has to be left behind. I always took the full amount of Australian rations, I like what's in them and on top of them I take my pick of American rations; this way I always have enough to eat.

What is impressive about the American ration system is, with every one hundred meals, comes a supplementary pack, an unbridled indulgence by our standard. This supplementary pack is a cardboard box, about 500mm square, jam packed with all sorts of goodies like cakes of palmolive soap, safety razors and blades, cans of soft drink, cartons of cigarettes, sweets, M&Ms, hershe bars and gum. An Australian platoon has no hope of using up the quantity. To top it off, there are cigars in the pack. At the end of the day you can sit at the back of your shell scrape, cigar in the mouth, looking like General Patton. There is no doubt about it, the supplementary pack is a real bonus.

It has taken Australia the best part of a hundred years to get to the point where they now have the system to make life better for the digger in the field, somewhat commensurate with the country's ability to do so.

During the 1st World War, Australia had the highest standard of living in the world. Notwithstanding this, we didn't have the developed systems to deliver to the troops what the country was capable of delivering in the way of good food. As a nation we learnt very little from this, perhaps thinking that the Great War was indeed the war to end all wars as it was said at the time. If so, then there was no need to develop the system to a higher standard. Alas, along came Adolf Hitler and Tojo. Again bully beef and only bully beef was a daily feature on the diggers menu. In 1942, the Americans entered the war and nothing was too good for their people in uniform. But we did learn something between 1939 and 1945.

A quarter of a century later along comes Ho Chi Minh and General Giap. By now our ration packs are just starting to reflect the fact that we've learnt something under the heading of product development and standards. Even so, we still lag behind the Americans by the proverbial country mile. If we can learn something from the Americans then here it is.

Having said this, I'm confident any post Vietnam War dispatch of Australian troops will see them issued with combat rations consistent to the standard Australians expect their fighting men and women to have.

We cook our food on small fold out stoves using Hexamine tablets (Hexamethylene-Tetramine) for fuel. We also use fuel, which comes in American ration packs, a small cake of compressed methylated spirits, which is blue in colour, more easily ignited, and burns away faster and with less odour than Hexamine. The best fuel of all, however, is C4 plastic explosive . . . but more about that later.

To cook our rations we place a small piece of fuel on our stoves and bang the can of our choice on our knee to put a dent in it. We place the can on the stove and set the fuel alight. After a while, the dent commences to come out from the build up of heat and the contents of the can are cooking nicely in their own juices. Once the dent is almost all the way out we take the can off the stove and carefully pierce the top with our opener, making as small a hole in the lid of the can as possible, allowing the pressure in the can to vent out.

Once the pressure is gone, we open the can and eat the contents. If you don't keep your eye on the can while it is cooking, the can swells beyond its normal size, expanding to the point of exploding. Apart from the loud bang, scaring the hell out of your mates nearby, everybody cops a serve of meatballs and spaghetti – or whatever – which they hadn't ordered.

For the first couple of weeks in 1 ARU we did only short distance reconnaissance patrols to get us acclimatized. It is now getting on towards the end of the dry season, the days are hot and humid and the perspiration drips off you from head to toe. Your shirt is wet all the time from perspiration as is the tops of your trousers at the waist. At first I couldn't see myself surviving, I thought I'd simply melt away like a bit of butter on a hot griddle. It's necessary to carry four bottles of water every day – any less and you'll suffer badly from thirst.

You resist the strong temptation to put your water bottle to your mouth and gulp down the entire contents in one go. Some of the blokes can't manage and have to negotiate a deal with their mates. Water is more valuable than money. Money, there's plenty of, water no. One bloke, Pte. Brian Harrison, was always thirsty. Every day he runs out of water at about midday. Initially, we were quite happy to allow him a small swig on one of our bottles. It paid to keep a close eye on him, though, so that he wouldn't back pedal into your bottle and glug, glug, glug, your bottle was empty. We were happy to help him out, but eventually we all jacked up, we felt he could manage his intake of water better and we started to charge him $10 for a pint bottle of water. Poor old Brian had no option but to pay or die of thirst, but after a couple of weeks he was able to manage his water a lot better and it was a win-win situation all around. Brian became self-sufficient in water, and we'd become rich from selling it to him.

On formation of the platoon on my arrival at 1 ARU, I was given the task of carrying the M60 machine gun. Being larger than average was a sure fire way of being considered for the machine gunners job, provided everyone in the section is happy for you to carry it. The weight of the gun alone is sufficient to knock a number of the section out from carrying it. It's one thing to know how to operate the gun, which everyone is well trained to do, but it's another to carry it all day through the jungle.

My way of carrying the gun was to have the same type basic pouch on my belt used by the other section members for stowing ammunition. I filled this pouch with other items and rested the main part of the gun on the pouch. This transfers a lot of the weight of the gun from your arms to your waist.

Each individual has his own preference for the way in which he carries the gun; the main thing is, whatever way he carries it, he needs it to be in a firing position and he needs to be able to carry it all day.

One discipline that has saved the lives of a lot of diggers is the strict removal and banning of rifle slings. Each man carries his rifle in the ready position all the time. There's no exception to this. Your ability to bring your rifle into action immediately is the difference between life and death in a lot of instances. This contrasts starkly with our American allies. They carry their rifles or machine guns on the shoulder, behind the neck across their shoulders and in any other manner that takes their fancy. The South Vietnamese soldiers also carry their weapons any way they like. It looks – and is – extremely unprofessional, slack as hell and really serves to highlight the difference in standards between the Australians and everybody else. This always-at-the-ready position gives us a distinct advantage against our enemy who's often carrying his rifle slung on his shoulder.

Seeing the Americans carrying their weapons in a slack fashion, I was reminded of a 2nd World War comic strip of 'Bluey and Curley', two Australians at war in the Middle East. One day, Bluey and Curley on their own captured fifteen thousand or more Italian soldiers. They were marching their prisoners back, four abreast across the sand dunes, the line of prisoners stretching back miles as far as the eye could see. Bluey allowed one of the prisoners to carry his rifle for him. Along the way, Bluey turned to the prisoner carrying his rifle and said "Giovanni, if you don't stop dragging my rifle butt in the sand, I won't let you carry it for me."

After a few days of our arrival at Nui Dat the platoon left on a full day patrol heading off towards a village called Hoa Long. The patrol was an introduction to the local people and for us to have a look around as well as checking the IDs of the people we came into contact with. It isn't what you'd call serious work but it was a job to do, and I guess someone has to do it. We were following a dusty track which the locals used to drive their ox carts along. Two women wearing conical hats and three small children were seen coming towards us along the track. The diggers spread out to both sides of the track as if to envelope the group as they approached. Lance Corporal Ross asked me and another soldier to check their ID cards. The women are wearing thongs and are dressed in peasant garb of shiny black pyjama pants and shirts of sorts, which suggest at one time, long ago, they were white but they're now filthy. There is no collar to the shirts but they're pinched in at the waist to give some shape. Nor are they tucked in, they fall to just below the top of the pyjama pants. There's two little pockets on their shirts, one on either side and they're both pinned with a safety pin to secure their ID cards and other valuables. As they approach, the women know they have to show their cards and they stopped a few paces short of me. One of them, turning her head slightly and tilting it forward a little, let go from her mouth a solid stream of red gunk, which hit the ground in a great splatter. Bloody hell, I thought, what have I got here, she's bleeding profusely from within. She stood tilted forward, dribbling and working her bottom jaw up and down to make sure it was all gone. I didn't know whether to look at her or the bloody mess on the ground. If I'd been any closer my boots would have been splashed. She lifted her head and looked at me with her mouth wide open, showing a mouth full of red and black teeth. You would have sworn only moments ago that she had all her teeth taken out, but they're still there, in a black and bloody looking mess in her mouth. I couldn't help but think that here before me is the real meaning of the word "hag". We soon learnt how popular chewing betel nut was for them and being something similar to the South American Indians chewing coca leaf.

The kids, by contrast, looked reasonably healthy, although any suggestion they'd had a wash or bath since being born was just not credible. A pungent odour arose from them that reminded me of a canvas tent rolled up while still wet and left to go mouldy. Their flawless complexions intrigued me, though. I thought, how can anyone living in obvious squalor, on a diet of what I suppose to be fish and rice, have such flawless faces. I wondered about this many times. Their clothes, though, were another story. Their shirts are made from the cloth our ammunition comes packaged in. Ammunition is packed into cloth sachets before being put into the ammunition cases. These sachets are imprinted with large lettering, denoting the type of ammunition. For example, 7.62 Ball, Smokeless, Rimless. The villagers get hold of these discarded sachets, open up the stitching and, by using about half a dozen or so of them, knock up a shirt for their kids. In terms of fashion, they're well ahead. It's funny looking at their shirts, adorned with the words 7.62mm, Smokeless, Rimless, Ball. The kids are bare-footed, and are wearing filthy shorts.

The women tender their ID cards for inspection. Looking at the photograph on the card, it's difficult to reconcile it with the woman standing before me. Apart from the fact they all look the same to us, there is no way of telling whether their age appears to match the date of birth on the card or any other detail for that matter. We just looked at the cards and let them go. Anyway, villagers from Hoa Long are assumed to be communist supporters at the very least.

Every now again we are reminded by a downpour of rain that the dry season was coming to an end. One day, with monsoonal rain threatening, our Platoon Sergeant – who'd previously done a tour of duty with 1 RAR as part of the 173rd Airborne Brigade – got it into his head that we should do a patrol to experience a tropical downpour. We left the wire and patrolled an area to about 1.5 kilometres from the base. The skies opened up and down came the rain. It literally bucketed down, limiting visibility to about forty metres or so.

Our sergeant had us just prop there, spread out in a defensive position. It took about two hours for the rain to stop. We were saturated to the bone ten times over. The sergeant pulled us in from our positions, and said, "Now boys, get used to having a wet arse because in a few weeks every day will be like this." I had to hand it to him. He didn't spare himself from a wet backside, copping it just like the rest of us.

There is no way to prevent yourself from getting wet. Our army-issue camouflaged raincoats are no good. If you put them on, the humidity has you sweating on the inside. You got just as wet from perspiration anyway. If I'm to get wet I'd rather the cleansing rain than perspiration any day. The only thing a raincoat does is keep you a little warmer. Apart from anything else, it is not practical to carry a raincoat and even less practical to use one. We just got wet and put up with it. You don't get cold – the rain is more of a nuisance than anything else.

In our second week we were given the job of protecting American and Australian Engineers on land clearing operations. Land clearing is designed to clear a wide buffer strip of land between the large towns and the jungle preventing easy access and withdrawal of communist forces in and out of the towns. The Tet Offensive mounted by the National Liberation Front six weeks earlier saw their communist forces take over and temporarily hold large provincial towns, like Baria and Long Dien. Easy access by the enemy to and from the towns through nearby jungle is a problem for our forces. Large land clearing operations is thought to help overcome this. Our job, as Infantry, is to position ourselves on all sides of the bulldozers as they work forward clearing as they go. This means from time to time we have to move forward through the jungle to new protective positions. All in all, it's a reasonably easy job. The weather is still mostly hot and sunny but we're in the shade of the jungle where it's nice and cool. Keeping an eye out is better than slogging your guts out somewhere with a heavy pack on your back.

But we do have our problems. One day, I positioned my machine gun in a spot, which I thought was a reasonable distance in front of the bulldozers. The jungle was as thick as it gets. Taking the packs off our backs, we settled down to what we thought would be a good half hour before we'd have to move forward again. Suddenly, a bulldozer, the largest Caterpillar I'd ever seen, and only about ten metres away, came through the jungle heading straight for us. There was no way the driver could see us through the scrub. It looked like we were gone for all time. I picked up the gun and bolted, leaving my pack and two belts of linked ammunition behind. Protection of the machine gun was paramount. There was no time to grab my pack and ammo. The three or four other blokes with me did the same. We just managed to get the driver's attention before he drove over our gear. He scared the living tripe out of us, we weren't sure if he had an inkling we were there and it was his idea of a bit of fun, or whether he genuinely didn't know where we were. From then on we decided the biggest threat to our safety was the bulldozers and from then on we moved well in advance when the nearby clink, clink of their tracks suggested we did so.

The Enemy. The forces opposed to the Australians in Phuoc Tuy comprised three components: Main Forces, Provincial Forces and Village Defence Forces.

The best trained and equipped are the main forces being the 274VC Main Force Infantry Regiment numbering around twelve hundred, mostly North Vietnamese Army Regulars, and the 74th North Vietnamese Army Rocket Regiment and the D-65th North Vietnamese Army Engineer Battalion. All these main force units operate not only in Phuoc Tuy but also in the adjoining provinces of Bien Hoa and Long Khan. They're full time fighting organizations, well trained and well equipped.

The Provincial Forces are engaged in operations at the local district level and opposing us are the D440 and D445

Provincial Mobile Battalions. These units are manned by regular soldiers, and amongst their ranks is a large body of North Vietnamese regulars.

Down the scale in third place are the local guerrilla force units and, generally speaking, they operate part time and are not as well trained or equipped as the aforementioned units. These part timers often carry weapons left over from the 2nd World War or the Indo China War. Their activities, apart from engaging us in combat from time to time, include observation, carrying messages, informing on anti communist village members as well as acting as guides by virtue of their local geographical knowledge. There are not too many places we can go in the Province without the locals counting us and recording our direction for passing on to higher command. They're also well skilled in setting traps and using such devices as panji pits – pits staked out with fire-hardened bamboo spikes. The spikes are coated with all manner of things from human excrement to regular poisons. There is no shortage of anecdotes which also has them staking out poisonous snakes to the roofs of tunnels and caves.

VC tactics are designed to terrorize the local village population into co-operating. Their co-operation is sought for a wide range of support from finance, provision of food stores, enlisting young men and women into the ranks and providing information etc. The VC guerrillas systematically eliminate village chiefs or anybody else for that matter who resists in any way. Women and children are not spared if their deaths can serve a useful cause.

About three weeks in, we were engaged on road clearing. On one occasion, the platoon boarded a Section of Armoured Personnel Carriers and left Nui Dat heading towards Baria and proceeded up Route 15 towards the border of Phuoc Tuy and Bien Hoa. It was noticeable that the road was virtually devoid of all traffic. Normally there is a lot of road traffic heading south to the markets in Baria. This created a strong feeling amongst us that something was wrong. We proceeded cautiously, keeping a sharp lookout, not knowing whether we would be ambushed or some other similar shock was awaiting us. The three APCs, each carrying a section of infantry, continued up Route 15. About eight kilometres north of Baria, we came across the problem. The APCs went into a defensive fish-tail position, backing up to one another suitably spaced in the form of a triangle with their guns facing out at 12, 4 and 8 o'clock.

On the road – dead – was a man with his hands tied behind him. He'd been executed by beheading. It appeared only one blow had been struck to the back of the neck, sufficient in force to decapitate the man. Adjacent to the body, at the side of the road, driven into the ground, was a small freshly cut branch of a tree made into a stake. The stake was about 15mm in diameter, one metre long. The bark was peeled down about 150mm from the top and left hanging in six strips. Obviously, this was a message stick of some kind and no doubt the purport of the message known to the local populace.

The dead man was middle aged, about forty-five years old. We assumed he was from the hamlet about one hundred metres opposite from where he lay. There was no movement of people in the hamlet. It was very quiet and a foreboding atmosphere seemed to hang around. He looked as if he made a living riding a pedicab carrying freight or something similar. His strong thighs were consistent with the Vietnamese engaged in that industry. The Platoon Commander and the APC Section Commander, supported by a section of infantry, made their way to the hamlet to find out what this was all about. A few minutes later they returned with four men from the hamlet, one driving a Lambretta – a three-wheeled scooter and cabin vehicle commonly used as a taxi. On arrival at the scene, they backed the Lambretta up to the body and the four men proceeded to lift the dead man into the back of the vehicle. There was one man on each leg and arm. The man's head was only attached to his neck by a thin strip of skin about 10mm in width. When the body was raised from the ground and halfway into the Lambretta, the piece of skin gave way and the head fell onto the ground with a sickening thud. I was watching this, standing only two metres away. On hitting the ground, the head rolled like a soccer ball dribbling towards me. I jumped out of the way. One of the men, Peter Hollingworth, still sitting atop the APC, seeing this said, "Christ Stan, I thought he was going to have you".

"So did I, that's why I jumped out of the way," I replied.

The Vietnamese nearest the head went to pick it up, hesitated and looked at me in a strange way as if to enquire, what shall I do with it when I pick it up. I shrugged my shoulders in a manner, which suggested it wasn't my problem, and left him to get on with it. He stooped, picked up the head by the hair and hurriedly put it beside the body in the Lambretta.

The Platoon Commander and APC Section Commander, a Sergeant, questioned the men to find out what had happened. They said he'd allowed his daughter to recently marry a South Vietnamese soldier and, according to the VC, he should have allowed her only to marry a VC. For this crime the punishment was death by a public beheading. This form of execution is common. From what we're told, their religious beliefs hold that, in the event the head is separated from the rest of the body, both parts of the spirit eternally wander the heavens looking for the other part.

The villagers have little defence if any from the VC, who descend on them in the dead of night to terrorize, kill and exact whatever they want from the village. Obtaining support from all the rural villages is a key element in the strategy of the Viet Cong as dictated to them by their masters in North Vietnam.

Once a village population is firmly in the grasp of the Viet Cong, they can then be isolated from the influence of the South Vietnamese Government. When this is achieved on a wide scale, the VC consolidate their position in the area, pending a step up to the next phase in their plans.

The next day the platoon was placed at the disposal of the army engineers. Jumping aboard a truck, we were taken down to the concrete mixing plant near Luscombe Field Airport, given a shovel each and divided into gravel, sand and cement shovelling teams. The gravel, sand and cement is shovelled onto a large tray lifted by motor and cable to the top of the mixer and poured in. Once mixed, a tip truck backs up to the mixer and the concrete is poured from the mixer into the back of the truck. The truck driver, his load slopping about in the back, drives away to where it is needed. There are two or three of these trucks coming and going all day. For each batch we're required to shovel quite solidly, counting the shovelfuls as we go. The gravel shovellers have the hardest job, but we swapped around a lot.

Perspiration pours from our bodies, however, there's no shortage of water. The work is hard, but no-one seems to mind too much and there's good humour amongst the gang. The buildings at Nui Dat are made of western red cedar weatherboards with corrugated iron roofing. Most are rectangular in shape. The concrete pours are for the floors. The army engineers have a large-scale building program going on in the task force base as well as doing civil works outside. After a couple of days on the concreting gangs, two infantry sections boarded a TCV (troop carrying vehicle) for a job of guarding the engineers working on a school at Baria. There wasn't anything hard about this job. All we had to do was space ourselves out with our weapons handy. The hardest part was actually getting there. The TCV had two rows of seats back to back down the middle of the vehicle.

This configuration enables the diggers to sit facing out to the sides. Alongside the driver in the cabin stands his offsider "riding shotgun." His body protrudes through the porthole in the roof of the cabin, giving him vision all round.

Once out the main gate of Nui Dat we cock our rifles and check to ensure the safety catch is on. The road from Nui Dat passes through the town of Long Hoa, a few kilometres to the south. Long Hoa is not a particularly nice sort of town. The buildings reflect a poor standard generally, and it's very much a town at the lower scale of the Vietnamese social order. (True, there are a lot of villages and hamlets even further down the scale). Australians who have previously had some experience of the townspeople are of the view the place is full of Viet Cong. Once the driver hit the outskirts of the town he put his foot down. There's a water tower situated to the north of the road and regularly VC snipers climb the tower and take a few shots at any Aussies passing through. This day, a burst of fire, the sharp crack, distinctive of an AK47 momentarily startled us, even though we half expected it. The driver jammed on the brakes forcing us to hold on to the seats as hard as we could until the truck came to a stop.

Jumping off the truck, our Platoon Commander orders us to take up positions immediately. It was only a few seconds before we were deployed and after this bloke on the water tower. Moving forward with two sections, each covered by the other, it wasn't long before we were in a position to secure the area around the water tower. But our man has gone, no doubt seeking refuge amongst the crowded townspeople. After a good look around we returned to the other section left to secure the truck and jump on board again.

I was sitting at the rear of the truck and, as the last bloke jumped aboard, I gave him a hand up. No sooner was he on the truck than the magazine from his rifle fell off and onto the ground. On impact, the base plate came off, the spring shot out and all the rounds from the magazine spilled onto the ground. As quick as a flash, a woman from the crowd jumped forward and gathered up the rounds into her apron as though they were gold sovereigns, and then she was gone. No doubt the 7.62mm SLR rounds, which agree with the 7.62mm enemy AK47, will be put to use by the VC.

About twenty-five minutes later, we arrived at the school in Baria. The school is of solid masonry buildings with tiled roofing. It can easily be seen that at one time it was a very good structure, perhaps in the French colonial period fifteen years earlier. It may even have been a school for the French colonial children. The buildings are still sound, but neglect over the years has seen the condition fall away.

At the front gate stands a solid masonry and brick structure similar to a very good quality kiosk. It's no longer used and the kids climb up and sit on the counter. Passing the kiosk you enter onto a quadrangle about the size two tennis courts and upon which the kids gather to play, talk in small groups and have their lunch. This area is not paved and has a sandy surface.

Around the sides, save for the front entrance, are the classrooms. These are well constructed, with long tiled floor verandas. The rear walls of the classrooms form the boundary of the school. The classrooms are rudimentary and the kids sit at long bench type desks facing a single blackboard at the front.

The army engineers are refurbishing the school and doing general maintenance work where required. All we have to do is spread ourselves around a bit and just keep a bit of an eye out. Once we picked our spot on the verandas in the shade we shed our packs and make ourselves comfortable. Having nothing else to do, we dipped into our gear for the necessary requisites to make a brew of tea or whatever.

At recess, the school children come out of classrooms and hang around us. The "Uc Dai loi" (Vietnamese for Australian) always attract the kids, simply because we have nice things like lollies or even an apple which we always freely hand around. Strangely, they know what an apple is and have a name for it although I don't recall ever seeing one amongst the people. The children wear the typical primary school dress of silk black pyjamas and a white shirt. Their little white shirts, however, are not pinched in at the waist. Footwear is invariably a pair of thongs.

One little girl, only a slip of a thing, probably about eight years old but much smaller than an Australian kid of the same age, always comes up to me for a chat and to satisfy her curiosity. At the end of recess a little bell rings and the kids hurry off and form up in two's outside their classroom door. The teachers ask them to be quiet and on a command the children march very orderly into their classroom. Actually, it's very refreshing to see some order we can relate to in what is otherwise a country where order is an absolute scarcity.

At every morning and afternoon recess, the little girl comes out to talk to me. At lunchtimes she comes out and goes to her bag hanging on a peg on the veranda and from her bag she pulls out a small green bundle and comes to where I'm sitting. In the bundle is her lunch, which is wrapped around with banana leaf, widely used in Vietnam for wrapping food and around which is a small rubber band holding it all together.

When she unwraps her little lunch parcel she shows me what she has, a small amount of rice with what smells like fish oil mixed in with it. We sit down together and have our lunch, me giving her bits and pieces of my rations, like half my chocolate bar and apple that I always bring with me. It's surprising that, with a little effort and the use of sign language, how well you can communicate, especially with the kids, who for the most part, have all picked up a few words of English.

The army engineers are accompanied by a Eurasian lad, who they've taken under their wing and are looking after. I was told he's an abandoned leftover from the war against the French. It's a good gesture by the engineers, who do so much good work amongst the people, improving their lot by making roads, water reticulation and a whole variety of civil works such as rebuilding schools, orphanages, hospitals etc.

We've been at the school a few days and the engineers are nearing the completion of their work. By now, I'm well and truly good friends with the little girl. She has a European first name, which is not altogether uncommon.

On our last day at the school, she came forward with a lovely little gift of a small piece of embroidery work of a flower. The petals and stem of the flower is done in red cotton, the stamen in yellow and the leaves blue. In the top right hand corner written with a red ball-point pen is her mark of eight out of ten given to her by her teacher. I was surprised to see a fine piece of embroidery work done by such a young girl and it serves to highlight the need to teach the girls a worthwhile skill that they can carry into adulthood in the knowledge that their school years are limited. By the number of children you observe around the towns and villages you can be excused for coming to the conclusion there are no schools at all. For every child in school, there's probably fifty not. Young children generally stay home and help their parents in whatever their livelihood is. I'm quite sure the embroidery work done by the girl is important to her and I want to respond in kind.

I didn't have much on me apart from cans of food, but searching through my pack I came up with a cake of Palmolive soap still in its paper wrap. Soap is an absolute luxury to the Vietnamese and will be ideal in return. The little girl took it and smelled it. A smile came across her face as she put it in the little pocket in her shirt. She placed her two hands together in front of her neck as if in prayer and slightly bowed her head as to thank me. This was one of the very few times in Vietnam that was simple and innocent and I've always held it a treasured memory.

The next day we went for a patrol outside the wire at Nui Dat. The day was hot and humid, not a cloud in the sky. I'm intrigued by days like this, which are exactly the same as the one before. The perspiration pours from us, our shirts are soaked in sweat all the time.

The woop woop birds, as we call them, are calling out their regular loud calls, as they do every day. The call of the woop woop bird serves as a strong reminder we're in another country, not that you need reminding . . . everything else about the place reminds you of that. The loud cry of this bird, which is about the same size as an Australian Currawong, can be heard quite a distance away. It starts off with a drawn out spaced series of woop woops picking up speed with each woop woop until, in the end, the call is a continual woopwoopwoop-woopwoopwoopwoopwoopwoopwoopwoopwoop. It's call is as loud as that of a peacock.

There was what I thought was another bird making a strange call in the camp, but I could never see it, until one day, a mate told me it was a geckoe lizard and they're hard to see because they change colour to the environment they're in. From then on I kept a sharp lookout until eventually I did see one; it changed colour from brown to green as it crawled up a banana tree.

A short distance into our patrol we came across some kids looking after their Brahmin cattle grazing in the fields. A couple of kids were stretched out, napping on the backs of the Brahmins. As we approached, the kids remained on their animals, kicking them with their bare feet in the flanks, steering them towards us they then hopped off. With tongue in cheek, we suggested to them they were VC. Pointing at them we said, "You VC, you VC"

The kids, patting their chests replied, "No VC. No VC".

After our little bit of fun, which the kids also enjoyed, one of them said, "*uc dai loi* number one, you got cigarette."

"No no, *uc dai loi* number ten, we have no cigarette," I answered.

The kids chorused back, "No no. *uc dai loi* number one, he got cigarette."

We always ended up giving them a cigarette.

If there's one thing the Australians and Americans have achieved in Vietnam, it's turning the kids into seasoned smokers before they're eight years old, not to mention their proficiency at giving you the fingers up sign. Surely, they must have learnt these rude gestures from the Americans. Although, once they gave us the fingers up, we feel compelled to give it back likewise.

Furthermore, they're the worlds best at botting cigarettes. Quite often they take one on offer, light up, and ask for another, putting it in their pocket to take home to Papa san. Other times they break it in half, smoking one half on the spot and taking the other half to Papa san. Or, if you give only one cigarette between two kids present, they break it in half and share it. Lighting up, they take a big draw then protruding their bottom lip they let the smoke out through their lips, drawing it up into their nose and down into their lungs. I've never seen anything like it. They're good smokers for eight year olds. Their disposition towards sharing is amazing. At this time I'm not a smoker, however cigarettes come in American rations, a packet of four with every meal, and I generally have a few packets on me to trade. Sometimes, I give a kid a whole unopened packet of four, notwithstanding the possibility his father in a day or two could be smoking them at his VC hideout in the jungle. The smiles on the faces of the kids is good to see though.

The Brahmin cows were about ten metres away grazing quietly. I asked one of the kids if I could have a ride. He went over and brought the beast over to me. I swung my leg up and over and got on its back. That's when the fun started. The cow went crazy and I realized straight away it was unfamiliar with this two legged on its back. There's not the strong musky odour she is used to coming from this rider, but rather a foreign odour, not to be accommodated. The damn thing flung its head around from side to side, butting me in the thighs. "The things gone crazy!" I yelled.

I didn't know whether to stay on and take my chances or jump off. Either way, it was going to be the winner. I didn't get the chance to jump off, as it happened. Arching it's back, the animal jumped to a great height, using all fours. It kicked out both its back legs together and sent me flying through the air. It seemed I was flying five seconds before I hit the ground, sprawled out not knowing if I'd sustained an injury or not. My thighs hurt the most from a series of good head butts. Everybody stood around, laughing their heads off and Pte. Maplestone said, "Sorry Stan, no prize mate, you didn't last the full eight seconds."

"Bullshit! It must have been ten seconds at least," I replied.

The cow took off, taking the other members of the herd with it. The kids weren't worried – they spend all their time with their cattle and know they can catch them at any time.

The Vietnamese don't leave their cattle to graze out at night. They bring them out of their enclosure situated right next to their homes for the day and take them back of an evening. Other livestock, such as pigs, live with them in a pen as part of the house. It's common to see a pig-pen with two or three pigs in at as an extension or part of the daily living area of their houses. The pig-pen isn't large, about three metres square at the most, but part of the house nevertheless. Chooks are free to wander in and out of the houses as they please. It seems the family consists of pigs, chooks, cattle, the odd dog, kids, a few cows, mama san and papa san, all in together.

I must say, though, rats are not welcome. One day, I saw an old bloke coming out of his house holding a dead rat by the tail and at arms length. He walked over towards his neighbour's yard and gave it a good fling in that direction. It landed in his neighbour's coffee bush and got hung up there, upside down, on a small fork in the bush. He looked at it for a moment, a little concerned as if contemplating what he should do. After a few seconds he turned around and went back inside his own place. I couldn't help but smile as I thought how it'll intrigue his neighbour, leaving him to ponder how a rat could climb up and die upside down in his coffee bush.

Approaching the perimeter of Nui Dat, represented by concertina wire, five rolls wide and three rolls high, you can't help but notice how difficult it is to see into the camp. The whole of the task force is situated in a rubber and banana plantation, which allows good vision out, but looking in is another matter. It's difficult to see anything at all. The tents and buildings are set back about one hundred metres from the wire. Trees, brush and scrub has been cleared outside the wire a further fifty or sixty metres, and even much further in some places, preventing anybody from creeping up unseen to the wire for a better look into the camp. The exits and entrances into the camp used by clearing patrols, standing patrols and other patrols are constructed in a way that reminds you of a maze. The path zig zags through the five rolls of wire . . . it isn't a case of just walking straight in. The exits and entrances are directly in front of a machine gun, slowing down any enemy rush through the wire.

The topography of the base is undulating with one distinct hill, namely Nui Dat Hill, which is the home of the SAS and upon which a permanent lookout is maintained. From the top you can see for miles around. There's only one other feature nearby, the Horseshoe, so named for its shape. The Australians maintain a permanent position on this feature as well. The task force is extremely well located and the land beyond the wire is generally flat, affording excellent vision and coverage. The soil within the base, and indeed outside, is deep red in colour. With the wet season coming on, the downpours every now and then seem to be turning the soil into a brownish red colour with a slight purple tinge. The coloured dirt gets into your clothing and it's virtually impossible to get it all out.

Fortunately, we don't have to do our own washing. The army has arrangements with a workforce of women in Baria who wash our clothes. Our trousers and shirts are numbered with each individual's laundry number. My number is K54 and all we have to do is hand our dirty laundry in to the Q store and a few days later give our number to collect it. Our jungle greens are worn all the time and they have a smell which is impossible to get out. In actual fact, the smell, sponsored by the tropical humidity, pervades every nook and cranny of our gear. Even items stored in our large metal trunks are affected. If you don't regularly clean your belongings they go mouldy very fast from the humidity and any metal objects are prone to rusting rapidly.

The next three days we spent at Nui Dat on various work parties. Footpaths are being put down using crushed rock won from the task force quarry. The oncoming wet season, evidenced by a build up of clouds, threatens more each day. The red soil, once wet, sticks to your boots like wet cow dung. The camp will be in a shocking state soon without paths to walk on.

The following morning, we assemble early for a three-day operation around a small town called Ap Lo Gom, north west of the Long Hais. The Long Hais are a chain of hills and deep valleys and a sanctuary for the VC due to its natural defensive topography.

The Viet Cong use their bases, many well hidden deep underground in natural limestone caves supplied by running underground streams, within this rugged mountainous complex to launch attacks against the nearby towns to the west and coastal towns to the south. Nobody enjoys going near them due to the large number of mines and booby traps they've put in place to protect themselves. 3RAR have been giving the Long Hais a going over. Prior to them moving in, the feature was bombarded with artillery, and bombs from B 52 bombers were dropped to soften up the enemy positions. The assault on the Long Hais is a large scale affair involving 2RAR as well. We've been told a number of Australians have been killed and wounded by mines and enemy small arms fire.

About eighteen months earlier, the Australians put in a minefield stretching from the southern part of the Horseshoe to near the coast in the south, a distance of about twelve kilometres. I've heard the minefield contains about thirty thousand mines but whether this is true or not, I don't know, however, it sounds right given the extent of the minefield. Viet Cong sappers have breached the integrity of the minefield, lifting mines to take away and resetting them for use against the Aussies. It has become a double bladed weapon, being a nuisance for us as well as them. A number of our blokes have been killed or injured by our own mines.

The area we're to patrol for the three days is a hot, barren, dry, sandy coastal plain. The scrub is, in the main, chest and head height. There are very few trees of any substance. Vision is quite good and our job is to block any VC escape routes from the Long Hais if they get through the 1RAR and 3 RAR blocking positions. Not long into the afternoon patrolling an area fairly close to an RF (Vietnamese Regional Force) outpost, the Platoon Commander sends a hand signal down the line for a ten-minute smoko and brew. Very few words are spoken on patrol. Most messages are conveyed by field signals.

The bloke in front of me, Brian Tobin, peels off to the side a few metres. I move forward a few metres, peeling off to the same side as him, looking for a spot to drop my pack. The two in front of us are the section commander and forward scout. They more or less stopped where they were. I take out my water bottle and pannikin, make a brew of tea and sit on my pack to enjoy it. I was just finishing off when the signal came up the line to saddle up again. I waited a minute, letting everyone get themselves sorted. I was never anxious to be the first, as this meant standing around with the machine gun in arms. I happened to be looking at Brian Tobin picking up his pack when something off to the left caught my eye. As he picked up his pack, swinging it round to put on his back, I noticed a leaf about one and a half metres on his left come up with it. I thought that's strange, and moved forward a couple of steps to take a closer look.

"Bloody Hell Brian! Don't move, for Christ's sake don't move your feet or we're both fucked."

"What do you mean Stan, what's going on?"

"You're right on a booby-trap. Just keep both feet where they are, under no circumstances move." I spoke in an agitated and excited manner.

"Jeez! Are you sure? Are you sure?"

"I'm dead certain mate, just don't move."

I moved forward the rest of the way to him and said, "Now, don't move, but look straight down, you'll see some fishing line six inches off the ground. Just follow it with your eyes to that bush over there and you'll see a hand grenade wired to trunk of the bush."

"Fuck me! " he said, unable to say any more. His vocabulary had suddenly dropped to two words, "fuck me, fuck me." He was temporarily frozen to the spot but, when he gathered himself, he realized he could step away from the line and hurriedly did so.

"Fuck me! That was close! I was almost a goner, another step and I would've been a goner, Stan."

"Yeah, you and me both mate. Shit! We were lucky!"

"How did you see it Stan? I must've been sitting right on the bloody thing."

By this time, the section commander, Bill Ross, knew something was wrong and was looking at me as if to say, "What's wrong?" I gave him the signal to come to me, which was the index and middle finger of the left hand put on the upper arm of the right arm. I then lifted the left hand to the top of my head patting it a couple of times, which means come here. Two fingers denoting two chevrons for corporal. Bill Ross was about twenty-two metres away and he sensed something was wrong. He came up to me and asked, "What's the matter Stan?"

I waved him back. "We've got a bloody booby-trap here, Bill"

"Shit! Where Stan?"

"Right there. Look at that bit of fishing line going into that bush and you'll see what I mean."

"Jeez! You're right mate, I'll get the boss up."

Bill put his two fingers on the left shoulder and patted his head, this signal being conveyed down the line of diggers until it reached the platoon commander. In less than half a minute he was on the spot. He passed Brian, who was still sitting down saying, "Fuck me! Fuck me! That was close."

The first thing the boss saw was Brian's distress, not yet knowing what the problem was. "Are you alright Brian?" he asked.

"Yeah boss, but only just. Fuck me!" he said shaking his head from side to side.

Bill pointed out the grenade to the boss, who said, "Shit! Who saw it?"

"Stan did."

The boss turned to me and said, "How'd you see that Stan? It's so well concealed."

"Well Sir, I didn't see the grenade at first or the fishing line, what caught my eye was a leaf hooked on the line coming up from the ground. Brian was actually sitting on his pack. When he put the pack on the ground it pressed the line to the ground. There was insufficient give to pull the pin the rest of the way out. Had he taken one more step we would've both gone up."

A close look at the grenade revealed the pin pulled halfway out. The boss said, "Hell! How lucky can you get? I bet those RF in that compound over there put it out to stop the VC."

"Maybe the VC put it out to stop the RF," Cpl. Ross said.

"Yeah, they could have, but they know the RF are too lazy to be wandering about out here."

It didn't actually dawn on me at the time how lucky we were. It sort of just happened and that was it. I really thought no more about it. The grenade was the familiar pineapple jacketed grenade, common in World War 2, and in extremely good condition. It still had a very new look about it, indicating it hadn't been there long. It was sleek and bronze brown in colour. It had a long tapered neck leading to the pin.

The boss secured the grenade by inserting the pin through the second pinhole and tying the lever down with some nylon perimeter cord for added safety. An infantryman's war is the area fifty metres around him, but for the rest of the day it was hard to get the men to lift their heads. We were all continually looking out for booby traps. Our war had reduced to a few steps around us.

Nothing much happened for the next two days. Of an evening we harboured up for the night in a position on a track, which afforded us the opportunity to set up an ambush. We very rarely harboured up for the sake of harbouring up to spend the night. The Viet Cong claimed the night as their own in which to move around unseen. We claimed the night as our own in which to set up ambushes to knock him out of the war for good.

In the tropics, there's no evening as we know it in Australia and it's necessary to have your ambush site determined by about 1700 hrs each day at the latest. By the time you've set up the ambush and squared away your own position in which you are to spend the night, and have had your evening meal, it's getting to be around 1800hrs and near last light for the day. During the night, the platoon's three M60 machine guns are manned at all times with the first two hour shift starting at 1800 hrs. The shifts are organized by each section commander and maintained on a rotating basis.

If you're on the first shift, commencing at 1800 hrs. going through to 2000 hrs, your shift the following night is from 2000 hrs. until 2200 hrs, and so on. This method permits you to get one full nights sleep every seven days or so. During the first few hours of a night you entertain yourself looking up at the stars and watching the satellites go over. It's surprising how many you see when you have nothing to do other than look for them.

The night harbour and ambush routine is easy to adopt. Generally speaking, if you've been bush bashing all day, the heat, humidity, stress and weight of your pack has taken its toll and you're happy to call it a day as soon as it gets dark. Furthermore, ambushes both day and night require absolute quiet and we never speak too much unless it's necessary. When there's a need to communicate we go quietly over to the other person and speak softly. When it gets dark we go to our position and rest or get some sleep until picket duty.

We're always on the lookout for the enemy, never knowing when we'll encounter them. Many times we hear them before we see them. Sometimes we hear them and don't see them at all, they just clear off as if they have an inkling we're there. Whilst not conscious of the stress that goes with the necessary vigilance, it nevertheless has a cumulative affect on you at the end of the day.

The infantryman's work is extremely physical and you need to be able to withstand daily rigors of heat, humidity, perspiration, dirt, rain, mud, myriads of mosquitoes, a variety of biting ants, scorpions, snakes, centipedes as big as a school ruler, a heavy pack, shortage of water at times and only the ground to sleep on. Then overlay this with a cunning enemy, soldiering in his own back yard and who'd like nothing better than to kill you . . . it's no wonder we feel tired at the end of the day. The night has its own discomforts too. The need to do picket on the gun interrupts sleep, the noises of the jungle, wild animals such as pigs rooting around in the dark sometimes only a few metres away and nearby artillery firing all night on harassment and interdiction missions mean sleepless nights. Quite often we're buggered from lack of sleep even before the day starts.

At first light in the morning our day commences. We need to be breakfasted, toileted and packed up and ready to leave the position on the Platoon Commander's orders. Most of the day's heavy work is done in the mornings. This is not always the case though – there are enough unforeseen factors and invariables like torrential downpours or finding an enemy bunker system that makes the afternoon the hardest part of the day.

Returning to Nui Dat is always refreshing. Once we've cleaned our rifles we look forward to a shower, putting on some clean clothes and enjoying a nice cold beer or two at the boozer. The ORs (other ranks) canteen is the focal point for the unit. Here we mix and talk to men in the other platoons. When on operational duties platoons quite often work independently of one another and there's not a lot of contact with the other two platoons in the company, save for the occasions when we harbour up as a company and even then there is very little contact if any. Each platoon has its own area of responsibility within the harbour. It's never a case of individuals just wandering all over the place talking to their mates in other platoons. The boozer gives us the opportunity for get-togethers.

Each unit has its own open-air theatre. Films are shown nightly and are well attended. Other forms of entertainment are the numerous card games in the lines where we can gamble away a few dollars or participate in a game of Crown and Anchor run by entrepreneurs in the unit.

I brought thirty dollars with me from Australia when I came to Vietnam. After six weeks I have thirty-five dollars, a profit of five dollars. I was fortunate enough to win ten dollars one night at crown and anchor. I still have the ten dollars Brian Harrison gave me much earlier on for a pint of water and another digger paid me five dollars to do a picket on the machine gun for him. Furthermore, I'm about ten dollars in front from playing poker.

I must confess, I'm no card sharp but some of the fellows are bloody hopeless and generally good to pick up a few dollars from in a game of cards. With nowhere to spend money, they feel a bit inclined to sometimes throw caution and good judgement to the wind. Moreover, some of them can be egged into making foolhardy bets because money is not a problem.

We're able to buy a tax-free can of beer at the boozer for fifteen cents or a "goffa" (can of soft drink) for ten cents. For those who smoke, a carton of cigarettes costs one dollar twenty cents, again tax-free. You can live like a king for ten dollars a week.

Word gets around that there's a card game in such and such tents. Those interested gather there and buy chips from the banker. We have a bet limit of one dollar per bet. There's never enough hard cash to go around and, if you're short, you write out an IOU to the bank for satisfaction next payday. On a real bad night you can lose thirty dollars but that's about it. However, more often than not, a bad night is followed by a good night and you're square again. It's a lot of good fun playing cards, the conversation at times wanders away from the game but the humour is good.

Once the conversation got onto fireflies, which are quite common around the camp. Fireflies generally stick together like a flock of birds and they come and go. Stretch Harvey commented to the effect that the VC use fireflies at night so they can see the bloke in front when travelling through the jungle by saying, "Well, they catch half a dozen or so, put them in a clear bottle which they sling over their back, and the nog following behind just keeps following the glowing bottle."

"Ooh bullshit!" remarked Harrison. "I gotta hand it to you, Stretch old mate, you come up with some beauties."

"No! Fair dinkum! I've been told that by a good mate in 3RAR and he's not one to bullshit, especially to me."

Pte. Tobin joined in, saying, "Tell me Stretch, do you think these fuckin' fireflies would glow if they're not happy?"

"How the bloody hell would I know mate, anyway, what's that got to do with it?" replied Stretch.

"I don't know mate! It's just that maybe if they're not happy, locked up in a bottle getting carted miles away from home – well, then maybe they don't light up their arses."

"Jeez, Brian! What sort of bullshit are you coming out with? Look! All I know is they light up their bloody arse in the dark, so it just stands to reason you could follow the glow in front. Anyway, fireflies don't know whether they're happy or sad."

"Crap mate! Even a fuckin' donkey knows when it's not happy, anyway, we're all donkeys otherwise we wouldn't be here and I know when I'm happy or sad," said Tobin.

Listening to this exchange, my thoughts went back to the hopeless night in the rain forest at Canungra. I joined in and said, "Well, I've been in the scrub at Canungra on a totally pitch black night and you couldn't see your hand in front of your face, not a thing, the VC have to have some form of light, that's all I know."

"A torch Stan! A bloody torch mate!" said Tobin.

"What! Carrying torches, you're fuckin' mad Tobin," said Kline, who'd been quiet up until now.

"Nobody here amongst us idiots knows anyway, let's get on with the card game. Whose deal is it?" asked Stretch.

We've just been informed to pack our gear for an operation down at the southern end of the Australian-laid minefield west of the Long Hais. Our role will be to protect the army engineers as they endeavour to dismantle a section of the minefield. It's common knowledge the VC has bridged the minefield and extracting dozens of mines to use against the Australians. The mines laid are M16 Anti Personnel Mines.

These mines, commonly called jumping jacks, come in a metal outer jacket. They have three metal prods at the top of the mine and, when stepped upon, the mine, made of cast iron, is propelled out of the metal case to about waist height, where it explodes. The cast iron shatters into thousands of small pieces, sending shards of shrapnel in every direction. Those not killed by the mine suffer horrific wounds, losing arms, legs, eyes, buttocks etc.

We've heard on the grapevine that the VC have lost a number of their mine lifters, probably as a result of the mines that have been booby trapped when laid.

As I understand it, every sixth or seventh mine is booby trapped with an M26 fragmentation grenade set directly underneath the mine. If someone tries to lift the M16 mine, the hand grenade will go off in their face before they have time to insert the pin into the mine to make it safe.

The TCVs (troop carrying vehicles) arrived on time to take us down south to the minefield. The Armoured Corps were there with a number of APCs and centurion tanks. They have rigged up a centurion with four steel booms, one on both sides at the front and the rear. The booms are angled upwards at about thirty degrees. They have a heavy steel cross member at the end of each set and hanging down from the cross members are heavy pieces of chain which connects to horizontal steel RSJs that have welded to them lengths of heavy chain coming out at right angles. The idea is for the tank to proceed in measured sections up and down the minefield, with the RSJs at the front and rear dragging along the surface of the ground setting the mines off as the tank passes over them.

There is nothing for the infantry to do other than watch the proceedings unfold before us. Several complications have set in. The ground surface is all sand and the tanks are continually sinking down into the sand to such an extent that another tank has to come in and try to extricate it from the sand bog. There are occasions when the second tank also becomes bogged in the sand and a third is called in to assist. This is taking a lot of time and very few mines are being set off. Another problem creating havoc is that, instead of the steel RSJs setting off all the mines, they're dragging a lot to the surface and leaving them exposed on top of the sand. This unsatisfactory result necessitates other engineers to go into the minefield on foot with mine detectors to deal with the mines. In theory, the idea is sound but the sand is simply not conducive to centurion tanks.

To further compound the problem, the tank with the booms is getting hell knocked out of the tracks as the mines explode underneath. All in all, there's concern amongst the Engineers and Armour that, despite best efforts and given the danger inherent in this operation, it will be best to abort the process and try and come up with something new and effective. After a few days the operation was halted and we returned to Nui Dat.

We're now into the last week of April and, for all intents and purposes, the wet season is here. The skies are now more grey than blue and the Indian summer is getting pushed aside. The rain we've already had is evidenced by the new growth of grass and the landscape everywhere around is starting to turn a little green.

A number of men have marched out as reinforcements to 1 RAR and 2 RAR.

Today is the 8th of May 1968 – and what a bugger of a day it turns out to be. The platoon went to the range to fire our weapons. I'd handed in the M60 to the Armourer a few days before as I'd identified a fault in the mechanism. So I could carry a weapon while the gun was being repaired, I drew out an SLR but didn't fill the magazine with rounds. I took the rifle to the range and filled up with ammo there for a shoot. Later that afternoon, at about 1700 hrs, three or four of us were keeping the picket company as he did his shift on the machine gun overlooking the wire. For some obscure reason, which I'm unable to explain, I fired a shot from my rifle out over the perimeter wire. I'd forgotten I'd loaded the weapon when at the range. It was only a matter of thirty seconds or so and an NCO was on the spot to charge me for an unauthorised discharge.

The effect of this was to front the OC who promptly handed me fourteen days field punishment and fourteen days loss of pay. For the next fourteen days I was required to report to the duty sergeant two hours before commencement of the working day and then again at the end of the working day for another two hours extra work. Field punishment didn't preclude me from going out on operational patrols or anything else the platoon was engaged on. I just didn't get paid for it. All in all, I had to do four hours extra work each day as well as not getting paid for the fourteen-day period.

The duty sergeant gave me all sorts of extra work to do for the first couple of days or so, then he hit upon a grand idea, which was to have me paint all the buildings in the company army green. To carry out this task I was provided with paint and paint brushes, plus a spray gun and compressor needed to do the job. After a few days, word got around the company that I was good at re-painting steel trunks. Diggers from all over were bringing up their steel trunks to me for a quick spray job. It was the first time I'd got myself into deep shit since signing on but I did deserve it, and was more than glad when the fourteen days were up. The next time I shoot out over the wire I'd better come up with a dead VC.

3 RAR is operating in the north, having just relieved 2 RAR at Fire Support Base Anderson in Bien Hoa Province. They'd only arrived at Anderson when they were re-deployed to Binh Duong Province in an area known as AO (Area Operations) Surfers, about forty kilometres north of Saigon.

Around this time I happened to be over near the task force helipad and I could hear the regular thump, thump, thump of a lot of helicopters. I walked to the top of a rise to see what was going on. Suddenly, two rows of American helicopters, twenty metres apart, ten choppers in each row, one behind the other, came in over the rubber trees. They hovered over the helipad for what seemed only about six seconds to enable two companies of diggers in operational kit to scramble aboard.

As soon as the last man was aboard each helicopter, they lifted up and flew off. These were followed by another twenty helicopters only seconds behind them. They also hovered for about six seconds and another two companies jumped aboard and they also lifted as one and headed off following the first twenty choppers. In this twenty or so seconds, with meticulous timing and precise organization, a whole battalion of rifle companies was airlifted and on the way to the AO.

It was common for us to be airlifted at platoon level on three helicopters or even a company on ten helicopters, but the four rifle companies of a battalion was a sight to see. It's obvious a big operation is underway somewhere, the skies are alive with helicopters coming and going with stores slung underneath. Chinooks are also in the air carrying huge amounts of stores in their rope cargo holders slung underneath the aircraft. It seems you only have to look to the sky and you'll see Iroquois helicopters with a 105mm pack howitzers being transported forward to a fire support base.

Back at 1ARU we're told the VC are making large scale incursions into Saigon and, furthermore, there's reportedly a number of enemy regiments in the AO. The movement of 1RAR and 3RAR north to Binh Duong Province on 21/04/68 was the commencement of Operation Toan Tang and both battalions were heavily engaged in contacts with the enemy.

On the night of 12/05/68, 1RAR and 102nd Field Battery located at fire support base Coral were subjected to ground attacks by a large force of enemy supported by mortars which was then followed up by a further attack on 15/05/68. 3RAR Mortars and 161 Field Battery provided fire support from their position in close proximity to Coral.

On the 24th May, 3RAR redeployed further north into a fire support base called Balmoral with the objective of locating and destroying enemy bases. A troop of centurion tanks from C Squadron 1st Armoured Regiment joined them the following day to assist shore up the perimeter defence. There are four tanks in a troop and they arrived just in time in view of the large-scale enemy assault on Balmoral on the 26th May. The enemy, estimated to be a battalion sized force of the North Vietnamese army, commenced the attack with a heavy barrage of small arms, rocket propelled grenades, mortar bombs and heavy machine gun fire. The enemy pressed their assault for about an hour until they finally withdrew, taking a lot of their dead with them. Notwithstanding their failed attempt to destroy Balmoral, they girded their loins for a second attack using a larger force.

The second attack was launched in the early hours of the morning on the 28th May. The Australians met the attack by throwing into the battle infantry rifle and machine gun fire, mortars, artillery, centurion tanks using canister, and helicopter light fire. The enemy broke off the attack after a couple of hours leaving more than forty of their dead behind. During these two attacks 3RAR lost five men killed and a number wounded. Immediately after the second attack on Balmoral, I was called to the orderly room at 1ARU and told to pack my gear and march out to B Coy 3RAR the following morning joining them as a reinforcement.

Chapter 3

3 RAR after the Battle of Balmoral

✦

Joining a rifle platoon as a reinforcement isn't without its problems. Invariably, the platoon is a tight-knit unit, which relies on the trust and strength of its members as a whole in order to do its job. The men are always together in the boozer, in the lines and, more importantly, when out in the jungle; they are always in close proximity to one another, working as a highly-trained team. They rely on their own skill, training, initiative, and one another. They have only their personal weapons with which to engage the enemy.

The camaraderie and mateship is particularly strong. This is true of the whole Australian army, but those of us in infantry see ourselves in the aura of a special light. Together, and at the same time, we get soaked to the skin, covered in leeches, get boils, footrot, fungicidal crotch, stink to high heaven, get hungry, thirsty and get shot at for good measure.

As a reinforcement, you're required to join this team, take a former member's tent space in the knowledge he has perhaps been killed or wounded, and take on board all the sensitivities that go with the departure of a friend and the introduction and acceptance of you, as the new man.

Considering all these factors, I made up my mind that I wouldn't be in the lines of my new platoon when they returned to Nui Dat in a few days time.

There is one thing you have to learn in this man's army, and that is to keep out of the way of a combat unit when they return to camp after an operation. The men are tired, thirsty and quite simply don't want to be fucked around by experts. It's as simple as that. There's a very descriptive term given to some, and that's "pogo"(personnel on garrison operations). Notwithstanding the important work that pogos do, the combat soldier, nevertheless, sees himself at the top of the tree. He represents the sharp end of the stick as to what the army is about. There's no more honourable work than that given to the combat soldier who goes out into the jungle, seeks out the enemy and destroys him with his personal weapon. He lays his life on the line and is acutely aware of where he stands in the army, at the top of the food chain, so to speak.

At the end of an operation, and having put up with all the physical deprivations that goes with the lot of an infantryman, he's not in the mood to gladly suffer the approaches of a pogo, even though the pogo has an important job to perform in his own right. The combat soldier is quite prepared to overlook this aspect and sticks it up the pogo for the time being, at least, until he gets a chance to clean up and relax for a bit over a cold beer. Then, and not until then, should the pogo show his face.

The Aussie combat soldier is quite adept and highly skilled at putting the pogo in his place. Practice makes perfect and the most common expression is, "You pogo bastard!"

However, this simple and straightforward welcome is always drawn out and slowly spoken with each word emphasized so that it sounds more like, "Youu Pogoooo Baastaard."

To be called a pogo is quite derogatory and, as a general rule, is only trotted out when circumstances deem it appropriate. When the combat infantrymen are talking amongst themselves, it is quite freely used to describe everybody. The infantryman is acutely aware that he can call any non-combatant a pogo with absolute impunity, simply because he occupies the high ground in military roles. The infantryman uses the term light-heartedly, with tongue in cheek or, if needs be, garnishes it with venom, dependent upon the circumstances.

As a newcomer into the platoon, I didn't have to worry about being called a pogo. My challenge was to slide into the platoon as seamless as possible to become a fully-fledged accepted member of the team.

My arrival at B Coy 3RAR was brought about by the battalion completing a hard operation and characterized by losses of dead and wounded, losses caused by frontal assaults on the battalion's defensive position at fire support base Balmoral, and other heavy enemy contact on platoon and company patrols in the AO. With this in mind, I decided to lie low for a while when the battalion returned to Nui Dat.

Kapyong helipad, within the precincts of the battalion's position at Nui Dat, is about 120 metres west of B Coy administration buildings. Returning to the Dat, 3 RAR troops disembark from the choppers at Kapyong helipad and walk to their respective companies. In the case of B Coy, they walk down the main road, past the admin buildings and then peel off towards their platoons lines. By this time I'd actually been posted to six platoon but hadn't actually moved into the lines as such because I didn't know what section the platoon commander would end up appointing me to. I decided that I wouldn't be in the lines when six platoon returned but would report to the platoon commander about three hours later. This would give time for the diggers to clean up, relax, have a beer, and to settle down before I turned up as a reinforcement. This was a wise move because one look at the returning men left me in no doubt they were stressed to some degree and not altogether in a tolerant mood.

Later that evening, I reported to 2nd Lieutenant Morgan. We exchanged a few words in which he welcomed me to six platoon and directed me to Corporal Mooney's tent. I stopped outside the front of the tent and said to the first digger I saw, "Excuse me mate, I'm looking for Corporal Mooney."

"You're in luck, he's right here," and yelled, "Hey Ken! There's a bloke here to see ya."

Corporal Mooney came out and I said, "Corporal Mooney, my name's Stan Sutherland, I'm a reinforcement to your section."

"Well Stan, we're bloody glad to have you aboard, we've been hard pressed of late so let me introduce you around. This is Brian Mckenzie, our forward scout, we call him Shorty."

Shorty stood up, came towards me a couple of paces and offered his hand. I said, "Pleased to meet you Shorty." "Same here" he said.

"This bloke here is Rex Marsh, he's from South Australia but you'll get used to him, Rex carries the M79," Mooney said.

"G'day Rex" I said, shaking his hand firmly.

"Now this other bloke here is Brian Gibb, he's our machine gunner, we just call him Gibby."

"G'day Gibby, pleased to meet you," I said, also shaking his hand vigourously. "Likewise Stan" he replied.

"There's a few other blokes but they're still up in the boozer, but Gibby here will show you where to doss down in his tent which is just over there," Cpl. Mooney said.

"Thanks Corporal."

As I turned towards the tent Mooney said, "Look! We're all as one here, just call me Ken, but before you go, where're you from back home?"

"You probably haven't heard of it but a little town in the north east of Victoria called Yackandandah."

"I'll be buggered! I'm from Dederang, only fifteen kilometres away," Mooney replied.

"Come with me, I'll show you your digs," Gibby said.

As I went with Gibby, I thought to myself, I'm off to a good start – they seem a good bunch of blokes.

For the next three weeks, B Company didn't move far from Nui Dat and mostly we were engaged on land clearing protection, TAOR (tactical area of responsibility) patrols and convoy protection up along Route fifteen into Bien Hoa province.

Convoy protection is interesting in so far as most times we're mounted on APCs. The American drivers in the convoy are mostly African American and without exception, as far as I can see, the fuel tankers are all driven by African Americans. They hurtle along flat out. Nobody can really keep up with them and, as a general rule, we position ourselves at strategic points along the road.

A lot of land clearing has been carried out along the sides of the road back to about sixty metres from the road's edge. This provides good visibility. On one occasion, the VC made a fire lane through which to shoot at us from the western side of the road. They fired a couple of bursts as we passed. There was dead ground immediately to their rear, which allowed them make good their escape into the jungle. No damage was done, the convoy didn't pause at all and the drivers just kept going with the foot down.

Fuel tanker after fuel tanker comprises a lot of the vehicles in these convoys and I thought to myself, driving one of these could get hairy, particularly if the VC fire RPGs into them. At times, a light fixed wing aircraft flew overhead up and down the road looking for signs of enemy.

I'd now been in Vietnam a little over three months, Australia seems far away and pushed to the back of my mind to such a degree that it's almost an abstract memory. Living on the job day in day out seems to take over your mind and any thoughts of a former life are vague and distant. This is all you know now. This is your life today, tomorrow and so on, nothing else matters, any other life in the past, or in the future, is inconsequential.

Your commonsense tells you there is another life to go back to, however the thought is so remote and distant that it's not worth thinking about. This is you now, in this man's army, this is what you do, now and into the future.

We've been told that tomorrow we'll be going up Route 15 working with the armoured corps, both tanks and APCs. The operation is known as "Ulladulla" and for all intents and purposes we'll be under the operational control of C Squadron 1st Armoured Regiment, which is the centurion tank element of the armoured corps. Our job as infantry is to position ourselves in support of the tanks and virtually take over a long stretch of Route 15 in a show of force at the least.

We moved out on the morning of 25th June aboard APCs, a section of infantry to each APC. We ride on top of the APC, four diggers to the left of the cargo hatch and four to the right of the hatch, sitting on ammunition boxes. We loathe sitting in the bowels of the carrier below deck for a number of reasons. Firstly, it's hot and claustrophobic. The smell of diesel and fumes tend to make you crook as a dog after a while. Secondly, you have no fix on your environment, no orientation to speak of. If you have to dismount out through the rear door or ramp, you won't have a clue where you are or, worse still, where the enemy is. And feeling crook from fumes, heat, and no sense of orientation is not a good start to a fire-fight.

The risks of riding on top, as opposed to inside, are risks the infantry prefer. Some can stand up with their head and shoulders out through the cargo hatch but there's only room for half the section to do this at any one time. Sitting on top, in the fresh air, able to see where you're going is far more preferable. A section of infantry on top gives the APC crew commander another eight sets of eyes on the lookout all round.

Everyone on board has a good appreciation of the environment and can readily see any potential spots that danger may come from.

About three kilometres north of the village of Phu My there is a road which goes north-west to the banks of the Song Thi Vai river. At this point, the river is quite estuarine and about five hundred metres wide. A curfew exists from dusk to dawn and anybody caught out after dark is fair game. On the first night, some sampans, quite large ones, came chugging up the river to be met by the searchlights of the tanks as they came around the bend in the river. The sampans had nowhere to go and were like sitting ducks. A good sportsman doesn't shoot a sitting duck but, in war, a sampan loaded with supplies for the enemy is fair game. The tanks saw to that.

The centurion is a good-looking tank. I stepped one out and it worked out to be about nine metres long and three metres wide and about 2½ metres in height. The turret is set in the centre and the long gun barrel protrudes well beyond the front of the tank and, as far as tanks go, they're large; but they have a graceful appearance and, despite their size, they're quite sleek.

Once the tanks had the sampan in their searchlights it was done for. The main guns were loaded with high explosive rounds and, *bang*! no more sampan. Seven sampans came along during the night and all were blasted out of the water.

For the infantry it's interesting working with the tanks, and indeed the armoured corps as a whole, particularly in light of their firepower. The shot most favoured by the infantry is the twenty-pound canister. This has a giant shotgun affect that cuts a swathe through the jungle or open ground to warm any infantryman's heart. When an infantry company works alone in the jungle it's all hard slog, tanks are more or less restricted to the edges of the jungle and can't penetrate into the depths where we have to go. Jungle operations are a hard slog day in day out but that is where the enemy bases are, so we have to go in and ferret him out. Working with the Armoured Corps tends to make us mounted infantry. We can cover far more ground, riding in style. As the diggers say, a third class ride is better than a first class walk.

Riding on APCs all day is not physically hard for the infantry. The combination of armour and infantry provides more fire and man power. As for the infantry, we benefit by the extra firepower. Some APCs are armed with .50 calibre guns and others have twin .30 calibre machine guns. The tanks carry armour piercing, high explosive and canister rounds. They also have .50 cal and .30 cal machine guns. This extra heavy firepower was more than welcome in the defensive positions of fire support bases Balmoral and Coral a few weeks earlier.

One thing is for sure though – when you're working with the armour, everybody for miles around knows you're in the neighbourhood. Tanks creak, groan and clink along, making a hell of a racket, and the APCs have the continuous resonance from their diesel motors. Both combined put out a strong signal, "Here we are."

From the armour's point of view, they like having infantry around, particularly at night when the infantry can protect their flanks. Provided they know where we are, it gives them an added sense of protection from that direction, especially from close up rocket attacks. Infantry prefer to be dismounted and away from the armour, but it's good to know they're handy and nearby if all hell breaks loose. Armour makes too much noise for us, and they stand out silhouetted at times. At night, the tropical moon throws a strong light and more so on a full moon letting you see quite a distance. To me, it seems there is always a lot of clanging, metal on metal, albeit a lot of troopers put their London runners on at dusk.

When the sampans were heard on the river with their little motors chugging away, the tanks started up their auxiliary motors to run their big searchlights and traverse their 84mm main guns; this action tends to shatter any piece and quiet.

When you have a sampan on the sit and a twenty pounder on your side, the noise goes with the job. The sampan's motor makes its own din and tends to cancel out the noise from the tanks, especially when the tanks are five hundred metres or so away.

Infantry rely on stealth and quietness, notwithstanding the different cultures, both forces combined pack a punch. The enemy, well aware of this, will generally only engage if he thinks he can inflict damage without getting hurt too much himself. He has to readily have at his disposal firepower and manpower if he wants to fight against tanks and APCs as well as infantry. This makes it difficult for the Viet Cong. Armour is always moving about the country unless it's employed for base defence as in a fire support base or similar defensive position. Time is needed to muster a sizeable well-armed force with heavy weapons. Enemy movement is by foot and therefore it takes time to get a suitably sized and armed force to where it's needed. In spite of these problems there has been times when the enemy has made a stand and fought against the tanks.

After the sampan engagements, we patrolled around the countryside for the next five days. The only thing we came across were woodcutters who used the wood to make charcoal to sell in the larger towns. Their kilns stand about head height and are approximately two metres across. The walls slope inwards, meeting in a dome at the top. The wood is put into the kiln and set alight, and, at a point where it's burning well, the opening is blocked up. A small hole at the top lets the smoke out. When the charcoal is ready, it is allowed to cool and the villagers bag it up and then wait at the side of the road for transport to take the charcoal to the markets.

Today we came out of a jungle area and passed through a section of prickly bamboo, which gave way to rice paddies. We emerged from the bamboo. My section was the lead section and we were walking between the edge of the rice paddies, which are now full of water and the bamboo. About forty metres away a farmer was ploughing his field. The plough was being drawn by a single water buffalo. The farmer, seeing us, and knowing his buffalo would go crazy once it got a smell of us, stopped ploughing and he went to the front of the buffalo and took hold of its nose ring to control it. As we neared, but still a good twenty metres away, the buffalo started going berserk. The farmer couldn't control it, he lost his grip on the nose ring and the buffalo knocked him over, trampling him underneath before bolting. The plough went over the top of him, ploughing him like compost into the field.

At first we thought the farmer might have been badly hurt but a second or two later he emerged from the mud and slush and stood up, dripping mud from head to toe. He reminded me of my mother making lamingtons by dipping pieces of sponge cake into a bowl of melted chocolate and then holding the cake above the bowl until the excess chocolate dripped off. When we saw that he was able to hobble to catch his buffalo we continued on our way in the knowledge we'd just won another heart and mind.

Being the end of June it pours rain every day, generally commencing mid to late afternoon. The water lies in big pools, sometimes six inches or more deep and many metres wide and long. There's no way to avoid the water, your boots and feet are wet twenty-four hours a day. Small streams in the dry are now rivers and we wade across up to our armpits holding our rifles above our heads. There is no chance to dry out before nightfall so you're wet all night. You sleep wet and you get up wet, that's how it is.

The combination of perspiration, humidity and continual wet makes you stink. At night you hop into your silk and put your head in to escape the mosquitoes, but then you can't sleep because you stink so much and you can't stand yourself so you poke your nose out of your silk so that you can breathe fresh air. The atmosphere hums with myriads of mosquitoes waiting to get their chance at you and you hope they don't find your nose. All sorts of noises prevent you from sleeping and, although you're tired, sleep doesn't always come that easy. Then it seems you just get to sleep and someone is shaking you for picket duty. What a bugger!

While you're sitting on picket the mosquitoes get a good crack at you. We carry small plastic flasks of mosquito repellent to rub all over our shirt sleeves and shoulder areas of our shirt as well as face hands and neck in an attempt to ward them off but this gives only limited success. You sit on the gun, getting eaten alive by mozzies, the repellent adds to your overall smell.

When patrolling during the day, we stop for a spell and sit on our packs to avoid sitting on the wet ground. If you continually sit on the wet ground the cheeks of your backside end up with little sores, itchy little sores. What a bugger! Leeches pick up your body heat and you watch them heading your way, bringing their back half up to their front half until their body is arched, then the front half extends forward heading towards you. You survey the scene out to about two metres, you count a dozen or so, all anxious to be the first to draw blood. Again – what a bugger! In this man's army though, you put up with it and get on with the job.

We arrive back at Nui Dat late afternoon on 30th June. The men are anxious to clean their weapons, have a shower and get to the boozer for a couple of beers before the evening meal. Shorty comes over to my tent and says, "Stan, tell the Baron and Gibby there's a card game in my tent as soon as mess is finished, we want six players."

"Yeah, well count me as a starter Shorty, I'm feeling lucky and might clean up."

"Bugger you mate! I'm cleaning up tonight!" replied Shorty.

Meeting up with the Baron and Gibby, I tell them about the card game and they're anxious to play. We down a couple of beers before joining the mess queue. Everyone's in a good mood and looking forward to a nice hot meal of fresh food for a change.

It's surprising the effects of two small cans of beer upon you when all you've been drinking is lots of water, interspersed with the odd pannikin of tea or coffee. The four pints of water you drink on average each day flushes out your system and reduces your tolerance to alcohol. For fifteen cents a can it's really good value. For thirty cents you're close to drunk. Anyway, all the diggers in the mess queue are happy.

The evening meal completed, the card sharps gather at Shorty's tent for the big game. Rex Marsh volunteers to be banker. Everyone dips into their wallet for some MPC. MPC is Military Payment Currency and represents American dollars, the manner in which we are paid. The American military establishment worldwide is huge and the US government wants to limit American greenbacks circulating on world markets. The US dollar is by far the dominant world currency and it stands to reason that arms dealers are more than willing to accept US dollars as payment and quite often will only accept US greenbacks. This scenario becomes a double bladed weapon for the US, in that their own currency can be used to purchase weapons for use against the US military. One way to curtail the circulation of US greenbacks is to pay the many hundreds of thousands of US military personnel stationed around the world with a currency substituting for US greenbacks.

In the normal course of events, MPC should only be good for use in American military post exchange stores and other on-base facilities, however MPC circulates freely amongst the Vietnamese community at large. In my view, this can only happen when very senior US personnel have the ways and means of converting MPC back into regular US currency. MPC is traded on the Vietnamese market as ordinary US dollars, thus thwarting the principle. A couple of times a year at a predetermined time and date, all military bases are closed and all military personnel with MPC have to exchange it on base – say before 1600hrs – for the new issue of MPC. The new issue is a complete colour and design change so that no relationship exists between the new and the old. After 1600 hrs or the predetermined time as the case may be, your old MPC is totally worthless and cannot be changed for the new. By doing this, Vietnamese middlemen and bagmen are caught out on the float, unable to exchange the old MPC for which they have given good value to underlings in the market. We hear rumours of suicides and all sorts of drama with respect to MPC money traders caught out in the cold and who have lost everything. MPC is issued in notes commencing at the five cents level. This note is 105mms by 55mms and going up the range there is, ten cents, twenty five cents, fifty cents, one dollar and so on.

Our Australian dollar pay is converted into US dollars and entered in our pay book as US dollars. In drawing pay, we naturally receive US dollars by way of MPC.

The card game is about to start and everyone's busy buying chips from Rex, the banker. There's no electric power at this stage into the lines but we're informed the engineers are working towards achieving this. Meanwhile, our lighting is via a small fluorescent light powered by a discarded PC 25 radio battery. We bribe the platoon signalman to furnish us with his discarded batteries which still have a reasonable amount of power left in them. The signalman regularly changes his battery well before it goes flat. This prevents the platoon commander or senior NCO from having to contend with a flat battery at an inopportune time such as in contact with the enemy.

Our fluorescent light purchased from a store in Baria, the provincial capital of Phuoc Tuy, throws a good light for the game. The game decided upon is poker, a favourite, but every now and then the game switches to seven-card stud poker or pontoon. Shorty attends to the first deal, shuffling the cards at length.

Gibby pipes up. "For Chrissake Shorty! Don't shuffle the tits off the queen, get on with it!"

"You can all shut up, I'll shuffle as much as I like."

The game proceeds, everybody's feeling their way, placing cautious bets until they sort out in their minds how the game is going. After an hour or so there is no clear winner evident, but the bets start to get to the game limit of a dollar per bet. The conversation begins to wander away from the game, a normal feature. Rex Marsh interjects, "Look you blokes, I'm only a few dollars up at this stage but I'm determined to kick arse here tonight."

"Like General Giap, eh Rex?" I suggest.

"What are you talking about Stan, who the hell is General Giap?"

"He's our adversary mate, he's the man we have to beat! He's the North Vietnamese supreme military commander and he sees himself as an international arse kicker."

"He can bugger off, he's not going to kick my arse," remarked Rex.

"Nor mine," said the Baron

"Or mine," said Gibby.

"Well, it's his job to try and he's got a few things going for him," I said.

"What do you mean anyway Stan, by international arse kicker?" asked Shorty.

"Well, Vietnam's been dominated by the French as a colony of theirs for the last 150 years or so. Then along come the Japs during the Second World War, and they kick the French out. After the war's end, the French come back to reclaim their colony, the only problem is, the Viet Minh, who numbered in the many thousands also fought against the Japs and they were well armed. The French gave the Viet Minh one or two hidings but they were still able to take the French on at Dien Bien Phu in 1954 and win. Now Giap first fought against the French prior to the war, then the Japs, then the French again after the war, and now the Americans, Australians, New Zealanders, Koreans, even the Vietnamese who don't support him. If that's not international, I don't know what is."

" Shit Stan! How do you know all this? You're not bullshitting us are you?" asked Shorty.

"No Shorty, this Giap bloke wrote a book, it's simply called *Giap*. He even spells out in his book how he's going to beat us. I read it before coming to Vietnam."

"Well, it wouldn't be hard to beat the French, they're fuckin' useless! It's my deal, hand the cards over here Rex will ya," said the Baron.

Rex pushed the stack of cards towards the Baron and, as the Baron reached to scoop them up, he said, "We're a different kettle of fish, anybody can beat the French, Napoleon won their last battle for them, they've lost every bloody battle since, this fuckin' Giap bloke can't claim fame for beating them, everyone has."

"Yeah, I don't know, when you've been dominated by foreign powers for 150 years or so, you just want your country to yourselves, no foreigners telling you what to do, or the like. It's a pretty powerful argument from which to garner support from the people," I said.

"Yeah," said Shorty. "You're bloody right. Deal me two cards will you Baron. We'd be the same back home, no bugger wants another power making you lick their arse."

"Then what the fuck are we doing here – we don't want to push them around do we?" asked Gibby.

"No mate, we don't, but we have to pay our insurance premium," I replied.

"What fuckin' insurance premium Stan, what the hell are you talking about," said Gibby.

"Look, we're basically a small country, there's only about fourteen million of us, we need some big and powerful friends to help us out if we're ever in a jam, like the Second World War for example, we would've been buggered if it wasn't for the Yanks. It's simply a matter of you scratch my back and I'll scratch yours. Morality doesn't come into it, national survival has to always outrank morality. Those silly buggers marching down Pitt Street with their banners, they haven't a clue where we fit in the world. They have this naïve view that you can just step aside from the power play in global politics. They've got their heads up their arses that far they can't see for the dark. They wouldn't know the type of pressure the Yanks can put on us as a country. Now, I'm not saying they would, but they sure as hell could. For a start, they'd only have to sell down the Australian dollar if we don't toe the line. Australia is a large trading nation, if they did that, that's enough to fuck us. That's how they brought Great Britain to heel over the Suez crisis twelve years ago. If they can threaten to do that to the Poms, another nuclear power, they can sure as hell do it to us," I said.

"Jeez, Stan! It's good to have you in our section, someone who knows what's going on for a change, not like these dickheads here," Gibby said.

"If we're dickheads, how come we're winning and you and Stan are losing. You're the dickhead Gibby," said Shorty.

"Stuff you Shorty, anyway, I know where you're coming from, but why Vietnam?" asked Gibby.

I replied, "Well, Vietnam is just the battlefield, just like the Duke of Wellington picked a small town called Waterloo to do battle against Napoleon, so have the Yanks picked Vietnam to make a stand against communism. Nobody gives a stuff about Vietnam, or its people, it's the war against communism that counts. This is the battlefield and someone's arse has to end up being kicked, like on all battlefields. Our problem is the division back home on the war, politicians can sell the army down the river and if they do, where in the hell does that leave us?"

"Up shit creek without a paddle," said Shorty.

"Yeah, there's no bloody votes up shit creek, that's for sure," said the Baron.

"C'mon, all this bullshit is holding up the game. It's your bloody deal Stan, you started all this crap about Giap," said Gibby.

"Yeah that's true, but the bastard's just out there beyond the wire,." I said, pointing towards the perimeter only a hundred metres away.

Everyone turned their head towards the perimeter as if they expected to see Giap peering through the wire.

"Fuck Giap, I've got some money to win here, I'll cover you Gibby and raise you a dollar," said Shorty.

Everybody concentrated on the game and a few more hands were played out before anybody spoke a word other than on the game itself. Rex opened up the batting again. "Tell me Stan, do you support this war?"

"It doesn't really matter whether it's this one or some other bloody war, we can't let communism take over countries by the barrel of a gun. They're the ones that put up walls to keep their people in. If communism was so bloody good for everyone, why do they have to do that? Anyway, that's my position on the war. I don't want to be without a position, such as, I'm only here because the government sent me here. Bugger that, I'm a volunteer. I like to think I have a mind. The government has a position on the war and so should we one way or the other. I really wouldn't want to fight a war in which I didn't agree in principle. We're supposed to be the good blokes, but we're in this man's army though, and we have to obey orders, irrespective," I replied.

"Yeah, you're right mate, ours is to do and die not to reason why," said Shorty.

"Fuck me Shorty! Stan just told you, you have to have a position and he's right – it's good to know what you're fuckin' dying for," said Rex.

I said, "You know, during the Second World War, there was a Yankee general, Paton I think, who said he didn't want soldiers prepared to die for their country, he wants soldiers who were prepared to make the other bloke die for his."

"You're right, I must be a dickhead like Gibby said. Now, can we get on with the game here, no more fuckin' politics," said Shorty.

The game proceeded for another couple of hours until about an hour after lights out. By then the fluorescent was beginning to flicker and dim. Gibby said, "Hey Shorty, put the squeeze on the sig for another battery, this one's just about fucked, it won't last another game." Shorty, halfway out of the tent, turned and said, "I'll see what I can do."

I ended up being five bucks down on the night. The Baron was the winner, pulling up nearly twenty bucks in front.

He said, "Thanks to you blokes, I won't have to draw any pay next payday."

"We'll get it back next game, don't be too bloody anxious to spend it at the boozer, anyway, I'm buggered and hitting the sack," I replied.

The others also left to go to their tent. By this time the lines were quiet. Six platoon, apart from the picket doing his shift on the gun, had turned in for the night.

The following morning it was pouring with rain. The grass under the rubber is now about one hundred and fifty millimetres high and very green. The whole landscape's green, everything's green merging with more green. The days are very humid and the skies are grey overhead.

On 3rd July, the Battalion was airlifted by chopper to relieve 1RAR in AO Birdsville, in Bien Hoa Province. We've been deployed to deny access to an area called the rocket belt. The American bases at Bien Hoa and Long Binh are often rocketed from the east. Companies were positioned to act as blocking forces to inhibit the enemy's ability to rocket and mortar the bases. Platoons patrolled during the day but there was little contact with the enemy, which suggested the operation was successful.

After a couple of weeks we were re-deployed by chopper into the south of Bien Hoa. The Hat Dich, as it is known, encompasses a large jungle area, extending south well into Phuoc Tuy Province and westward across to Route 15 in the west of the province. In this large jungle zone the VC lay up in their bases, all their main and local force units, 274 VC Regiment, D440 and D445 Infantry Battalions are often in the Hat Dich. They feel relatively secure because the area is so large, and in here they can go about training, building bunkers, tunnels and fighting trenches etc. VC Bunker systems are extremely well camouflaged and cunningly laid out.

The enemy use this area for establishing staging camps from which to prepare for attacks against Saigon and Bien Hoa, as in the instance of the Tet Offensive six months ago. The VC has numerous networks of bunker systems and, if attacked, quite often pull up stumps and withdraw through the thick jungle to the next system. The only way for us to deal with this is by regular aggressive patrolling in force over a given period to all the grid squares in the zone.

Mini RAE (Royal Australian Engineers) teams with explosives accompany battalion operations and it's their job to destroy camps and bunker systems as they're found. We assist by ring-barking the trees with our machetes. Small tell-tale signs betray a bunker system's presence: saplings cut down to be used for shoring up the ceiling of a bunker, or making a planning table and seating.

Our section scouts are very good at picking up sign that puts us on notice a bunker system was probably nearby. Furthermore, the heavy body odour, an extremely identifiable characteristic of the Vietnamese, often raises the hair on our necks. This strong indigenous odour is a good indicator that a bunker system is nearby and probably enemy occupied. The VC odour varies in strength from bunker to bunker system and a strong, fresh odour often spells trouble ahead, raising our senses and alertness.

The Battalion was inserted by air into AO Yass. Fire Support Base Archer was established and secured by D Company. Artillery support located at Archer is provided by 161 Field Battery. A further fire support base, Hawk, needed to be established east of Archer and A Company moved out straight away to secure and establish it. Once Hawk had been established, Battalion Headquarters, D Company and 161 Field Battery left Archer and moved into Hawk. B & C Companies were charged with patrolling the area and laying down ambushes on significant tracks used by the enemy. There was a measure of success in that five enemy soldiers were killed between the 18th and 23rd July.

In one contact with the VC, 6 Platoon was the middle platoon in the company line when we came across the junction of two tracks. They were both well worn and by appearance, recently used. One thing about the wet season is that each day's rain washes away footprints. Therefore, if you come across a track with footprints on it, it's a safe bet they've been made in the last twenty-four hours or so. The company line came to a halt and we were ordered off the track ten metres but remained spread out. The company had a large footprint, probably extending to around eight hundred metres along the edge of the track. A lot of the troops in the middle of the line had no clue how far up the head of the column was and they were also unable to see the track as it wound in and out through the jungle and prickly bamboo. Prickly bamboo presents an impenetrable wall of vegetation denying you the ability to see through it.

I was standing, waiting for the company to move forward, when suddenly, immediately to my front at a distance of about ten metres, I heard excited voices speaking Vietnamese. The only person I could see to my right was Shearer Newton and he must have heard them also as he was looking straight at me.

I gave him the thumbs down sign to indicate enemy and both of us immediately went down on our knees, with our rifles at the ready. The voices, now more excited than a moment before, came from the same spot, which indicated to me they were propped for a moment. I slowly slid my pack from my back and edged forward in an attempt to see them. The adrenalin kick was severe and my heart was pounding in my chest so much I could actually hear it in my ears. I thought, "Shit, they're bound to hear my ticker."

I paused for a while to let my heartbeat subside to something near normal and also to collect myself. If possible, I wanted to engage the enemy with a degree of control over my emotions. I was conscious of the fact that I wasn't scared, but my feelings reflected anxiety and, perhaps, apprehension. From my position in the company line I wasn't expecting to come across the enemy and their sudden and close proximity took me completely by surprise. It only took a few seconds for me to collect myself, but it seemed like minutes. The enemy were still talking excitedly, which indicated they were aware that something was wrong and that we're in the area, although they had no idea where we were, and in what strength. I moved forward a little trying to peer through the scrub as best I could and, at the same time, careful to make no noise.

I was carrying an SLR and knew that I had to get a good clear shot. I'd moved about five metres and had their position fairly well pinpointed but still couldn't see them. Their voices were now a little more controlled and nowhere near as audible as a minute ago. I was now convinced they were aware we were nearby somewhere. My mind was racing as to what to do. I know where they are but can't actually see them. I thought, do I jump up and rush them, firing as I go? The element of surprise is on my side, but they're also alerted now and will be ready for anything. I made up my mind that I had to take the chance and surprise the hell out of them, shooting one first and not waiting to see the results, but immediately turning the rifle on the other. I slowly came to full height and gripped my rifle ready for the encounter. Suddenly, off to my left, a shot rang out, followed by some diggers yelling. The two VC near me took off. I only got the shortest of glimpses as they vanished into the jungle. Had they sprung my way, they were in for a shock. Shearer was ready as well as myself.

Their quick exit in the opposite direction was a lucky break for them, and perhaps even for us. Once all the excitement had died down, we found out it was a shot from another platoon eighty metres up the track, resulting in one VC killed. Obviously, there were more than just the two VC near me and Shearer. On closer examination, it was found that the dead VC was an enemy doctor. He was carrying a bolt-action rifle, about First World War vintage, but being a doctor, he probably didn't envisage fighting as such, and carried an old weapon never expecting to use it.

The Company was positioned for return to Nui Dat by chopper late in the afternoon of 23/07/68. As we quietly waited at the jungle's edge it wasn't long before the regular thump, thump, thump of the Iroquois helicopters could be heard coming in low over the prickly bamboo. The lead chopper came over the radio, "Ground-force one this is Hawk-Eye Two, throw smoke over."

"Hawkeye Two this is Ground-Force One, smoke thrown over."

"Aahh roger, Ground-Force One this is Hawk-Eye Two, I see yellow smoke, confirm yellow smoke, over."

"Hawk-Eye Two this is Ground-Force One, aahh roger, yellow confirmed, over." "Ground-Force One, this is Hawk-Eye Two, roger out."

Orders were given and the troops made their way to the edge of the landing zone. In a matter of a few seconds the company was airborne. Because of my long legs, I liked to get the seat on the edge, and, therefore, I was generally the last to scramble aboard. The choppers had no doors or the doors were slid back wide open to facilitate rapid boarding and disembarking. Sitting on the edge was like a ride at Luna Park. The chopper took off with its nose down and tail up suddenly gaining altitude and banking at the same time. You felt an urge to hang on but there was nothing to hang on to. The choppers gradually gained height to about six hundred and fifty metres, flying in two rows of five. The distance between each row was about sixty metres. It looked strange to just look across and see the chopper opposite full of soldiers, seemingly suspended in the air.

Looking to the ground, the rice paddies in various stages of cultivation and planting, presents a mosaic pattern of light and dark. The majority of fields are flooded, reflecting the sunlight in various colours of yellows and browns, set out in the rectangles and squares of the rice paddies. The average field seems to be about a half acre, with a few smaller, and a few larger. The whole countryside looks like a giant quilt of yellow, green and brown.

Flying in over Nui Dat, the only visible signs of civilization is various corrugated iron toilets and ablution blocks constructed in the open. Everything else is under the canopy of the rubber trees, or in amongst banana groves, now in full leaf. It's difficult to imagine the Dat as being home to thousands. There is little evidence to this effect from the air.

The choppers landed at last light of the day, the three platoons and company headquarters jumped off just as it was starting to rain quite heavily. By the time we were fifty metres down the road, you couldn't see more than ten metres in the deluge. I walked passed the company orderly room and peeled off left towards six platoon lines. The ground was covered in a sheet of red water. If you didn't keep to the track you fell into weapon pits situated to the left and right of the tracks. These were now full of water and quite indistinguishable. I was walking a few metres behind Private Routledge when, suddenly, he completely disappeared from view. The only thing

I could see where he was moments before was a bush hat floating on the water. Near the hat, was a swirl of red muddy water.

This photograph highlights the presence of weapon pits near the tracks to the lines. Pte Routledge fell into one during a monsoonal downpour.

Routledge's head momentarily came to the surface, and disappeared again under the water. He bobbed up again after a few seconds having got a kick off the bottom of the pit, but his heavy pack and rifle took him under again. The next time he came up I was able to lean across and take his rifle from him before he disappeared again. Without his rifle his hands were free to enable him shed his pack, which he pushed across to me on the next surfacing. Free of his load, he was able to get to the edge of the pit and I pulled him out. The pit he went into was an in-depth machine gun pit at least two metres square and, having never been used, it hadn't occurred to anyone that it was dug too deep in the first instance. It was well over Routledge's head.

"Christ, Stan! I thought I was going to drown, I couldn't get my bloody pack off, look at this mess, there's pits everywhere but you can't see a damn thing. It's just as well you were behind me."

"You just vanished mate," I said. "But your hat tried to swim for it – here, I've fished it out for you."

"Thanks, I'll shout you a can at the boozer later."

"Anytime," I replied.

I made my way towards my tent keeping my eyes to the ground watching each step. Once I got level with the first tent I knew I was right from then on as no pits were between the rows of tents.

The rain poured down for about twenty minutes accompanied by loud claps of thunder and sheets of lightning. Most of us just took our filthy clothes off and had a shower via the cool and fresh downpour.

We were able to have a few days rest. During this period Cpl. Ken Mooney came up to me and said, "Stan, you're probably already aware that Shorty is having trouble with the forward scout's job, he's smoking non-stop. The poor bugger never smoked at all until coming here, he reckons he's now up to sixty a day. On top of all that, his nerves are stuffed."

"Jeez! That's a lot of fags. I never smoked either but I'm only smoking four or five a day tops, and then I only puff on them. I smoke these bloody mild cigarettes, Winstons, I don't do the draw back though, it would kill me."

"Well, what do you reckon, will you take it on?"

"Yeah, look I'm happy, but are the other blokes in the section happy for me to do it?"

"As a matter of fact, I've already sounded them out. They reckon you're the best one amongst us for the job, and I agree with them."

"Well that's settled then," I said

That night, after a few beers with the boys, I wrote a letter home to my father asking him to buy a good pair of secateurs and send them across to me. Secateurs are important tools. They enable forward scouts to snip their way quietly forward through the jungle.

We were deployed again on the morning of 2nd August. A and B companies carried out an airmobile assault into a clearing in the jungle, now named Landing Zone Coolah. We were soon followed in by Battalion Headquarters and 161 Field Battery. C and D Companies were flown into "Wattle", a clearing some six kilometres north west of Coolah.

B Company established fire support base Coolah and A, C and D Companies patrolled in search of the enemy. Four centurion tanks joined us at Coolah for a few days and then moved on. The scene at Coolah was quite pretty in its own way. The fire support base covered an area about the size of two football ovals. The grass has grown to more than waist high and you can only see the upper part of the centurion tanks and their long 84mm gun barrels protruding. The artillery is in the middle of it all but not easy to see because of the long grass. When they fire their guns, however, large puffs of white smoke rise, contrasting beautifully against the green of the jungle and the blue sky. It seems much too pretty for a war scene.

Out in the jungle, the other three companies are going about their job, making a number of contacts with the enemy, killing five or six of them in the process. But, sadly, Pte. Campbell of D Company was killed by a sniper. The following day, they took on a defended bunker system and Sgt Carroll of 10 Platoon was fatally wounded by another sniper. Two other D Company diggers were wounded as well. After that, Alpha company clashed with a force of North Vietnamese, killing one who was carrying a wealth of valuable documents revealing future enemy activity planned for Phuoc Tuy Province.

Patrolling continued for a few more days and changed plans provided for 3RAR to move east, crossing Route two into AO Hammersley. The whole area is thick jungle and we marched in company strength. It was hard and slow going for two days. On harbouring up on the afternoon of the second day B52 bombers conducted a number of softening up strikes. Furthermore, New Zealand and American artillery was fired continuously into the area all night. We're a few hours march from where the strikes have been put in but the sound of the bombs exploding was an experience. A loud muffled noise like the drum roll of a base drum came our way, the dense jungle softening the noise, and it made us happy the bombers were on our side. I sat in the total blackness under the canopy thinking about what we will find when we make it to the area tomorrow.

In the early hours of the morning I was woken to do my picket and it was so dark and the jungle that dense, I had to crawl to the machine gun on all fours. Two hours later, when my picket was up, I woke my relief and went back to the gun until he arrived to take over. He arrived a minute later but I had a problem – I had no idea where I had rolled out my groundsheet for the night.

I didn't want to make any noise scratching around looking for it so I just picked a spot and lay on my back until daybreak. As it happened, it was only a few metres away, but in the conditions it may as well have been a mile. The company was all packed up and ready to move out by 0800 hrs.

There is some distance to go before we'll be in the BDA (bomb damage area). The thick jungle is slowing us down and we're not making good time. Three hours later we came across the first of the bomb craters. The blast of the bomb has peeled back the jungle to a distance of about twenty metres from the edge of the crater all the way around. The crater itself is about twenty metres in diameter and goes down into the earth like the shape of an ice cream cone. The depth of the crater seems to be approximately twenty feet and it strikes me that you could easily lower a house of average suburban size into the hole and the top of the roof will still be below ground level. We clambered over the jungle debris and found another crater and then another, and so on. The bombs have peeled back the jungle from around each crater and stacked it up in tight circular walls, making movement through the area difficult. The whole area is blasted to hell.

The monsoon rains fall every day and each crater already has water in the bottom from the rain earlier today. In a couple of weeks there will be a hundred or more swimming pools to choose from. You can't survey the scene unfolding before us without sparing a thought for the poor wildlife. We haven't seen any sign to suggest the enemy has even been in the area. We haven't even seen any dead animals, no monkeys, nothing. There's only jungle rolled back from the edge of every crater. We patrolled the area for three days and found nothing with the exception of a couple of contacts with the enemy, resulting in two enemy dead and another wounded. The whole exercise has been just one great big expensive waste of time and effort. The cost of the B52 strike alone must have been enormous. We were airlifted back to Nui Dat on 12/08/68.

Not a lot happened over the next week apart from a few routine tasks. Lance Corporal Peter Maher came up to me early one day and said, "Stan, be ready at 1700 hours for a standing patrol. There's five of us going out to the east for the night."

"What if I don't want to go?" I replied.

"Well, that's just too bloody bad mate! You're going!"

Every now and again you're selected for a standing patrol. These patrols generally consist of five men with an NCO in charge. Apart from the NCO, the others are an M60 machine gun group of two men, a forward scout and a rifleman carrying the radio. Standing patrols leave the task force after curfew in the fields and normally, we're trucked for a kilometre or so to the starting off point and then we make our way across country for approximately another kilometre where we look around for a suitable spot under cover to hole up for the night. The basic task is to keep our eyes and ears open for enemy movement. In particular, to report back by radio in the event we see a large enemy force moving on the task force. I always felt we were somewhat expendable, only five of us out there like sitting ducks.

This particular day we made across rice paddies, sticking to the bunds because the fields now have rice growing in about thirty centimetres of water. Our course took us around lots of clumps of prickly bamboo until we came across a creek. We looked around for a good clump of prickly bamboo to hide in which will give us good vision across the fields to our front. The rear view beyond the creek is compromised by bamboo; however, all things taken into account, it's a pretty good spot. We didn't want to get into our spot much before last light in case we were spotted by anyone. The machine gun was positioned and the rest of us spread out into defensive fire positions. The picket was organized for the night and we settled down to make a brew and have something to eat as last light gradually faded away.

In the early hours of the morning I was roughly awakened. "Stan! Wake up quick! They're coming towards us – they're gonna cross the creek, right behind us," PF (as we called Lance Corporal Peter. F. Maher) said, half whispering, half talking.

"What! Shit! Are you sure?'

"Yeah, bloody sure mate, they're carrying torches."

"Jeez! Are the others all awake?"

"I've just gotta wake Gibby and the Baron, I thought I'd better wake you first".

Given that we were ensconced in bamboo right on the bank of the creek meant that anybody coming across the creek had to be close to us.

Now fully awake, I whispered to PF, "Keep down, don't silhouette yourself against the skyline when you move across to them. I'm going to edge a little closer to the creek."

I pulled myself along with my elbows with my rifle held by both hands until I could get a good view of the creek. I peered into the blackness, expecting the enemy to be right on top of us by now, but I could see nothing, no enemy at all. Having wakened the other two, PF crawled back over towards me and, whispering loud enough so that I could hear him above the noise of the creek, he said, "Can you see 'em Stan?"

"Not a bloody thing. I can't hear anything either, apart from the creek."

We waited a couple of minutes but we couldn't hear anything suggesting enemy coming our way.

"You must have been seeing things PF, there's nothing out there," I said to him

"The buggers were shining torches across the creek – look, there's a torch light now!"

I looked at the shaft of light coming through the bamboo, hesitating a moment to make sure I was looking at what he indicated and said, "Shit PF! That's a bloody flare fired from Nui Dat."

"Bullshit! Are you sure?"

"Of course I'm bloody sure, you watch, as the flare swings from side to side under its tiny parachute it casts slithers of light through the bamboo. You may get a first impression of it being a torch light but on further examination it doesn't stack up to be a torch."

"Shit! What a bloody idiot I am."

"Never mind! We've all been caught like that with fire flies and flares but I must say, I've never scared the living tripe out of anyone as you just did to the four of us right now."

"Well, mate, if it's any consolation, I shit myself as well. I thought the buggers were coming right on top of us."

The others all commented about PF being some sort of dickhead and, with adrenalin coursing through our veins, it was almost daybreak before we could settle down again.

After breaking camp, and making our way back to the pick up point, we were glad PF had got it wrong and that there was no way we were going out on a standing patrol again with him in charge. All PF could do was suffer the jokes until we tired of the subject.

On arrival back at our lines in Nui Dat we were told to get our kit organized for a one-day operation to Long Son Island. Long Son is a small island just off the coast and only a couple of kilometres due north of Vung Tau Peninsula. You get the impression that you could walk to the mainland at low tide but with the island virtually surrounded by mangrove swamps you're also mindful that you'd probably sink out of sight in the mud if you attempted to do so. There weren't many battalion sized one-day operations but our visit to Long Son Island was one of them.

We were ferried in by Chinook, to the eastern end of the island on the morning of 23rd August. The only excitement our platoon had was when patrolling alongside some very tall bull rushes on our left, a Viet Cong, not knowing we were there, and us not knowing he was there, unexpectedly came out of the bull rushes within a couple of yards of Shearer Newton. Both Shearer and the VC got a hell of a fright. The VC took off back into the bull rushes before Shearer was able to line him up with his rifle. Later, riflemen of D Company were successful, killing one VC and taking possession of his AK47 rifle. Several small camps yielding food, equipment and ammunition were located during the course of the operation. We returned to Nui Dat in the afternoon.

Our platoon is assigned as the duty platoon. Being on duty involves a number of tasks around the company lines. Two other diggers from the section and myself are assigned to work at the ORs mess. This involves the setting up of tables for meals and doing whatever the sergeant cook asks us to do, such as assisting in serving the meals. At the end of each meal it's our job to tidy up the mess hall again, sweep the floors and wash up all the plates, pots, pans etc.

The three of us on kitchen duty seemed to be going well until one evening the duty officer came down to six platoon lines looking for the washing-up hands. We didn't seem to have much alternative to giving ourselves up and the three of us came forward, the Duty Officer berated us for a lousy washing-up job claiming the plates have a film of grease on them due to us not changing the washing-up water. He told us to get our backsides up to the mess immediately and wash up everything again. We made sure we didn't stuff up again for the rest of our duties.

For the next few days we remained in the company lines doing a few odd chores like cutting the grass around our tents and, in particular, the grass between the tents and the perimeter wire. These tasks were to be finished before the next operation commencing on 28th August.

Operation Diamantina is being carried out by us in the north east of the province, where the Song Rai River forms the eastern boundary. Also involved in the operation is a battery of the 2/35th United States Artillery as well as 161 Field Battery (New Zealand).

The U.S. field pieces are mobile tracked 155 millimetre guns, which can fire ninety- pound artillery rounds to an accurate distance of around fourteen kilometres. On a few occasions we camped inside the fire support base and trying to get some sleep when the 155s fire is anything but easy. The concussion picks your whole body up off the ground an inch or so and then you fall back down, jolting all the bones in your body.

Halfway through the operation, the platoon was patrolling along a track and our section was out in front. Suddenly, Rex Marsh disappeared – he was there one second and gone the next. We found him hanging upside down, having fallen victim to a Viet Cong snare. Snares are set to catch game and the size of the snare determines what sort of game they're after. In this instance it is most likely deer. While Rex was hanging there he was complaining bitterly about it not being good for his hernia. He got the hernia at the Battle of Balmoral when enemy mortars came his way. He dived head first into a weapon pit and, before he could sort himself out, another digger with size ten boots jumped in on top of him, giving him a hernia.

As he hung upside down, we discussed whether we should set our own trap, leaving Rex in the snare as bait.

Cpl. Mooney said, "You know what Rex? It's a bloody good idea, we'll set up an ambush and when the VC come along to check their snare we'll let 'em have it. You might have to hang there until evening though."

Rex was the only one who didn't think it was a good idea. Everybody else was for it.

Rex said, "Wait till I get you bastards, you're not going to get away with this! C'mon fellows be nice for a change and get me down."

We cut Rex down and gave him a minute or two to collect himself and then we went on our way again.

The following day we had another small distraction. I was the lead scout following up a track that had seen some activity on it but not anything significant. The undergrowth was particularly thick due to the preceding months of monsoon rain. On the left hand side of the track I noticed a VC marker. To the untrained eye the marker could easily have been passed by. It was a simple cluster of stones with another stone detached off to the left. This indicated a cache or the like set back into the scrub on the left hand side of the track. I gave the signal for Corporal Mooney to come up to me and when he arrived I showed him the marker.

"There's something around here on this side of the track Ken, but whatever it is they've got it in a good spot, the bush is as thick as buggery," I said

"I'll just get the boss up here to let him know what's going on, he'll sort us out for a look around. In the meantime, keep an eye out along the track – we don't want any bloody surprises."

The Platoon Commander, Lt. Morgan, was signalled to come forward. When he arrived he took a look at the marker, discussed it with us for a few seconds and deployed the platoon so that we could have a look around.

I continued to lead the section off to the left of the track, pausing every few metres for a good look in front of me. After a couple of minutes I saw what the marker was pointing to. Roughly twenty metres due left of the marker and well concealed in thick undergrowth, was a platform about two metres long and one metre wide. The top stood about a metre and a half off the ground. Pitched over the whole lot, similar to the fly of a tent, was a sheet of green plastic.

The stand was made out of thin saplings cut and lashed together with jungle vine. On the platform, protected from the weather under the plastic, were two large bags and two smaller bags. The large bags were the size of the standard Australian potato bag and were filled with rice. The smaller bags contained salt. The height of the stand ensured the goods would be out of the reach of wild pigs. We continued to look further into the jungle for other caches but this was the only one. It was common knowledge the VC maintained such supplies along tracks. These supplies of rice and salt are accessed by the VC as they require. The one at hand is capable of feeding a large force.

As a forward scout, my job amongst others is to keep a lookout for markers. Markers vary in style and layout. Sometimes sticks, sometimes grass and sometimes stones. Markers are not always consistent with the type of cache.

We cut open the bags and spread the rice and salt about on the ground. The next downpour of rain expected later in the day, mixed with the heat and humidity, would soon do its work.

During the operation a number of enemy camps were located. Food, weapons and ammunition were recovered and the camps then destroyed. Clashes with the enemy resulted in two of them being killed.

On the second last day of the operation Ken Mooney's section was in the centre when we stopped for our first five-minute smoko for the day and also to de-leech. I knew I had leeches on me, as you always do, however, I was not expecting what was revealed. I along with just about everybody else used rubber bands to put around the tops of our boots. We tucked the bottom three or four centimetres of our trousers up under the band. This made a snug fit around the bottom of the trousers and boots, which went a long way to keeping out a lot of nasties. Leeches, though, seemed to have no trouble getting under this defence and could suck away at their leisure until you decide to do something about it.

I pulled my trouser leg bottoms out from under the bands and lifted first the left leg up to get at the leeches. On the inside of the calf muscle, there was a mass of them, the size of a golf ball. Cpl Mooney was behind me and I walked back to show him. I said, "Have a look at this Ken, the buggers must be on to a good patch here. There must be ten or fifteen leeches in this one bunch."

"Shit Stan! I've never seen them bunched up like that before."

"Neither have I, but seeing is believing."

I hadn't smoked prior to coming to Vietnam but I had taken up the habit of just puffing away as did just about all other previous non-smokers. American rations provided a small packet of four cigarettes with each meal. My favourite was Winstons. They didn't seem as strong as others like Camel and Chesterfield. I lit up a cigarette and dabbed the lighted end on the leeches, which soon got rid of them. On that de-leeching, I got rid of about twenty leeches and resolved then to have more prompt spot checks as circumstances allowed. One of the problems with leech bites is they tend to itch as they start to heal. The worst thing you can do is scratch them because this makes them itch more and scratching them makes the wound bleed again. You need the wounds to heal as quickly as possible because in this man's army you get more leech bites every day.

Small pimple-like sores break out on the buttocks from sitting on the wet ground all the time. Again, these itch a lot if scratched, and the only way out is to pack your kit in such a way so you can sit on it during smoko breaks. Itchy leech bites and an itchy backside we can do without.

Some of the diggers suffer from heat rash from time to time. Me having dark skin, heat rash is not a big concern, however, from time to time I get a rash on the lower wrist and forearm where the skin is a little softer than the top of the wrist and arms. The platoon medic carries calamine lotion which soothes the rash.

All in all, we spent nine days patrolling in hot, wet and humid conditions. We were airlifted back to Nui Dat on the

5th September for a few days break to allow us tend our lines and have a little personal time out.

The following few days gave us a chance to write a few letters home, see to a few personal matters like going to the PX store, getting a haircut and visiting a few mates in other companies.

On one of these days we went to the range for a yippee shoot. The range is straight out in front of six platoon lines. These shoots enable us to get rid of old ammunition as well as check our weapons to see that they're working as they should.

The following morning I had to report to battalion headquarters for some small matter. Walking up the road out of B Coy lines, I did a left turn at the intersection to walk up the road that led to BHQ. Further up the road, walking towards me, was Major Bert Irwin, Company Commander, B Coy. Major Irwin was a good seventy-five metres away when I spotted him and we were the only two on the road. I thought, "Oh shit, I've got to do a salute on the march, what a bummer." There was no way out, no side track to deviate on, nothing. Oh well, concentrate, think back to your training and get it together. I braced up as I approached Major Irwin and by the time I had got to within twenty metres I was marching with shoulders back and arms swinging. I got to within about four metres of the Major and as my left foot hit the ground my right arm went out to the side and up at the same time my head turned sharply to the right. Looking the major straight in the eye I saluted him and said "Good morning sir" as I passed him by.

Major Irwin returned the salute and I thought I was home and away free.

"Good morning Private Sutherland, but tell me what was that."

"What was what sir?"

"That! That miserable demonstration for a salute on the march."

"I might be a bit rusty sir. I haven't had occasion to salute on the march for six months."

"Well Private Sutherland, we'll remedy that. When you finish your business at BHQ report to CSM Martin and tell him I said you need remedial training on how to salute on the march."

"Yes sir."

"Carry on soldier."

"Yes sir," I replied.

I went on my way and it occurred to me that the Battalion Commander has probably given Major Irwin a bit of a roasting over something and I was the poor sucker who happened by first, bearing the brunt of his anger and frustration. What bloody luck!

When I got back to B Company lines I reported to CSM Martin and told him why I was there. If I'd known what was in store for me I would have run the gauntlet and not done a damn thing. CSM Martin had me marching up and down the road in front of the orderly room practising saluting on the march for a whole hour. I felt an idiot. I don't know how many salutes on the march I gave to a couple of posts standing at the edge of the road, but it was more than enough.

My mates who happened to come by commented in all sorts of joking ways.

I resolved never to put myself in this position again. I'll spend time in the compound rather than be made look like a fool. However, in this man's army you soon get over having a bucket tipped over you and I resolved to move on and keep out of Major Irwin's way for a bit.

The Engineers have been working towards putting the power on to the company's lines. Tomorrow is the big day. Switch on is at 1600 hrs.

On the big day it was decided to have a game of cards to celebrate. We gathered in the canteen that afternoon after work to have a couple of beers and it was decided that this evening's game will commence straight after mess in my tent, which I share with Gibby and Baron Skell.

The card game commenced with poker, as was the norm. As soon as it got too dark to see, the lights were switched. We got a bit of a shock. Six platoon's lines lit up like Luna Park. We weren't used to light streaming out from every opened flap in our tents.

Gibby commented, "Christ, the bloody nogs will be able to see everything in here. In this light they'll even be able to see what hand I've got."

A few adjustments were made to various tents so that the light was contained, particularly the row that had their backs towards the perimeter wire. Electric power certainly made life a lot better and we soon got used to a brighter camp.

"Hey Stan, how are ya enjoying being forward scout?" Shorty McKenzie yelled from his tent.

"I can cope Shorty. I have to remember to put the safety catch back on after the section drops back though. The first time up front I forgot, but I was alright after that."

"Have you had any frights, mate?" he asked walking across to me.

"As a matter of fact I have. I nearly shit myself on that last operation, the day after Rex got strung up by the snare."

"What happened?"

"I was going along, the jungle was thick and we came into one of those areas where your sixth sense tells you to be cautious. You know Shorty, you've been there. You know what I'm talking about."

"Yeah, I know."

"Well, we're all moving quiet, everybody sensed danger and had their wits about them and their eyes peeled. I was moving cautiously. Suddenly, a bloody fallow deer saw me at the same time I saw it. The damn thing was only three metres away, it got a fright, I got a bloody fright and then it took off. It was so well camouflaged, but, Jeez mate, did I get a fright. I thought I was gone for all time."

"Yeah, you almost die. I've had it happen to me with monkeys, the bloody things have scared the crap out of me a few times".

"I tell ya what, though," I said. "I thought I'd had a couple of frights in my life before, but now I realize I only *thought* they were frights. I now know what a real fright is."

"When you can creep up on a deer Stan, you're doing well mate, they're about the hardest things of all to creep up on," Shorty said.

A few minutes later Cpl Mooney and the other members of the section came to the tent to join in the game.

"Hey Ken! Any idea when we're going out bush again?" asked Gibby.

"Na! But it won't be long, there's a bit of a rumour it's going to be a long op though. Just make sure you've all got your gear ready for a long op just in case," he replied.

"Christ, just what we need, a long op in this bloody weather. I'm getting sick and tired of having a wet and itchy arse all the time," remarked Gibby.

"Yeah, well a wet arse goes with the job," Ken answered. "Anyway, a few more months and we're out of here. Just make sure your arse doesn't get shot off in the meantime."

"Shit! A few more months is a life time here," said Rex.

"We must be coming due for a couple of days down at Vungas," added the Baron.

"Yep, after this next op we'll probably have a couple of days down there," Ken replied.

"Bloody beauty! We can all get pissed!" said Shorty.

"Yeah, and end up in the slot, specially after last time. The MPs will know we're coming and they'll be on the lookout for any drunken bums from B Company. They're not going to put up with any shit from us next time around," Ken said.

Shorty: "I still get a laugh when I think about the time we locked those Yanks in a bar and threw in a CS grenade. The poor bastards were as sick as dogs. It's just as well no one knew anything about it. The shit would have hit the fan if anyone buckled under the pressure and owned up."

"I can tell ya the Yank MPs were really pissed off by us," Mooney said. "If they weren't paired off with our MPs a few Aussies would have had a wrap over the scone with those batons they carry. The damn things are like bloody baseball bats."

"Look Ken, the Yanks are a piece of piss, all you've got to do is bullshit 'em mate. We leave 'em for dead. The Aussie MPs know when we're bullshitting but the poor Yanks, they don't have a clue. You know, it's the old story, bullshit baffles brains," said Shorty.

"That's alright Shorty, just don't get one of those baseball bats wrapped around your ears. We're not used to getting hit over the head with those damn things," I said.

"Any bastard that gives me a whack better look out, I'll kick him in the balls, after I regain consciousness that is," said Shorty.

Meanwhile, during this whole conversation, the card game proceeded in an orderly fashion and the men were thoroughly enjoying the night. Our last card game was about a month earlier and the whole company has been working pretty hard since. This was the first chance for a good social evening we'd had for a long time.

The next day we spent seeing to our gear on Ken's advice. Rumour has it a long op is coming up. That evening, Cpl Mooney, having just returned from an O group (orders group), called the section together in his tent to let us know what was happening next.

Gary Bullock

Allan "Shearer' Newton

G.P. "Baron" Skell

Cpl. Ken Mooney

Brian "Gibby' Gibb

Cpl. Ken Mooney (front) and Brian McKenzie

"Well boys, we're off to the outskirts of Baria for a week," he said. Baria is the provincial capital for Phuoc Tuy province and lies to the south of Nui Dat. The town was the stage of a lot of fighting by 3RAR, against well-positioned enemy during the Tet offensive some six months ago.

"Whatta we going to be doing there for a week Ken, checking out all the bars?" responded Rex.

"Nothing quite as exciting – we're going to be part of a defensive blocking force sitting on the outskirts of Baria."

Shearer: "I'm taking a couple of good books just in case we find ourselves sitting on our arses."

"I don't think we'll be sitting down too much, there'll be patrolling to do further out from the town, but given the whole company will be there, most patrols will be done at section strength and a few at platoon strength. But it's a good idea, take a book just in case," Ken said.

The next morning we boarded TCVs for the trip down to Baria. It took only half an hour to get there. When we arrived B coy was allocated the old Olympic Sports Ground. It had been a very good complex going back to the days of French control but no upkeep has been carried out since the French were kicked out of the place fifteen years ago. There is a fine grandstand and, off to the side of that, a basketball court. The sporting arena has a brick wall about two metres high all the way around. Six platoon is harboured up outside the wall on a bare paddock, beyond the paddock the rice paddies commence. Our defensive positions are more or less halfway between the wall and the paddies, a distance of about a hundred metres.

Our first task on arrival was to sort out our positions, which Lt. Morgan organized. This didn't take long. We were then organized into work parties to construct the Coy CP (Command Post) which is about four metres square and a little over two metres high and constructed with sand bags. It took us the rest of the day and well into the night before we had it completed. Filling and stacking thousands of sandbags is hard work in the heat and humidity – the entire platoon was worn out by 2000 hours when we finished the job.

Our first night was spent alongside shell scrapes we'd dug. The following morning the diggers set about building their own fighting bays above ground. There seems to be a competition amongst the blokes to build the best construction. There's also no shortage of architectural flair. Accessing sheets of corrugated iron and sandbags for the job is not a problem. We felt quite safe for there was no cover for any attacking force making their way towards us across the rice, which extends about three hundred metres in front of us. Furthermore, we have a troop of centurion tanks from C Squadron on our flank and a couple of rounds of canister will sort anything out coming across the rice. Without these circumstances there is no way the platoon's fighting complexes would have stood so high. Most are a metre and a half above the ground.

Cpl Mooney came to have a look at my bay. He said, "Shit, Stan! You'll stand out like dogs."

"I know, but this tank on my right is going to stand out a lot more and it's unlikely anybody will be looking at me with that there," I replied.

"Yeah, you're right. It's good to have them around at times," he said as he walked away on his rounds.

Later that day at about 1600 hrs a couple of young women came out from the nearest residential area three hundred metres to our rear. They were carrying little mats and soon made clear their intentions.

"Hey you *uc dai loi*, you want boom boom?" one asked

By this time there was a small gathering of diggers.

Again, the same girl said "*uc dai loi*, you want boom boom?"as well as giving a universally understood sign for sexual intercourse.

"How much for boom boom?" one of the diggers replied.

"Ten dollar, for boom boom." The girl doing the talking responded.

They both held their woven rice straw mats in front of them, hanging down like aprons.

"Ten dollar, buku too much." (Buku means plenty in Vietnamese)

By this time word had spread through the platoon that field service was on offer. Ten diggers were now concentrated in the group for negotiation.

"Shit, ten dollars, that's Vunga's prices. We're in the country now and they probably haven't had a wash for weeks. Five dollars is more than enough," Shorty said.

PF, holding up five fingers on his right hand said, "Five dollar."

The girls standing about fifteen metres away at the edge of the rice paddy had a small discussion between themselves and the talker then said, "OK. Five dollar."

Two diggers volunteered but within the perimeter is out of bounds and the only place available was in amongst the growing rice. The girls took the diggers (their names I cannot mention here because their mothers may still be alive) about twenty metres into the rice and lay down their mats. The rest of us stood there for a minute with grins on our faces, some of us shaking our heads. We didn't want to see any more, but as we walked back to our positions we couldn't help but take a look back at two sets of white buttocks rising and falling in the growing rice.

The wet season is only days away, it seems. Clouds appear in the sky on a daily basis. Of an evening the clouds on the horizon in the west, mainly clear away to reveal the most beautiful sunsets. The clouds remaining reflect back a collage of blues, purples and pinks.

We remained at Baria for a couple of weeks engaged in routine patrols around the area, then we went back to Nui Dat for a couple of days prior to doing a day long operation down near Cape St. Jacques. The nature of the task was a cordon and search of a reasonable sized town. We were trucked there aboard TCVs and when we arrived we found the streets of the town were set out in an organized fashion, probably French influence.

The cordon was put in before daybreak to ensure no-one entered or left the town. After daybreak, the townspeople were instructed by megaphone to assemble at the eastern end of the village. Once the townspeople had all assembled under armed control, six platoon was given the task of searching all the houses.

Going into each house with our rifles in one hand and our bayonets in the other, we methodically searched for weapons, ammunition or stores, which looked as though they could be of use to the enemy. Every house has a little bunker under the bed for the occupants to jump into in case of need. We opened drawers, looked in bins and utensils and generally had a good look around before going on to the next place. The aroma of a Vietnamese village assailed our nostrils in the confined space of their dwellings, which consist of planks of timber, corrugated iron and rice and palm thatch and an earthen floor. Most of the houses are single room dwellings, but some have two rooms. Definitely no conveniences like running water or power though. Vietnamese village people live a life of hardship that we can scarcely imagine. It is noticeable that in a lot of the houses there is at least one decent piece of furniture standing quite incongruous to the rest of its surroundings.

After I searched three or four houses I entered the next to find an old lady with no teeth confined to her bed. Dressed totally in the standard black pyjama style of dress, she looked to be a hundred years old. I looked at her a moment to make sure she posed no threat – like blowing herself up and me with her – and then I nodded to her in some form of acknowledgement. She lay on two slabs of timber set side by side to give suitable width to the bed. The planks looked about five centimetres thick. The bed was raised from the ground to a normal height under which is the family bunker. It beats me how she can lay on the planks with no blanket, padding or mattress to cushion her frail old body. A smile crossed her face revealing a lifetime of blackened betelnut gums. I wondered what was really behind the smile.

Placing myself in her position, I thought about how I would feel back home in Australia if an armed foreign soldier with total control over me simply walked in to search my home and basically do anything he wanted. I concluded that I would have an enemy for life, and no doubt it is the same here . . . especially as they have had to previously deal with the French, then Japanese, French again and now the Americans and Australians. How can it be otherwise? How can we win a war when we're compelled to search the houses of ordinary people? Our involvement in this war is too late – the seeds of loss were planted well before the Second World War and we're too late by far.

The town is set out in a rectangle, running west to east about two hundred metres in length. Three straight tracks acting as streets also run west to east dividing the town into residential blocks. On the northern side, beyond a strip of bamboo running the full length of the village, is a ditch where the villagers go to empty their bowels. The smell is horrendous but it is the most likely place they would put in some underground tunnels or caches, given the sensitivities of the *uc dai loi*. The area has to be searched.

We had the quickest look around amidst unbearable stench and a couple of times I gagged, as if to be sick, being that close to vomiting, I just couldn't get away quick enough. I thought to myself, "Christ! If they've got a cache there they can keep it." I don't know the full results of the search but at least one villager was detained.

When we returned to Nui Dat later that day I was glad to have a shower. The dirt and mud of the jungle mixed with sweat from the humidity and heat seems, by contrast, clean dirt, and is much preferable to the filth of the villages and towns. Too many cordons and searches and I'll be bound to get leprosy, I thought to myself.

The following evening, Ken Mooney came back from an O group meeting. He called the section together and opened up by saying, "Well fellas, the day after tomorrow we're going bush and I think we'll be out for quite a while. Make sure you've got good laces in your boots and the rest of your gear is in good shape. If there's any item not up to scratch go to the Q store and have it replaced first thing in the morning. Now listen in, here's the details. This is a joint operation of 3RAR and 1RAR. We'll be flying out at first light. Our job is to seize fire support base Cedar in an airmobile assault. It's B Company's task to seize and secure Cedar. When we've done that, D Company will fly in and then I guess the rest of the battalion will follow. Once D Company is in, we're going to move west to a clearing to secure a landing zone for D Company 1RAR. They'll come in immediately after 3RAR."

Pte Gary Bullock asked, "Where in the hell is Cedar, Ken, where are we going?"

By this time Ken had the map opened and he pointed to a clearing marked on the map in the north-west.

"Shit!" Pte. Bullock remarked. "That's up near the Firestone Trail, what a bastard of a place, full of bloody VC. And not only that, on the trail itself there's bugger all shade in a lot of places. It's as hot as buggery. I'm taking all my water bottles, even though it is the wet season."

I said, "Not only that fellas, the trail is heavily mined as well."

"Anyway, that's where we're going, otherwise known as the Hat Dich Zone. We've all been there before and we'll just have to make the best of it," Ken said.

We all dispersed back to our tents, making various comments about what we could expect . . . and none of it was good.

The next day we got our gear organized and took the last chance to write a few letters to family and friends. The following morning we got up before it was light and had a last check of our packs to make sure we had everything. It was still dark when we had a very early breakfast at the mess. After breakfast, we went back to our tents, hoisted our packs onto our backs and made our way up to Kapyong helipad to await the choppers. Once we got to Kapyong we painted our faces with camouflage sticks, light green, dark green, grey and black. Most diggers only used two of the colours.

It wasn't long before we heard the thump, thump, thump of the choppers coming in low over the rubber trees as they came to pick us up. Within a minute, the whole company was airborne. Having long legs, I boarded last and sat on the end of the seat with my back to the pilots. I never got used to the anxiety as the chopper lifted off and banking gaining altitude at the same time. I always felt I could fall out.

When we got to Fire Support Base Cedar we found the helicopter gun ships had arrived before us and were giving the place a good pasting with rockets and mini guns. The two gunners, one on each side of our chopper, opened up with their M60 machine guns firing into the jungle at the edge of the clearing. Once the place had been well shot up, the choppers lowered in height to a foot or so off the ground for a few seconds, just enough time for us to jump off, and then they were away.

Six platoon quickly gathered themselves under the command of Lt. Morgan and the section commanders and melted into the jungle at the edge of the clearing. Once in the cover of the jungle, the Company set about securing the area under command of Major Irwin. A few days into the operation B Company located a large enemy camp late in the afternoon. Artillery from 161 Field Battery was called in to soften the camp up. As it was late, the Company was positioned for the night.

Later, Cpl. Mooney was called away to an O group meeting. When he returned, he gathered us together and said, "Well, the bad news is six platoon is the first platoon into the camp tomorrow. Sorry Stan, you'll be leading us in," he said.

"Why not the good old spread-out lineal assault," I asked

"No! Apparently Major Irwin wants us to creep in like thieves in the night."

"Shit, that's OK for him, he's way back in the line," I remarked. "I'm going to be the first one to buy it."

"Anyway, there's nothing we can do about it, we've got the job and that's it," Ken said.

We retired back to our harbour positions and there was just enough light left in the day to organize a meal of rations.

For hours I lay awake thinking about my life and I was pretty uneasy about tomorrow. I had a bad feeling of what tomorrow might bring. I was quite sure my life was over and I thought about my family and worried for them more than myself. I lay looking up at the stars thinking about life in general. I got a little sleep, but not that much.

The next morning, straight after breakfast, we saddled up ready to go. Once the whole section was organized, I looked back at Ken Mooney to get the direction in which to proceed, even though I knew what it was. It was more or less the order to proceed than the direction. He said, "For Christ sake be careful Stan, take your time, every other bugger can wait." I nodded, giving him a wry grin, and set off in the direction he indicated.

All the camps I had previously come across were situated in thick jungle. This camp was no exception and there will be no indication where the first bunker will be encountered. The Vietnamese, without a shadow of doubt, are the world's best at bunker building. They do not disturb any jungle or undergrowth in establishing them. They're bloody good at it.

I knew I would come across the first bunker in about a hundred metres and it was all about spotting it as early as possible. I moved cautiously for what seemed to me to be about twenty minutes. I then spotted a very well concealed bunker off to my right at two o'clock. Kneeling down, I signalled, indicating to Ken the bunker's position and distance.

I thought, "Shit, I'm a bit late in seeing it and if I'm too close, I'll be in the cross fire of another bunker." I thought this even though it's next to impossible to have spotted it any earlier. I lay flat on my stomach and looked under the undergrowth. There is always about twenty-five centimetres above the ground before the undergrowth throws out leaves and branches. It is this gap that affords you the best visibility. I looked to where I thought the covering bunker would be and, sure enough, I could just make it out.

The opening from which the enemy fire is raised above the ground about ten centimetres. On top of that is a series of logs for the roof upon which has been placed about seventy five centimetres of earth, all very well smoothed out and camouflaged. If you weren't actually looking for it there is no way you would see it before you stumbled right on top of it.

The artillery had fired a lot of rounds into the system overnight and there were pockets of bamboo burning. Bamboo explodes like a gunshot when it burns. The stalks are divided into sealed sections every thirty centimetres or so and, under the heat from burning, each section explodes and it doesn't matter how logical you are, you still get a fright. Anything that goes bang under these conditions makes you jump. I removed a hand grenade from my belt and took off the insulation tape from around the lever. Having done this, I turned my attention back to the first bunker I saw and indicated to Ken that I was going to make my way closer to it. Ken nodded his head in acknowledgement of what I intended doing and he in turn signalled to Shearer, carrying the M60, to follow on. We both crawled on our stomachs, Ken about ten metres behind me. When he spotted the second bunker he pointed in that direction and gave me the thumbs up sign, indicating to me that he had it spotted and would cover it so that I didn't have to worry about it.

As I got closer to the bunker, I became a little more confident, even though I knew it was a tactic of the VC to allow you to get well into the system before they let you have it. Could this be the case here, I thought. I was comforted by the fact I wasn't following a track – that would be more dangerous. If the camp's not fully manned, they'd most likely be covering the tracks in and out. Furthermore, the artillery pounding might have convinced them to take flight. These thoughts were fleeting and my attention was fixed firmly on the bunker while Ken had its supporting bunker covered for me.

Bit by bit, I edged closer and resisted the temptation to pull the pin and throw the grenade in. Rather than do that, I looked around at the entrance to the bunker to see if any movement in or out had occurred since yesterday's rain. No leaves on the ground of the entrance had been disturbed so I passed by and moved further into the camp checking out bunkers as I came across them, noticing as well that the tracks connecting one bunker to the other were very low impact tracks. All the underbrush was tied back with fishing line. No underbrush was disturbed other than having been gently tied back out of the way. Once I was sure the platoon had a good foothold in the camp behind me I turned my head to Ken who signalled me to prop. The rest of the company moved in and set about seizing the whole camp.

The bunker system gives off the heavy odour with which we are very familiar. The rain doesn't wash it away, but actually seems to wash it into the ground, giving it a very heavy and wet type of smell. Their fire lighting areas are built out of brush to about waist height and built on a layout consistent with a public toilet block found anywhere in Australia. You walked in and around to get to the fire. This prevents any glow from the fire being seen from any direction. The system has a reasonably large assembly area, about five metres square, in which was a table and seats along each side of the table, all made out of small saplings lashed together with vines. This no doubt serves as their briefing area. Maps can be laid out on the table for reference purposes.

There's a few tell tale signs of what they eat, such as the odd empty can of mackerels and a few piles of banana skins. Today's menu from which to choose is rice, mackerel and bananas or, mackerels, bananas and rice. A discarded bra indicates females have been in the camp, and this is not unusual.

Their latrine facilities, of which there is a couple, are situated only a short distance out from the perimeter. They consist of a hole dug in the ground upon which is a covering of very small saplings lashed together like a miniature raft and extending beyond the edges of the hole. In the middle of the covering is a small square opening about ten centimetres square. Erected over the hole directly above the covering is a platform lashed together with vines standing on four small saplings for legs. The upper platform also has a square hole in the middle the same size as the one below. The hole in the top platform is directly over the lower hole in the cover at ground level. The person using the toilet squats on the top platform and directs his business through the opening on the top platform, which ensures it also passes through the opening directly underneath and into the hole in the ground. The platform is at a height that, when squatting down, the person's line of view is just above that of the undergrowth and he can look out a good distance, so getting caught with your pants down is mitigated as best it can. Their toilets give off a hell of a stink and diggers whose harbour positions are only a few metres from them genuinely have something to complain about. They're quick to let the section commander know that it's not their turn to be next to the shit pit.

Once a bunker system is under control it's necessary to man it as you would in defending it. It is not uncommon for the VC to walk into a camp, completely unaware of the fact that we've captured it. With this system under our control, Major Irwin positioned the company accordingly and six platoon was given the task of manning the southern perimeter from which there is a track going in and out of the system.

About thirty metres out from the first VC fighting pit the VC have sited a Chicom directional mine. These mines are filled with all sorts of metal objects – nuts, bolts, nails and anything else they can get their hands on. VC directional mines are circular in shape, about thirty-five centimetres in diameter and the front of the mine is concaved so that the lethal blast sends out its deadly shards of metal in a concentrated shaped pattern. Directional mines are command detonated by a small electrical current and an electric wire leads from a fighting pit to the mine but it is not connected to the mine, a horrible looking mine if you ever saw one. The mine was left in place by us for the time being.

Later that evening, virtually at last light, two VC came along the track carrying their AK 47s slung over their shoulders. Passing the mine still in place, nothing was amiss to them and they didn't give us a thought. They were fully clothed in North Vietnamese army greens and were wearing Ho Chi Minh sandals – footwear made from truck or car tyres in the form of thongs. They are quite popular with the enemy and we see a lot of them. (Looking at the sandals you think they're guaranteed to give thirty thousand miles of wear before a retread would be needed). Over their shoulders they wore a square piece of very light green plastic to protect them from the rain. The rain was falling only lightly following on from a downpour an hour earlier.

The trees were still dripping heavily and the Vietnamese, unlike us, feel the cold when it rains, hence they quite often carry lightweight plastic sheets about a metre square to use as raincoats. Once they got to within ten metres of the first pit we occupied, they thought in the poor light of the jungle we were VC just like them, and they started to walk towards us with smiles on their faces. Alas! Not so. Once they realized their mistake they got a hell of a fright and unslung their weapons in one quick flowing movement. But it was too late. They were dead before they hit the ground. The smell of blood mixed with pools of rainwater on the dank monsoonal ground of decaying vegetation permeated the air. The two dead VC looked to me like wax dummies you see in department stores. I thought to myself, what a waste of time their lives have been. They're dead but their mothers don't know it yet. Only their enemies know it and we are going to put them in the ground and nobody apart from us will know what happened to them.

Bodies start to decompose within about twenty minutes in the tropics. Large yellow and black flies soon descended on them, moving in and out of eyes, nose and mouth. The bunker system and VC toilets smell bad enough as it is and we don't want the smell of the dead as well. As we were staying overnight, a quick burial party was put to work. Shallow graves sufficient to take the bodies and a covering of about fifteen centimetres of dirt was the norm.

The next day the bunker system was destroyed. We did our little bit by ring-barking the trees with our machetes. This prevents re-establishment by the enemy at a later date. Being a large system comprising eighteen bunkers, it took the Engineers and Assault Pioneer Teams most of the day to lay the explosives for demolition. On operations of this nature, these teams are always with us.

I managed to talk them into giving me half a slab of C4 explosive . . . the best cooking fuel available. Just a small piece the size of one top finger joint is all that's needed to cook a meal and boil a pannikin of water for tea or coffee.

Once the company was clear of the bunker system it was blown up and we continued on our way in a heavy downpour of rain.

For days now we have continually been getting soaked and pools of water are on the ground everywhere, our feet have been wet for days on end. Yesterday at about midday, I got the first opportunity to take off my boots. Sitting down on the ground, I undid the laces and pulled off my left boot first. It gave a loud squelch as it came off my foot, letting the water out at the same time. Pulling my sock off, turning it inside out as it came off, a layer of skin from the whole of the sole of my foot came off with the sock. The skin was green and yellow and stuck to the sock as if it belonged. The other foot was the same.

I poured a liberal quantity of fungicidal foot powder on my feet and rubbed it all in until my feet were dry. After picking off most of the skin from my socks, I held them in my right hand and gave the socks a few good whacks against the trunk of a tree to get rid of the rest of the skin. That's what you do in this man's army.

A couple of months ago we had a change of socks brought out on the re-supply chopper. After changing our socks, we ditched our old socks in the jungle. A few days later we found an enemy camp, and there were our old socks hanging out to dry. We'd been followed by VC who had picked them up and had taken them back to their camp, washed them out and hung them up to dry. The VC found them very handy for carrying rice. This we learned from a VC subsequently killed in action and who had Australian Army issue socks on him full of rice. He'd filled the socks with rice, tied the socks off at the top, coupled them together and slung them around his neck to carry them. After that we refrained from ditching our socks.

During the course of the operation, a number of enemy camps were located and destroyed. A total of fourteen VC were killed over eight engagements. The largest engagement was by 4 Platoon B Coy when they engaged about eighty in an ambush sprung in the early hours of the morning. The battalion was not without loss and unfortunately Pte. Davidson of D Company was fatally wounded during a contact on 30th September.

During the operation we were re-supplied every three days by chopper. The terrain we covered was jungle of varying types. There was almost a week in which we patrolled high canopy jungle with only light secondary growth underneath. These areas are characterized by little daylight penetrating the canopy above. Patrolling beneath the canopy you can see a number of diggers in front of you compared to only a couple of diggers in other types of jungle where there's thick secondary growth. After a few days you get used to patrolling in poor light and when you emerge from such areas the bright light of the day hits you.

On one re-supply in high canopy and dark jungle we had to have axes dropped in by helicopter so that we could cut a clearing big enough for a helicopter to land. Our section was given the job. The landing zone to be was well positioned on the crest of a hill and we set to chopping down a dozen or so trees, stripping the branches off them once they were fallen. After about half an hours work the landing zone was suitable for a chopper to come in. I stood on the far side of the clearing we'd made and looked across the twenty metres to the other side. Where the clearing met the jungle there was complete darkness to about three metres above ground level. Visibility into the jungle beyond the clearing was zero.

On this re-supply we also received jerry cans of water for the company to fill their individual water bottles. Many times we crossed creeks from which we could fill up but there were occasions when we worked in areas where there were no creeks or rivers.

Back at Nui Dat, the Company cooks had been up very early that morning and baked fresh bread rolls, which they'd made up into salad rolls. They did this on a lot of re-supplies and we were always appreciative of their efforts. A nice fresh salad roll was a good break from combat rations. Along with the salad rolls came large cartons of flavoured milk, one for each man. Thirst was a constant companion on operations, no matter the season. A nice cold carton of strawberry or chocolate flavoured milk was a luxury. The only problem was our stomachs found it hard to accommodate it all. We invariably persevered to find we could not put our web belts back on after the indulgence.

On the 12th of October we were airlifted to the east of the Hat Dich Zone across Route 2 to near the Song Rai River. The Company continued on operations until the 21st of October when we returned to Nui Dat. All in all, we'd been out in the bush for a little over three weeks in what could only be described as hot, wet and difficult conditions. Walking back to our lines after we hopped off the choppers I thought to myself, "God, we stink!"

The next day the Platoon Sergeant came up to me and said, "In a few days time you're going to Saigon."

"Saigon, Sergeant! What do I have to go down there for?"

"I've put your name down for the Saigon Guard. A dozen of you from six platoon are going down so make sure you've got some clean clothes to take, you'll have to look half reasonable down there."

"Sounds good Sarge, at least it'll be bloody good to get away from here for a week."

"You're all leaving Friday morning. Just be ready to go when the time comes, that's all."

"Thanks Sarge, I'll be ready."

The aircraft flight to Saigon was uneventful. We disembarked and were met by a first lieutenant, a Canadian wearing an Australian Army uniform. I wondered how he got into the system. We boarded an army passenger bus to take us into Saigon. On the way in from the airport, the Canadian was giving us the do's and don'ts, nobody was listening though, the diggers were looking out the windows paying more attention to the sights of Saigon.

The bus pulled up outside a hotel in Cholon, the Chinese quarter of Saigon. There were a large number of Australian military personnel billeted at the hotel and it is also one of the places we have to guard. Other establishments are the Australian embassy and the Australian Army headquarters building. We were allocated bedrooms and given rosters telling us where and when we would be on guard duty. I was assigned to the very hotel we're staying in and I thought to myself, this will do me, I just have to walk out the front door and I'm at work and not only that, all I have to do is sit on my backside and wave the civilian traffic on. There is no parking or stopping outside the hotel for about forty metres up and down the street and anybody who tries to do so gets waved on.

The Saigon guard is a very sought-after job for infantry platoons. It gives us a week away from Nui Dat and the jungle and it is considered a holiday. Just imagine being able to have a shower every day for a week and wear clean clothes as well – what a marvellous thought it is, and we're going to enjoy it!

The rosters are two hours on and four hours off. The four hours off gives us plenty of time to wander round the streets and get a feel for life in Saigon.

The hotel I'm assigned to guard is situated on a very wide French-style boulevard. There is a service street directly out from the footpath in front. Beyond that, there's a three metre median strip with power poles and trees, then the main street, beyond which is another median strip and then a service road on the other side of the street. The street is at least sixty metres wide. The army has commandeered the footpath immediately in front of the hotel for the hotel's entire street exposure. This area of footpath is caged up with strong metal mesh and in front of the wire mesh cage are twenty forty-four gallon drums filled with concrete. On the inside of the mesh there is chest high sandbagged wall, three bags thick. Behind the sandbagged wall are two gun emplacements protected by thick concrete blast walls to the front and sides. People going up and down the footpath have to divert onto the service street when they get to the hotel. The thick wire mesh prevents people throwing in hand grenades, satchel bombs and the like. The guard on duty waves on any traffic that attempts to stop. Even the median strip has a roll of concertina barbed wire on it to prevent parking there as well.

Civilians entering the hotel are searched as soon as they enter. A lot are employed as housemaids, kitchen maids and dining room staff. A female searches the women on entering and a male searches the men. They're searched again on leaving the premises at the end of their shift. I was well settled in after a day or so and on my four hours off I walked the streets, dropped into the odd bar for a few beers and generally did the rounds. I brought with me my ration card, which enabled me to purchase two bottles of spirits each month and about four cartons of cigarettes.

It occurred to me that I could utilize my ration card by going to the American PX store, buying what I wanted and then flogging it on the black market. To do this is about as easy as buying a newspaper in Australia. I got hold of a bag from somewhere and went for my big buy up. On entering the PX, which is the same as a large metropolitan supermarket in Australia I was taken aback by the volume of cigarettes on the racks. It seemed to me that everyone else uses their cards to purchase cigarettes and on-sell them into the Vietnamese market. The Vietnamese are particularly fond of menthol cigarettes. One whole aisle of the store, fifty metres of it, is dedicated to Kool and Salem cigarettes. If you didn't see it you wouldn't believe it. I made my purchases and came out with six bottles of spirits and six cartons of cigarettes.

As soon as I was outside the PX, Vietnamese were on hand pressuring me to sell to them. It was prudent to not sell at this point as they're at the bottom of the chain and have to on-sell the goods upwards themselves. It's better to go higher up the chain, such as to a bar, where you get a better price. This is what I did. I bought a few cartons of cigarettes for a couple of dollars each and sold them for about $7.50. I bought four bottles of spirits for around three and four dollars a bottle and sold them for ten or eleven dollars a bottle.

Saigon strikes me as a modern day Sodom or Gomorrah, full of black marketeers, prostitutes, pimps, racketeers, scammers and beggars. You name it and Saigon has it, and lots of it. You wouldn't want an Australian city to fall into such an abyss. In the city square stands a pole and, from time to time, a black marketeer is tied up to the pole and shot in public.

When it was time to do my shift at the weapon bay in front of the hotel, I put on a helmet and flack jacket and took my own rifle but just lay it on the sandbags. There's an automatic 7.62mm self-loading rifle mounted on a bipod which remains in position all the time. I just have to sit here observing all sorts of traffic passing, military, pedicabs, pushcabs, barrows, motorcycles, taxis, trucks cars and thousands of bicycles.

It's interesting watching the daily life of Saigon pass by, but the events that fascinate me more than anything are the Chinese funerals. Some days two or three funerals parade by. If the deceased was a person of some station then the funeral procession is large and colourful. I've never seen anything like it. The cortege includes people wearing elaborate masks, others beating on drums, cymbals and others blowing long trumpets, making quite a racket so everybody knows they're coming. Some are regaled in a fashion like the Ku Klux Klan, wearing long white hats, which come to a sharp point a metre above their heads. The hearse is a very ornate hand-carved carriage drawn by horses, also decked out in colourful regalia.

After doing a few shifts observing the comings and goings, I noticed that one man regularly sits on the steps to an apartment house directly opposite. He wears only a pair of shorts and a singlet and invariably appears right on the dot of 1600hrs, sitting there for an hour to have a smoke or two.

Another man on my side of the street appears every morning with a small stool. He plonks it down in the middle of the footpath and sits on it to read the newspaper and smoke an elaborate type of pipe, the type where the smoker inhales through a long tube attached to a glass bubble holding water. This fellow also wears only a singlet and shorts. Where he sits is only three doors up the street on my right and, as the weapon bay is on the footpath itself, it's easy to look up and down the footpath to see what's going on.

During the course of the day I observe that a number of people wander out from the apartments across the road and walk to the gutter at the edge of the footpath to relieve themselves. They urinate and defecate in the gutter and I'm thinking to myself, "You don't see *this* in Melbourne, thank Christ!"

Another observation I made was the number of Aussie servicemen getting around town with a bottle of whisky or rum under their arm. The Aussies don't like being ripped off buying a glass of rum and coke at a local bar. They find it far more convenient and cheaper to take along their own spirits, to the chagrin of the bar owner. Bars often place an observer at the door to detect and prevent Aussies coming in with their own whisky or rum additives. The diggers find ways to sneak through and simply order a glass of coke and whisk their bottle from their pocket and put in the required amount of spirits. They can't see the sense in selling a bottle of whisky on the black market for ten dollars and buying a bottle back via mixed drinks for $80!

On the third day in Saigon, Shearer came up to me and asked, "When's your next shift Stan?"

"Not until tonight," I replied.

"Good! What's say we go out on the town for the day?"

"OK, I'm easy."

"Right to go now?"

"Yeah, let's go."

Going on a bar crawl, we'd call into a bar, tell the girls we're *uc dai loi* cheap charlies, and to leave us alone. In every bar there were always a number of American servicemen and I found them to be extremely generous and quite fond of Australians, but they're very gullible though and it's very difficult not to bullshit to them. After having a couple of drinks at about eight bars and sitting in the ninth, I noticed my slouch hat was missing and I said to Shearer one of the girls must have knocked it off when I wasn't looking.

"The bloody bitches! Don't worry we'll get it back," he replied.

The problem was, a missing slouch hat is associated with a profitable sale to some Yanks. There is no way you'd be able to convince the OC you simply lost it. The good leather general purpose boots the Aussies wear and slouch hats are the most sought after items by the Americans and they're prepared to pay big bucks for them. The boots the Americans wear are not a patch on ours.

I told Shearer: "I'll be in the shit if I don't get it back. I'll cop a fine and also have to cover the cost of a replacement one as well.

"Come with me Stan and don't worry, we'll sort these tarts out."

"Where're we going Shearer?" I asked.

"C'mon! Just to the front door."

We went down to the front door and turned around looking into the bar, which is long and narrow (nearly all the bars are long and narrow. The bar is down one side and a row of tables and chairs against the wall on the other side). "Whatta we doin?" I asked.

"We're gonna herd all these bitches, the whole twenty of 'em, down against the back wall and not let 'em go until we've got your hat back. Let's go."

The two of us made our way down the bar herding the girls before us. Some were sitting with Yankee servicemen but it didn't matter. We pushed and pulled them all towards the back. By the time we got halfway down the bar the owner was quite excited and yelling at us, something about us being "*uc dai loi* fucks causing big trouble." Looking at him going crazy spurred me on so I picked up a bar stool and waved it around above my head as if to smash up his bar. The owner, standing behind the bar, was swearing and saying, "You go. You go. You big trouble." He had his hands side by side flat on the bar "You go. You crazy," he kept on saying. I lifted the stool above my head and brought it down on his fingers, breaking a few in the process. This made him yell and scream and he was jumping up and down, swearing and cursing, half in Vietnamese and half in English.

Up until this time, the dozen or so Yankees in the bar didn't have the faintest idea what was going on, but they were starting to get annoyed. We'd turned the peace and tranquillity of the bar right on its head and had separated them from the girls sitting on their knees. Six of them got off their chairs and started to come towards us as though they were looking for a fight.

I thought to myself, "Shit Shearer! You've got me into this and now we're going to have to fight for our lives and I'm glad you're on my side." Shearer is from Longreach in North Queensland. He's a good soldier, prepared to be in anything and when he wants to be, is as wild as buggery. I thought if I'm going to have the injuries that go with the crap beaten out of me, I'll at least be able to tell Major Irwin I was set upon by half a dozen Yanks who stole my hat despite me putting up a good fight.

The bar owner, still screaming and swearing, was trying to hold up his broken fingers but they just drooped towards the floor. The Yanks looked as though they meant business and a few more started hopping up off their chairs preparing to enter the fray when it started.

By this time we had all the girls pushed hard up against the back wall. They too were screaming and calling us "crazy fuck *uc dai loi*!"

The first Yank opened his mouth and said, "What's the goddam problem here Aussie?"

Knowing we were in a tight spot and before Shearer could open his mouth to speak. I said, "This fuckin' noggy bastard is putting water in the whisky."

"What! Are you sure?"

"Yeah, bloody sure he's just ripped us off. More water than whisky."

The big Yank, turning to his mates, said, "Did ya hear that guys? This dink here's putting water, lots of it, in the whisky. He's just took these Aussie guys."

The owner of the bar, shaking his head, was swearing and denying everything

"Whisky, no have water. Whisky, no have water. *Uc dai loi* no good, he crazy fuck." He said shaking his head and nursing his broken fingers. The Yanks, however, were prepared to believe us and when the owner of the bar saw the look on their faces he ran down the back screaming and out through a door. A few of the Yanks made as if they were after him.

In the confusion, I said to Shearer, "Let's get outta here mate, forget my bloody hat, we'll go back to the last bar we were at until things settle down a bit."

We quickly walked out and went back half a dozen doors to the bar we'd last left. Sitting down at a table I said to Shearer, "Shit mate, I thought we'd have to fight like buggery back there. Those Yanks were really mad at the disturbance we caused."

With a big grin on his face Shearer replied, "No, we'd have beat the crap outta em! They looked like a bunch of remfs to me!" Remf (rear echelon mother fucker) is the American expression for the equivalent of our pogo, but I find it a dreadful form of swearing.

A Yank, seeing us come in, wandered over to our table and asked, "Were you guys in here not long ago? About half an hour ago?"

"Yeah mate" I replied.

"I've been waiting for you to come back, I thought you would, I've been looking after a hat that belongs to one of you. You guys walked out before, leaving it on a chair. I'd hate to lose my hat and I guess you guys are the same."

Three hours later, the three of us staggered out of the bar. The Yank went his way, quite pissed, and Shearer and I started walking back to the hotel. I was pleased I'd got my hat back and more pleased my face wasn't rearranged getting it.

Walking back, I said to Shearer, "That poor bugger with his fingers broken. I didn't mean to hit them so hard with the stool. All the screaming and yelling made me mad and, as it turns out, he had nothing to do with my missing hat."

"Don't worry Stan, it's Karma mate."

"What do you mean Karma? He didn't do anything to me."

"No! Not to you, but to some other poor bugger in the past. You're just the instrument for squaring up. Karma works like that."

When I got back to the hotel I went to my room to sleep it off for an hour or so before my guard duty started.

A couple of days later I went for another stroll about the city. I found the street stall vendors interesting. Some just have simple kerosene burners upon which they cook a concoction of frogs and rice, fish and rice or vegetables and rice. I find the smell is more than anything I can handle in the way of food. They often use a strong fish sauce called Nuoc-Nam, which nauseates me.

I got back to the hotel at 1600hrs to find a lot of military police there and more turning up from all over the place in their respective vehicles. There were American, Australian and Vietnamese. I had no idea what was going on. An Australian

MP, a rather tall and solidly built sergeant, said to me, "What happened, soldier?"

"What do you mean what happened? I don't know what happened?"

"Where you from, soldier?"

"Nui Dat. 3RAR. Sergeant," I replied.

"What are ya doing down here then?"

"I'm on what they call the Saigon guard."

"Well, you must know what happened. We believe one of you blokes did it."

"Did what? I don't know what the hell you're talking about."

"One of you blokes shot and killed a civilian across the street."

"Shit! Well it wasn't me. I didn't even hear a shot. I don't know anything about it."

"No, you wouldn't would ya? You blokes from Nui Dat never know anything about anything. It's always the bloody same. Nobody knows anything when there's trouble. You blokes from Nui Dat, you stick to one another like shit to a blanket. I better take down your name and number anyway." He took out a pen and notebook from his pocket.

"Pte. S.B. Sutherland 368592 Six Platoon, B Company 3RAR," I said.

"So, you don't know anything Pte Sutherland?" he asked again as he wrote down my details.

"Nothing Sergeant."

"Why am I not surprised?" he said as he walked away.

I was rather pleased with myself. The sergeant was sure I was covering up for one of my mates, however I genuinely didn't know anything about the incident at that stage and I was glad I didn't have to be untruthful about a serious matter such as shooting dead a civilian. I was glad I could answer his questions honestly even though he didn't believe me. Furthermore, I didn't particularly want to find out the details. I thought it best to not ask questions and remain totally ignorant in case the matter blows up later.

The one observation I did make was that the bloke who used to sit religiously on the step to have a smoke directly opposite never turned up again. I heard that a digger accidentally placed his rifle down too hard on the sandbags at a weapon bay causing it to discharge. The discharge occurred at the time of day when the civilian across the street sat out on the steps to have a smoke.

The Saigon guard returned to Nui Dat by aircraft and we were glad to have had a week off. It seemed more like a week's leave than work. None of us had spent time in Saigon before and it was unlikely any of us would spend time there in the future. After a few days at Nui Dat I was sent down to Vung Tau on R & C (Rest-In-Country).

My accommodation for the five days is in the town of Vung Tau itself. The Army has taken over a former hotel, which in the days of the French would have been an up-market establishment. It still is because the army engineers have done the place up. The paintwork is good, the rooms have ceiling fans, the dining room is good and it's a fine place in which to stay. The hotel is only a short walk from the town centre. Everybody staying at the centre wears civilian clothes to give it a holiday atmosphere.

On the second day at breakfast I noticed a pretty Vietnamese girl serving at the tables. I gave her a nice smile. After breakfast I said to her, "What your name?"

"My name Le Hoa," she replied.

"Le Hoa, I think I love you very much. I think I no can sleep any more. I think I have to go see Bach Si." ('doctor' in Vietnamese).

"What you name?" she asked

"Stan. My name Stan."

"Ah Satan," she replied

"Stan," I said again.

"Yes Satan," she said, unable to run the s and t together.

"Satan, you can swim?"

"Yes I can swim."

"Today, I finis work at four o'clock. We go for swim OK. You wait for me outside at four o'clock OK."

After that exchange I thought to myself, I'd better buy some bathers. This wasn't a problem, there's a shop in the centre, which sells such items. When 4 o'clock arrived I was waiting outside and Le Hoa appeared with a big smile on her face. She hailed a Lambretta and we hopped in. I didn't have the faintest idea where we were going but the further we got out of town the more uncomfortable I became. I was also conscious of the looks we were getting from the locals. An *uc dai loi* alone with one of their girls is not a welcome sight amongst the locals and, as the Lambretta passed, they stopped what they were doing and looked at us. Le Hoa had to be conscious of this as well I thought.

She eventually asked the driver to stop and we got out. I paid the driver well, putting a smile on his face. (The generous payment for services, particularly by the Americans more so than the Australians is distorting the economy. A Vietnamese tradesman working for the Vietnamese is lucky to earn any more than $25 a month. When the Yanks or Aussies pay five dollars for a taxi drive, which is really only worth fifteen or twenty cents, a ripple effect spreads through the economy, inflating the price of goods beyond the scope of the locals to pay. The large numbers of foreign servicemen throwing their money around has had a bad affect on the country overall).

Le Hoa took me down to the beach and I was the only white man around. This looks a bit dicey I thought, me out here all on my own – and unarmed.

We went into dilapidated individual change boxes on the edge of the beach. The boxes give you enough room in which to change and they're fitted out with showers. The showers have seen better days though. I thought the French colonials would have made use of them and they'd not been serviced since 1952. We had a swim for a good half hour or more and then came out. Going back into the change boxes we had a shower with fresh water and put on our clothes.

Le Hoa hailed another Lambretta and we hopped aboard. I was thinking it won't be so bad going back but I realized we were going even further out from town. We got a lot of hostile looks, but eventually, to my relief, we ended up back in Vung Tau.

We walked around looking at a few shops and, passing by one, her eye was taken by a pink handbag on the counter of an outside stall. I asked the stallholder how much. But he indicated he was not going to sell it to me because I was with a Vietnamese girl. I told him that if he didn't sell it to me I would *caki-dau* him, at the same time drawing my index finger across my throat, a well-understood universal sign. He said something to her in Vietnamese, which I took from the look on Le Hoa's face to be derogatory. I made a move as if I was going to kill him by strangulation and he decided it was better for his health to be nice. The bag cost eight dollars.

Later on, we went to a Vietnamese restaurant for a meal, which I knew to be a big risk. Le Hoa was also conscious of my concerns. The word hygiene or the practice of it had not yet established itself in Vietnam and the typical Aussie stomach is just not strong enough to handle a Vietnamese meal prepared under local conditions. The most likely consequence is a dose of the "Quick Step" as the Yanks call it.

I decided to take the risk, and, as it turns out, it was OK, but I was careful, sticking to well boiled noodles and vegetables. I gave meat dishes a miss.

After dinner, Le Hoa took me down a few streets and side streets to her home, which she shares with her sister. It seems to me that others also share – the room is divided by screens. I was a bit worried about staying the night. Being on my own in the back blocks of town anything can happen. The night was punctuated by dogs barking and gun shots. If a dog barked too much a shot was fired to shut it up and it was hard to get any sleep at all.

The following morning Le Hoa went off to work at the R & C Centre. I walked with her to the centre and I told her I'd see her at lunchtime. When I went up to the dining room for lunch, word had already spread amongst the other girls. They looked at me and giggled – they couldn't stop looking and giggling.

I spent my time with Le Hoa. She's a great girl. She knows I'm from Nui Dat. I told her I'd come back to see her. She said, "Satan no come back, he go home to Australia and no come back."

"Le Hoa. I come back for sure. Satan come back," I replied.

At the end of my five days I caught the convoy back to Nui Dat. The week in Saigon followed by another five days in Vung Tau gave me the chance to have a good rest and a look around. It was also good to get away from active operations in the jungle for a while.

When I got back to the lines at Nui Dat there was a noticeable absence of troops in the company lines. On enquiring as to the whereabouts of the men, I was informed that most of them were in hospital with malaria. Bravo Company was down to about forty men fit for duty. This in actual fact rendered the company unfit to mount company operations. Consequently, we remained at Nui Dat doing small patrols and other limited tasks. The high incidence of malaria was put down to staying overnight in enemy bunker systems. It's well known the North Vietnamese have a problem with malaria and we end up getting infected by the mosquitoes in their camps.

One evening, in the last week of October, I was on picket, sitting inside the Six Platoon machine gun bunker. The platoon has two machine gun bunkers for picket duty. One is used in the dry season because it is a pit with no roof and the one I'm in now is used in the wet season because it has a roof because it rains every day and quite often at night as well. I'm on my own, sitting here in the dark, just looking to my front. In actual fact, there is nowhere else to look, the bunker is built up completely on three sides. The front facing the perimeter wire is the only way you can see out. When you stand in the pit your shoulders are at ground level. There is a forty-centimetre gap, between ground level and the roof, enough to shoot and see through. The night is quite dark but a little bit of moonlight bathes the area outside the perimeter.

Snakes get under the floorboards of the bunker and make their home there. They quite often come up from under the boards, scaring you half to death.

Sitting there quietly, I thought I heard a noise. It sounded like a high-pitched clink like metal on metal, but light metal. I strained my eyes in the dark until I spotted movement. Once I was sure of what I'd seen I picked up the bunker telephone and rang through to the Platoon Commanders tent.

"Lt. Morgan speaking."

"Lt. Morgan, it's Private Sutherland calling from the platoon bunker. I'm on picket sir."

"What can I do for you Pte. Sutherland?"

"Sir, there's movement in front of the wire. I'm sure there's VC there picking up brass."

"Right! Thanks Private Sutherland. I'll be right down."

Lt. Morgan was in the bunker within a matter of seconds. His tent was no more than forty metres from the bunker. "What have you seen?" he asked.

"Straight out in front sir, at this end of the rifle range, I've caught glimpses of people stooping to pick up brass. You have to look hard. It's dark but every now and then you get a glimpse of them in the moonlight when the moon comes out from behind the clouds."

"Ah yes! I just saw something then. This is what we'll do. I've got my rifle so you pick up the gun and we'll quietly make our way down to the wire, but we'll keep about thirty metres apart. Keep an even line with me though, we mustn't get in front of one another."

I picked up the gun and put two hundred-round linked belts across my shoulders. There are about forty rounds in the lead load on the gun and that will do for a start. We made our way down towards the wire. Proceeding in a half crouched position we could see movement outside the wire but how many of them were there picking up brass, we couldn't tell. Every now and then, we'd hear the clink clink of the brass as it went into their bags.

We got to within twenty metres of the wire and suddenly a flare went off and there was a helter skelter of VC into a ditch that ran down the side of the rifle range. It seemed to me there were three of them picking up the brass. Within a second they were all gone. Surprised by the flare, there was no time to actually target anyone, nevertheless, I used the whole lead load in one solid burst, raking the range area from the waist. The flare was their signal to clear out. Obviously, they'd had someone on watch.

In the past, when we went to the range, I was amazed that we never picked the brass up after a shoot. It was so unlike the army to leave the brass where it lay. Each unit which used the range for practice should have been made to pick up their brass. The Viet Cong have taken advantage of this, picking it up by night.

Later the same night at about 2130 hrs, lights appeared out in front. The lights moved from left to right across our front and at times remained motionless. Again, I called Lt. Morgan to the bunker.

"What's the problem now?" he asked

"Those lights out there sir, there's three of them. What do you make of that? They've been moving across our front and back again for the last ten minutes or so."

"Yes, I see. I dunno, but they shouldn't be there."

"They look a fair distance from here, sir. I'd say six or seven hundred metres at least, it's hard to tell in the dark."

"I'll get in touch with our CP. They can then get onto the Battalion Command Post and let 'em know up there and they'll probably put some mortars into the air."

Lt. Morgan rang through and told the CP what was going on. Within a few minutes mortars and flares were fired. The lights soon disappeared.

We later learnt that the VC fasten kerosene lamps to long poles. They hold the poles in the air so as to be seen by us. This tactic is used to draw our machine gun fire. They then take a note of our machine gun positions on the perimeter.

On the fifth of November the advance party from 9RAR, the battalion relieving us, arrived. There was not much more for us to do. Battalion sized operations were now finished and so were company ones for that matter. We spent the next couple of weeks tidying up the lines and getting our gear put into our trunks for the return journey home.

On the twentieth of November, truck after truck of 9RAR soldiers started arriving at Nui Dat and truck after truck of 3RAR blokes were being transported to Vung Tau harbour. HMAS *Sydney* was anchored about 500 metres offshore and we were ferried out by landing craft. On boarding the ship we were given hammocks and assigned sleeping quarters. Six platoon was allocated just behind the fo'csle and we slung our hammocks and settled into our spot.

The closest toilet and shower block, which the sailors call the heads, was at the very front of the ship and only through one steel door for us. All the soldiers on board, and there must be nine hundred of us, were given coloured discs for meals. Red disc holders eat first shift and green disc eats second shift. The next meal it's the other way around. Sailors and soldiers combined number close to two thousand. Providing three meals a day to this number would be no easy task, I thought.

The diggers didn't have much to do but each was assigned to at least one day of duty for the trip.

On the fifth day at sea I was assigned a job of dixie-bashing down in the galley. There were six other diggers assigned as well as me. It was our job to work under the supervision of the sailors working alongside us. There were about six of them as well. We had to report at 0700 hrs. It was a strange day, right from the start we were faced with a stack of greasy pots and pans a mile high. We worked like buggery, thinking that was all we had to do for the breakfast pots and pans. We'd just get to the end and another great load would come in and we'd have to start on them. All day there was no end to greasy pots, pans, baking dishes, boilers and saucepans. They came in by the score. When we came across a baking pan that looked too hard to clean a sailor took it from us and threw it out the porthole into the sea. This happened about twenty times during the day. The navy must have plenty of pots and pans and the seabed between Australia and Vietnam must be covered in pots and pans. We didn't finish dixie-bashing until about 2000hrs.

The first few days of the trip were interesting. The sea is very calm, almost like a mirror. Small fishing craft not much bigger than canoes can be seen and I wondered where they've come from . . . there's no land in sight anywhere.

The ship pulled into Singapore and was boarded by customs so they could go through our gear. Our bags were all lined up for us down in the hangar and we stood by while the customs officers rummaged through. I didn't think my bag search was all that diligent. Mostly I think they were looking for weapons and other accoutrements of war.

The escort destroyers darted from one side of the *Sydney* to the other. Sometimes they dropped depth charges for practice, the underwater blasts making great plumes of water rise from the surface. The destroyers, in comparison to the *Sydney*, which was formerly an aircraft carrier but now used as a troop carrier, seemed like small motorboats.

Once we got down past Christmas Island, the wind came up, making it difficult and uncomfortable to go upon the flight deck. The seas became rougher, making it tough for the diggers. The sailors on the other hand never had it so good. We were allowed two cans of beer a day but most of the diggers were not feeling good, mainly due to the daily pills they were taking to kill the malaria in their system. The affect of the pills and the rough sea put us off our beer. The sailors were more than happy to help out.

When the ship was off the West Australian coast the ship went into deep troughs only to rise again on the next swell. We spent a lot of the time in our hammocks to mitigate the effect.

Going to the heads (the toilet) or a shower is an experience. There's a foot of water on the floor and, as the ship rolls from side to side, the water goes with it in the form of a wave about fifteen inches deep. If you had a surfboard you'd be able to ride the wave crossing the floor.

Walking around the ship has become difficult and we do less of it. Our highlight of the day is meal times. The diggers who'd just spent the last twelve months eating combat rations more often than not struggle with the large meals dished out. The quality of the meals is excellent. Meat and vegetables are fresh and you can't help thinking, "These bloody sailors have it easy." I think they realized it as well.

The *Sydney* berthed at Fremantle to let the West Australian diggers disembark on leave. Sailing into Fremantle, the Battalion lined the decks – it was a magnificent sight and the men, seeing the first Australians waiting at the wharf, waving their Aussie flags to welcome us home, felt a deep sense of pride.

We spent four hours in Fremantle, giving us the opportunity to go ashore and have a look around. Most of us just went to a pub and had a few beers. I went with John Sanders and a couple of other blokes to a nearby pub. John, whom we called

Sandy, was wounded twice in Vietnam. He was sitting quietly not saying much then, after a prolonged silence, he said: "Tell me Stan what are you going to do now. We can't just sit around Woodside when we get back off leave."

"Dunno Sandy. I've been thinking I might try to get back to Vietnam."

"Me too mate, we'll work on it after we return from leave. I hate peace."

"Do you have any ideas how we'll bring it about?" I asked.

"Na! But we'll think of something. We'll agitate. In this man's army, if you want to get anywhere, ya gotta agitate."

Sandy was a good bloke to be around. He loved the army and the fact he'd been wounded on two separate occasions was like water off a duck's back. He was as game as they come, always happy and prepared to be in anything, and it didn't matter whether the 'anything' was trouble or not. He'd never let you down, but it's more likely you'd be finding yourself standing by him than the other way around.

At the end of our time ashore we returned to the ship. The ship left Fremantle late afternoon and the next day, entered the Great Australian Bight en Route for Adelaide. As large as the *Sydney* is, it just disappears down giant troughs only to bob up again to then go down again. It was the same all the way to Adelaide. HMAS *Sydney* pulled in to Port Adelaide on the 20th November 1968.

On disembarking at Adelaide we had time to meet our families before forming up for a march through Adelaide. My mother and father were there to meet me.

The crowds lined the streets and banners with "Old Faithful" written on them hung from shops as we marched with rifles at the shoulder to a warm welcome home. South Australia is the home base for 3RAR and the people of Adelaide view it as their own unit.

After the march, the Lord Mayor presented the Commanding Officer, Lt. Colonel J.J. Shelton, with the key to the city.

I handed in my rifle and I left with my parents for home and some leave.

Chapter 4

In between tours

✦

A few days after Christmas, I made my way back to Adelaide and then up through the Adelaide hills to the camp at Woodside. I'd never been to Woodside before and it struck me as hot and barren.

I reported to the orderly room and they told me where I'd be quartered in the camp. After drawing my gear from the Q Store I went to the barracks to settle in. There were only about twenty or so of us that had reported in from leave at this stage and we had nothing to do. Each morning at about 0900hrs we jumped aboard a TCV, which took us to the nearest public swimming pool to spend the day swimming, much to the horror of the locals. The impact of twenty raucous, fit young diggers, full of confidence about life, is far too much for any country swimming pool to handle. We took over. The vehicle called back at 1600 hrs to take us back to Woodside.

This went on for a couple of weeks. More and more diggers started returning from leave and WO2 Gary Martin, who was acting RSM, began waiting at the front gate. As the soldiers returning from leave came in through the gate sporting long hair, he promptly arrested them and had them marched to the nearby Guard Room. There they remained until a haircut was organized. WO2 Gary Martin was our CSM in Vietnam and for the moment was acting RSM until the Battalion RSM returned from leave.

Sandy came back from leave two weeks after me, and one day I said to him, "What are we going to do about getting back to Vietnam. I think we should talk to Gazza (CSM Martin) and see if he can help us."

The following morning at 1000hrs we went up to the front gate and, sure enough, that's where we found him. He saw us making a beeline towards him and said, "What do you two scruffy blokes want?"

"Seeing that you ask sir, Sandy and I want to go back to Vietnam. It doesn't matter so much if you're scruffy there," I replied. "We thought you might be able to help us."

"It just so happens I might. The regular barmen from the sergeants' mess are still on leave and I'm looking for a couple of barmen for a week or so to fill in until they get back. You two blokes can at least look presentable and if you do this job right for me, I'll see what I can do to get you back to Vietnam. No promises though."

"What do you reckon Sandy?" I asked.

"That'll do us fine. When do you want us to report to the sergeants mess?"

"1600 hrs. Today, sharp."

"Yes sir," I said. "Thank you sir. We'll be there."

On our way back to the barracks, Sandy asked. "What do you know about pulling beer Stan?"

"Absolutely nothing Sandy. Absolutely nothing mate, but I think I'm about to learn."

Later, we went to the sergeants' mess, arriving there ten minutes early. There were only eight sergeants in the whole camp at this stage. At most times there were only four to six in the mess for lunch or after work. For a while all we could pour was froth but eventually we got the hang of it.

"How are we going to keep the piss up to half a dozen sergeants Sandy?" I asked tongue in cheek.

"I dunno mate, just pour like buggery, I suppose."

On the seventh day working as a barman I was called up to the orderly room about 1000hrs and, when I reported in, I was told that tomorrow I'd go to the School of Infantry at Ingleburn in New South Wales to participate in a Basic Instructors Course for Corporal, a course set by Army Head Quarters. Sandy was also on his way.

I arrived at Ingleburn a couple of days after leaving Woodside. The course was not scheduled to commence until the 13th of March, giving me a few days to settle in. On the thirteenth we were off to an early start. First we were introduced to the five warrant officers conducting the course. I glanced over to them and they all looked as though they had a low threshold for nonsense. Furthermore, their jaw lines looked as though they were set in concrete . . . a tougher looking bunch I'd never seen before.

The course consisted of three components. Subject A was weapons and field craft. Subject B was drill and Subject C, military law. The course was full on every day and we worked until late at night as well. We were required to look crisp and neat at all times and this meant putting on two sets of freshly washed and starched greens every day.

Most of the blokes on the course are from 3RAR, with a few from other units as well. There are twenty-seven of us on the course and the emphasis is on being instructed in how to instruct. We've been divided into three groups with nine men to a group. Each of us in turn gives a lesson to the others. The warrant officers are tough but fair. They sit to one side observing and cutting in at times to give constructive criticism. The subject matter of the lesson to be delivered has to be studied the night before. You have to be fully conversant with the lesson material prior to its delivery to the group.

Yesterday, I was giving a lesson in drill. The subject was how to present arms. The class was standing facing me in a line eight metres out in front of me. After delivering the preamble it was down to commencement of movement.

I yelled, "Squad, on the order Present Arms, the drill is broken down to three movements. These movements are characterized by a time count of one, two, three, one. On the command of one you will thrust the rifle from the shoulder position to six inches in front of your chest. The rifle will be held perpendicular six inches in front of you. The rifle will not shake. It will not wobble from side to side. You will hold the stock firmly by your left hand grabbing the stock at the same time it reaches your front. The thumb of your left hand will be around your near side of the stock. Your fingers will be close together on the far side of the stock. Your body will remain upright. Your shoulders will not move. Your right hand will remain firmly on the pistol grip. We will now practise this first movement. Squad . . . ready!"

The diggers braced up for the command.

"Squad One," I barked.

The squad executed the movement.

"Six inches I said, not six bloody feet. The rifle is to be six inches in front of you. What a mess!"

A few started grinning, more started to giggle and the infection soon had everyone giggling, including myself. The trouble was, we all knew one another so well and we could see the funny side of it. The Warrant Officer, a Second World War veteran, was standing to the side watching me deliver the lesson and he had no sense of humour at all. He ripped into me, and the class as well. That was my only stuff up for the whole course.

Laughing at the wrong time has always got me into trouble throughout my life, going right back to my school days. There was one occasion at Kapooka while being inspected in the Guard Room by the officer of the Guard. He was a strange looking fellow but the recruit, Victor Attard, who was standing to attention opposite me was Maltese and he had very poor eyesight, necessitating the wearing of very thick glasses like the bottom of a coca cola bottle. I looked at the officer then at Attard and him, being short and dark with his thick glasses on, he looked just like a Jap out of the last war. It was all too much for me and when the officer came to inspect me I had a grin on my face a mile wide. From then on it just went from bad to worse and I copped some extra duties, but there was no way I could stop myself from laughing. But because Attard was right opposite me, the infection spread to him and he burst out laughing just because I was. He didn't have the faintest idea why I was laughing though. Victor Attard made me laugh on other occasions as well, particularly at the rifle range. He was hard pressed to even see the butts let alone the target.

Our instructor for military law is Major Irwin, my former Company Commander in Vietnam. It is good to see him again. One of our assignments in military law is to deliver a totally unrelated lecture. The subject I was given to research and deliver my lecture was the major tribes of Nigeria. Fortunately I could draw books from the library and study up on it. The lecture went well.

My brother Lance, who's in the Royal Australian Navy, always lets me know when his ship is berthing at Garden Island and I arrange to meet him on weekends at Royal Naval House, commonly referred to as Johnny's. Situated in Grosvenor Street, Johnny's is handy, particularly for sailors who can walk up from Garden Island dockyard. I go in by train from Liverpool Friday nights and book myself into Johnny's. Mostly, it's very thirsty sailors who book into Johnny's but it's also available to the army and air force as well. At Johnny's, a bed for the night costs one dollar. The accommodation is dormitory style and the linen is washed and beds made daily. On paying your dollar you're given a ticket with your bed number on it. You have to make sure you hop into the right bed. The shore patrol came around regularly and they're given a list of the bed numbers sold. If they find someone in a bed that hasn't been paid for they take a personal article – your trousers or false teeth for instance. The trouble is, this tends to have a ripple affect. The non-payer wakes up to find his shoes gone and then looks around to find some poor bloke still asleep in bed from a hard night before and then he takes his shoes.

Johnny's has a late night bar and bistro and it doesn't close until about 0400hrs. Up until then you can always get a drink and a meal. In the centre is an open-air area known as the snake pit. It can be rough at times and the Shore Patrol calls in quite regularly to take away drunk sailors causing trouble.

Around the corner from Johnny's, in George Street, is a good pub called the Brooklyn. They have a small bar area but somehow they manage to fit a live jazz band of three in there. Lance and I generally get there at about 1000 hrs. Saturday morning. When we think it's time for lunch and perhaps we should leave the pub to get something to eat, a nice young girl comes around amongst the patrons with an assortment of freshly-made salad rolls. A nice ham and salad roll costs forty cents. What is the point of leaving when lunch is handy? So we don't and in the end, late at night, having spent the whole day at the Brooklyn, we stagger around the corner to Johnny's, find our bed, and turn in.

One night we did this, climbing into bed about 0100 hrs. Lance woke up at about 0800 hrs and asked, "Hey Stan! Did you see what I did with my shoes last night when we came in?"

"Yes! You put them alongside your bed up the end there, on the floor near the wall."

"Well, the bloody things are not there now! Some bugger has pinched them. The shore patrol has probably found a bum in a bed not paid for and has taken his shoes. The bugger's then looked around for a pair in replacement and latched onto mine."

"What are we going to do? It's Sunday morning, everything will be closed," I said.

"The only thing I can do is go to the scran bag and ferret through it until I find a pair that'll fit me."

Fortunately, we managed to find a pair – they were a bit worse for wear but at least they got Lance out of trouble.

I met up with Lance quite a few times during Corps training at Ingleburn and then afterwards, when I was in reinforcement wing during early 1968. We always ended up having too much to drink. Quite often, though, we were led astray by Tug Wilson, a sailor mate of Lance's.

Another brother, Douglas, is also in the navy, but in the Fleet Air Arm branch and he is stationed down at HMAS Albatross at Nowra. Every now and then I hitchhike down there and spend the weekend with him and his wife, Rose-Marie.

On the second last day of the course we worked up until 2230hrs. The blokes were tired and just wanted to crawl into bed. The next morning we were woken half an hour before usual. The Warrant Officers came through checking our rifles to find that none of us had cleaned our rifle before turning into bed the night before, we were too done in. Nobody thought the instructors would raid us. Rust on a rifle is commonly referred to as GI's gold. We were all put on a charge of *"neglect to the prejudice of good order and military discipline"* for having a dirty rifle. This charge is the most common in the army and it virtually covers all misdemeanours. All that has to be done is add the misdemeanour to the end of the clause. The next day we were marched in to front the OC. Each of us received an admonishment.

A few days after completion of the course on 03/04/69 we had to present ourselves before an allocation board. We know that most of us, if not all, will be posted to a Recruit Training Battalion or a Corps Training Unit. When it was my turn to go in to the board, I was met by a Major sitting at a desk and a Sergeant standing on his left, about a metre and a half away from the desk.

I marched into the office, stood to attention before the desk and saluted the Major. His peak cap was on the desk obviating the need for him to return the salute.

"You're Private Sutherland?" The Major asked.

"Yes sir."

"And where would you like to go, Private Sutherland?"

"Back to Vietnam sir," I replied.

"Did you hear that Sergeant? This man wants to go back to Vietnam."

"I heard him sir," the sergeant responded. "He's only been back in Australia from Vietnam four months sir."

The Major, examining the documents in the file said, "Four months eh, yes I see. You were with 3RAR."

"Yes sir."

"Why do you want to go back to Vietnam, Private Sutherland?"

"I joined the Australian army as a volunteer sir. I volunteered because of the Vietnam War. If there wasn't a war on sir, I wouldn't be here. I have a little over twelve months to serve in the army and that's what I want to do sir."

"You do realize you might get killed?"

"Yes sir but that's a risk I'm prepared to take."

"Do you realize you came second out of twenty seven on the Basic Instructors course?"

"No sir. I didn't know where I came."

"You did very well, you're to be congratulated."

"Thank you sir."

"Very well then! Sergeant, this man's off to Vietnam. Put him down for that."

"Yes sir. Vietnam it is for him."

"Thank you sir," I said.

"You're dismissed Private Sutherland, and good luck."

I saluted, about turned and marched out of the office with a big grin on my face.

On the first of May I was promoted to corporal and posted to reinforcement wing Ingleburn. During the following weeks we were mainly getting ourselves prepared to go to Vietnam. Documentation had to be completed and kit readied. There was not a lot of soldiering to do. Every second day I took a group of soldiers on a five-mile run to keep their fitness levels up. The weather was nice and living in a marquee with the sides rolled up at this time of the year was good.

I went home on seven day pre-embarkation leave. On my return from leave, I was advised the time and date of the Qantas charter flight taking me, and a plane load of others, to Vietnam.

Chapter 5

Back to Vietnam

✦

. . . as a Section Commander

I boarded the plane at 2000hrs on the tenth of June. This flight had little impact on me compared to the first. Arriving at Tan Son Nhut, the sights were all familiar. The tropical heat had little impact on me and we didn't have to wait long for the connecting flight by C-130 aircraft to Nui Dat. The plane arrived and we boarded sitting on seats this time, along each side of the fuselage.

Twenty five minutes later, the plane touched down at Luscombe Field Airport at Nui Dat. When I got off I looked around for the identification badges of 1ARU vehicles. Seeing them, I went over and as soon as all the troops for 1ARU were on the TCVs, we made the short journey to 1ARU.

I handed in my AB83 to the orderly room, got my instructions and went to settle myself into the lines once again. I noticed this time though that 1ARU is a little more civilized, the paths we commenced making with crushed rock a year ago are now all concrete. Apart from that, nothing else has really changed. Over the next two weeks we got acclimatized and took various patrols out through the wire to familiarize the new arrivals into the country. There are a few road escorts to do up Route fifteen but nothing much more.

On the 28th of June, having completed all the necessary skills back in Australia for group nine, a rise in pay was the pleasing end result. The only difficulty I had at the time was in qualifying for air photography. In studying a photograph taken from a great height by aircraft, for the life of me, I couldn't recognize a cemetery, even though every town has one. Despite this, I still managed to pass.

About midday, on the 29th of June, Major Ted Chitham OC, B Coy 9RAR, came around to 1ARU looking for a reinforcement corporal. A few minutes after he departed I was summoned to the Orderly Room to be informed I was being posted to 9RAR and to report to the Orderly Room B Company at 1630 hrs that day.

I was handed my AB83 and then I went to my tent to organize my gear. That afternoon I reported to B Company Orderly room, handed in my AB83 and was informed to report to Lt. Langler in four platoon lines. I was further instructed that, before doing so, I was to attend an O group meeting that was commencing in a few minutes time. I went to the O group and listened to Major Chitham briefing NCOs on an operation commencing at daybreak the next day.

I was thinking this doesn't give me much time to introduce myself to Lt. Langler and, more particularly, the men I will be leading tomorrow as their new Section Commander. I knew from my previous experience of joining 3RAR as a reinforcement, the men would have their reservations with respect to a new Johnny-come-lately Section Commander. They will naturally think they're getting a clueless corporal who's never been in the country before and most likely will not be able to tell shit from clay when it comes to jungle operations.

At the conclusion of the O group I went to the lines and met up with the Platoon Commander, Lt. Langler, who shares a tent with the Platoon Sergeant. I nearly died when I saw that the Platoon Sergeant was none other than Tom Cross, who had obviously been promoted to Sergeant from Corporal. Tom was the regimental drill instructor who delighted in giving recruits a hard time when I was a recruit at Kapooka.

I pretended I didn't recognize him. I saluted Lt. Langler and introduced myself. I was pleased Tom Cross didn't recognize me, but how could he, I thought, all those thousands of recruits, passing through Kapooka . . . none of the instructors would remember a once-upon-a-time low-life face. After a few words with Lt. Langler, he directed me to my tent saying, "Your tent is just across the way there Corporal and you're sharing with Corporals Wakefield and Tonkin."

I went across to the tent and went in. Allan Tonkin and Barry Wakefield were both sitting. Barry was writing a letter and Allan was attending to some gear of his. I introduced myself.

Barry was the first to speak. "Well Stan, I hope you like it here. We've got a couple of no hopers but in the main they're a bloody good bunch. That's your corner there." He pointed to a spare bed.

Allan joined in, saying, "Yeah, you've got a couple of hard cases. They're good soldiers out in the bush but bad news back here."

"Par for the course then Allan," I replied.

Both Allan and Barry were a little surprised by my reply.

"Where have you come from?" Allan asked.

"I've just come from 1ARU but I was in these same lines with 3RAR last year – I was down in six platoon then."

"Shit! Allan remarked. "Did you hear that Barry? He knows his way around, he's been here before, that's good – that's really good."

"Your diggers will be glad to hear that Stan, that's for bloody sure. They've been a bit apprehensive. The platoon has been hit pretty hard. First we lost Sergeant Jeff Duroux – he was killed in January – and then only a few weeks ago we lost Paul Reidy from a mine in the Long Hais."

"I can understand their apprehension Barry. I'm glad you told me. Where will I find them?"

"All your blokes are in tents in a line, more or less straight with this tent."

"I'd better go and see them and let 'em know what's happening tomorrow,." I said

"Yeah, mate, we'll catch you later," Allan replied

I made my way down to the first tent belonging to the section. The first digger I came across, I said to him, "Before I introduce myself can you go and get all the blokes in the section to come up to this tent."

"Right Corporal." He hurried from the tent.

A minute or two later everybody was assembled and I asked them to take a seat anywhere they could find. Once they were all seated I looked around at them and could see some measure of anxiety on their faces.

"My name's Stan Sutherland and it's my pleasure to meet you blokes. You've been working as a team for the last six months or so, at least most of you have. This is good. I also understand you'll have some apprehension about getting a new Section Commander. This is only natural, particularly more so if the new Section Commander is fresh from Australia and has no prior experience of Vietnam or the jungle. If I was sitting where you blokes are, and I thought I was getting a new Section Commander straight from Australia, I'd be saying to myself, 'I wonder what sort of an arsehole this bloke's going to be?' I'm no different to you fellows.

"Now, as for me, I'm pleased in walking down to the lines here to see that nothing much has changed since last year.

"What do you mean Corporal?" One digger asked.

"Well, I was with 3RAR last tour and I was on the trucks going out the gates when you blokes were coming in. The only difference is, when with 3RAR, I was down in six platoon lines, but now I'm up here in four platoon, still the same Company lines though."

"You mean you're back here for a second time?" another asked.

"Yes only five months or so between tours."

"Shit! There's no way I'm coming back here again – when I'm out of here, I'm out for good," another remarked. The others also commented to the fact they won't be back for a second spin.

"OK fellas, can we just run around the tent and everyone give me your names. We'll start here." I pointed to the man on my right.

"Colin Shaw," he said.

"What do you do Colin?"

"I'm a rifleman."

"Good. Next."

"Vic Patrick. Rifleman."

"Stoney. Forward Scout."

"Jim Martin. Gunner."

"Haydn Watt. Jim's number two."

"Klaus Cimdins. Rifleman."

"Peter Wynd. Rifleman."

"Jeff Strawbridge, they call me Strawbs, I used to carry the gun but now Jim's taken over from me."

"Ian Henderson. Rifleman."

"Phil Whittaker. Rifleman."

"OK men, thanks. I'd like to spend more time just having a chat but, because we're going out tomorrow, I'll have to defer that and I guess I'll catch up with you individually over the next few days. We leave at first light by chopper for Operation Matthew. We're going to be out for nearly three weeks in an area of the Hat Dich, east of Route Two and north of the Courtney rubber. It'll be raining on us day and night so make sure you take plenty of foot-powder, perhaps even a spare set of dry socks if you can carry them. I've been up there a few times and I'm sure you blokes will have been there yourself by now. If so, you'll know the jungle is very dense, with lots of leeches and the like. Our job is to locate enemy bunker systems used by the VC, both main and local forces. Our aim is to destroy the bunkers and kill the enemy in and around them. The area of operations is known as AO Tom Thumb. It will be dark when we get up at 0430hrs. Breakfast is at 0500hrs. We leave the lines at 0600hrs. I suggest you pack your gear tonight. You don't want to be mucking around in the morning half asleep and trying to pack. In the morning, all I want you to be doing is checking to see you have everything. Before you go though, who carries the M72 and M79?"

Lyle O'rreal

From top: B Company cooks, Bob Russell far right; Lindsay 'Fisherman' Bryan; Ron Pearman, Tony Seychell and Jack English after an op.

Colin Shaw

Terry James, Ted Hamilton and Terry Godde

Haydn Watt —asleep with Jim Martin and John Arnold

Ron Pearman, Tony Seychell and Jack English after an op

Jim Martin

Phil Whitaker and Bob Davidson

Haydn Watt

Terry Godde and Bob Plummer

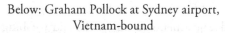

Below: Graham Pollock at Sydney airport,
Vietnam-bound

"I'm carrying the M72," said Ian Henderson.

"And me the M79," said Strawbs.

"Good. I'm just making sure we've got them, that's all. Any questions?"

The diggers passed a few light-hearted comments amongst themselves and Jim Martin said, "No questions Stan, is that it?"

"Yes that's it, I'll see you all in the morning then."

The men filed out of the tent and I followed and went to my own tent to get myself sorted.

There's always a certain type of quietness and calm in the camp when we get up in the dark to make our last preparations for an operation. The diggers say very little to one another. Every now and then you hear "have you got this?" or, "have you got that?" as they check their gear with one another. Each man quietly thinking and wondering how the commencement of the operation will unfold.

After breakfast, we returned to our tents, made last minute checks and adjustments to our packs and webbing belts and then made our way to the Company assembly area. The Company assembles on the road between the boozer and the Q store. Once the three platoons plus company headquarters are assembled, about 95 of us in all, the OC gave the order to make our way to Kapyong helicopter strip to await the choppers. This morning, it's just on daybreak as we walk up the road laden down with heavy packs, knowing the choppers will be along in a few minutes. There are still a few diggers putting camouflage paint on their faces at the last minute.

The platoons and company headquarters gather in their respective positions on the edges of the airstrip. Shortly after, we hear the thump, thump, thump, of the choppers, ten of them in two rows of five, flying in low over the rubber.

In just a few well-coordinated seconds, the choppers touch down, the diggers clamber aboard and the ten choppers lift and head towards the LZ in the AO. On the way to the LZ we are joined by fast flying helicopter gunships armed with 2.75 rockets and four M-6 kit 7.62mm machine flexguns with a total of 6000 rounds and two door mounted M-60 machine guns with 1500 rounds each.

The choppers carrying the troops are armed with door gunners, one on each side of the aircraft. They're alert to any activity in the jungle at the edge of the LZ and ready to open up with their mounted M-60 machine guns if necessary.

As we approach the LZ the gun-ships fan out circling the LZ, ready to suppress any hostile fire. The troop carrying choppers all come in together and hover slightly above the ground. The troops square their packs on their backs to balance themselves and jump off, remaining on their feet. Taking up defensive positions, we immediately make our way into the thick jungle at the edge of the LZ.

Major Chitham soon has the Company organized and ready to move out. Four Platoon is the second platoon to move off. We've gone only ten minutes into the jungle and shooting starts. I run, my legs are a little sluggish from being in a cramped position on the chopper. I see a log and I dive down behind it. My mouth gets full of dirt from the dive and for the first time since coming back to Vietnam, I ask myself, "What the bloody hell am I doing back here? I could be nice and comfortable back home in Australia. You idiot!"

I put these thoughts out of my head and say to myself , "You're in Vietnam now, in this man's army, get with it."

The next day the Company came into contact with enemy and, in a brief contact, Pte. Gordon Sorrenson was killed. Blood trails and packs were located in a sweep through. The five VC packs found on the track after the sweep through were left on the track and four platoon was given the job of putting in an overnight ambush on that part of the track. My position in the ambush is at the rear and I don't have a good appreciation of the lay of the land and all I can see in front of me is a wall of thick and almost impenetrable jungle. Banks of claymore mines are being put out and we've all dug our personal shell scrapes. I'd just finished digging my scrape and Tom Cross came around to put a claymore out in front of me. I was watching where he was siting it and said, "That's a bit bloody close Sergeant. You make sure you angle it right. I don't want my head blown off by the back blast."

"Corporal Sutherland, I've been putting these things out for years, right back to Borneo times. You'll be right, but then again if not, you'll be dead."

He finished putting the claymore out and he went on his way. The following morning quite early I'd just had something to eat for breakfast and the only thing apart from a wall of jungle for me to look at was the claymore. I sat at the back of my shell scrape having a smoke and looking at the claymore and thinking, I hope that damn thing doesn't go up. No longer had that thought crossed my mind when it was detonated, sending debris everywhere. I got a mouthful of dirt and rubbish from the back blast and, diving head first into my shell scrape, I let off a solid burst of a full magazine from my Ml6 into the jungle in front of me. It seemed like a good idea at the time. I quickly reversed the magazine and clicked in the other magazine attached to it by insulation tape, but I didn't fire any more because I couldn't see anything apart from jungle to fire at. A few leaves were still fluttering down from the explosion of the claymores as the dust and smoke cleared.

Apparently VC came along the track and, spotting the packs, suspected something was wrong because they would have known that the *Uc dai loi* would not leave their packs there from yesterday. Knowing we always take away packs and weapons, they skirted the ambush set for them and appeared in front of Lawrie Smillie. The VC saw Lawrie at pretty much the same time as Lawrie saw one of them, the only problem though, Lawrie thought it was Lt. Langler and didn't open fire. The VC, on the other hand, fired a burst at Lawrie and one of the rounds went through the handset of the radio and then through his shoulder.

Tex Bruce was sitting next to Lawrie with his back against a tree having breakfast. Tex is one of the most relaxed diggers in the entire army, nothing fazes him and, when a round smacked into the trunk of the tree only a foot above his head, all he was heard to say was "Shit – the bugger nearly got me!" Lawrie, being a tough bloke said in reply, "Well Tex, the bugger *did* get me, but only in the shoulder, but shit it stings a bit!"

The claymore mines were fired and when a sweep was put through the area – a thong with a lot of blood on it was found in a dry creek bed. There was a heavy blood trail leading away into the jungle, and we concluded that the VC would die from loss of blood anyway and we didn't follow it up. Lawrie needed to be evacuated, so we packed up and went to a clearing about half an hours march away. The medevac chopper was called in and Lawrie was winched aboard.

2nd July. It's Lyle Orreal's twenty first birthday, and he's celebrated in style with a carton of strawberry-flavoured milk that came in on the resupply chopper. I went up to him and said, "Happy birthday Lyle from all of us in Four Platoon. It's a bugger of a way to celebrate your twenty first birthday, mate, but in this man's army, it's as good as we can do today."

"Yeah, thanks Stan. I'll bloody do better next year, don't you mind about that mate."

For the next few days we patrolled in platoon strength, looking for suitable tracks to ambush as well as any signs indicating bunker systems might be nearby. Nothing of any consequence was found on these patrols. It rained every day though and we were always wet.

There are still some settling in issues to contend with. Stoney, the forward scout, has got to get used to me and what I want. This will take a couple of weeks, I suspect. Klaus Cimdins is on his last operation before he goes home and would much prefer to be anywhere but here. The poor bugger's got problems with his piles and he's also in need of a dentist.

I've been informed that some of the blokes think that I consider them slack. This might well be and, on the other hand, maybe they're testing me out by being slack on purpose to see what they can get away with. Klaus and Sergeant Cross have something in common – they both hate the scrub.

On the sixth of July D Company contacted enemy and L. Cpl. Richard Abraham was killed and Pte. Malcolm Spice wounded.

9th July. Four Platoon left the company harbour position to patrol through dense jungle. My section led the way out. I was keeping close watch on my compass because of the thick jungle. The Platoon Commander kept correcting me and I knew that the level of correction meant one of our compasses was out. I didn't say anything but was quite sure I was on the right bearing. The next section led by Allan Tonkin took over and they had the same problem. After a couple of hours, Barry

Wakefield's section then took the lead, and he was continually corrected as well. The three of us were of the view the Platoon Commander's compass was giving him false readings. Perhaps he's holding his compass to close to a pouch filled with ammunition or even his rifle. That can distort readings. There were no land features from which to take cross bearings to determine our exact position.

By the end of the day we were lost. The Platoon Commander had no idea where we were and neither did we. It's coming on late afternoon and pouring with rain and here we are lost in the jungle. No landmarks to see, only dense jungle on all sides. Lyle Orreal, our platoon medic, noticed the Platoon Commander's heightened level of stress and he said to him, "There's only one thing we can do sir. If we want to get back to the rest of the Company today, they have to know where we are so they can give us a bearing and to do that we need to fire a rifle. There is nothing else we can do other than to report in to Company headquarters by radio and tell them our predicament. What do you think about that sir?"

"Yes I think you're right Lyle, we probably only have an hour's daylight left at best and we need every bit of that to get back. We can't afford any more time." The Company was contacted by radio and were asked to stand by with a compass to get the bearing of the rifle report. A single rifle shot was fired into the air and CHQ took a compass reading on the report. Once we were given the reading a back bearing was calculated and compasses set so that we could make our way to the Company harbour position.

We approached the Company position near last light. It was still raining and visibility was poor. We knew the bearing we had to march on but the distance was an unknown factor, although we could make a good guess.

As we approached, we came across another platoon that had just left the harbour. I don't think they saw us but we saw them. At first we didn't know whether it was enemy or our own blokes. I looked across sideways to Jimmy Martin. He'd knelt down ready to fire. He looked at me and I gave him the friendly sign. Jim was quite distressed by the event. It was the closest thing to providing the circumstances for a shoot out between our own men and we were shaken up by the experience. This is a danger in becoming lost and approaching the company harbour from the wrong and unexpected direction. We were not expecting to bump into another platoon and they wouldn't have been expecting us to be coming in from that direction either. They may well have been informed by CHQ to keep an eye out for us coming their way but we weren't to know that. We weren't to know they were even there.

On the twelfth of July C Company came across a village. The inhabitants were women and children, suggesting an illegal village. The absence of men indicates they're away with their respective VC units. On the same day D Company met an enemy force in a bunker system. Cpl Bruno Adamczyk and Pte Beresford Edwards were killed and Sgt. Des Cochrane was wounded.

The following morning we joined the company on the edge of a bunker system one of the other platoons had found. Major Chitham has given his briefing with respect to sweeping through the system. Four platoon is lined up, each man is about eight metres apart ready to sweep through. We're waiting for further orders and Sergeant Cross yells out, "Fix bayonets."

The word passes down the line to fix bayonets and I can hear the very distinguishable clicks as the bayonets are clicked home on the fitting beneath the rifle muzzles.

A minute later we're given the order to advance. Sergeant Cross has positioned himself immediately on my left and we advance keeping as straight a line as possible, not an easy task in jungle. The first bunker is located inside fifty metres and Sgt. Cross pulls a pin from a grenade. We'd already removed the insulation tape we use for added safety from around our grenades and we now have the grenades in our pockets for easy access. Sgt Cross yells, "Grenade" and throws it into the bunker, a few seconds later a muffled explosion is heard. I followed soon after throwing a grenade into a bunker on my right. After the grenade went off I hesitated and moved to have a look inside the bunker and Sgt. Cross yelled out to me, "Keep in line Corporal, you don't expect to find anyone alive in there, do you?"

I knew I'd done the wrong thing and with nothing else coming into my mind I said, "I'd hate for you to be shot up the arse Sergeant that's all!"

"You keep in line and let me worry about that!" he replied.

The system is a very large one. The ground slopes gently uphill as we advance but the Company soon has the system within its control and the next task is to set about destroying it. This took the rest of the day.

15th July. Today we were paid a visit by a two star Divisional Commander from the American Big Red 1 Division. He came around the troops in the afternoon and was escorted by Lt. Col. Alby Morrison and an entourage of officers.

On the 17th July B Company flew out by chopper to secure FSPB Dampier. The following day the rest of the battalion joined us.

On the 18th July, Operation Hat Dich commenced. Some of the men complained about boils starting to develop. We put the incidence of boils down to water we'd taken from a creek somewhere in the last week or so. 2 Platoon A Coy, contacted enemy on the first day of the operation, killing three of them.

19th July. Lt. Langler has had enough of Stoney as forward scout of one section and relieved him of the position. The job has now gone to Vic Patrick.

Over the next week, companies came in contact with small groups of enemy and a number of bunker systems were located and destroyed. The battalion sustained a number of dead and wounded.

By now, nearly all of us have got large boils the size of cherry tomatoes on our bodies. The area around the boils is inflamed and sore. Jimmy Martin has a large boil on the webbing between two fingers on his left hand. Another bloke has a boil in between two toes, making it difficult for him to walk. I've got two boils, one on my left jaw, and another on the right side of my back where the pack rests. The boil on my back is painful and I try to take the weight and pressure of my pack off it by walking in an awkward twisted fashion to tilt the pack from my right over to my left side. To see me walking through the jungle like this would make anyone think I'm severely handicapped. There's nothing we can do about them except wait until they burst.

The Battalion returned to Nui Dat at the end of July. Most of the men's boils had burst by then. When my two burst, relief was immediate, but they left holes in my hide big enough to put a marble in. I was amazed how quickly the soreness disappeared and a few days later the wounds were almost completely healed.

1st August. The men are glad to be back at Nui Dat for a spell. Most are on their ear after only having two cans of beer and they will go to bed tonight to sleep in a regular bed for the first time in a month. Lt. Langler has taken out a TAOR patrol of twelve men and those of us left behind are sorting out our gear for the next operation, which starts tomorrow.

I went down to a tent occupied by Haydn Watt, Jeff Strawbridge and Martin Bink for a yarn. The conversation got around to a TAOR patrol about six weeks ago and in which Strawbs shot a VC. I said to Strawbs, "How was it that he was able to come right up to you before you saw him?"

"There were ten of us on the TAOR, Haydn and Binky here, as well as Jimmy Martin, Arab, Paul Snell and a few others. Lt. Langler inspected us as we went out through the wire. He wanted to make sure we all had our camouflage paint on. I'd just put a dab of green on the end of my nose and as I passed Lt. Langler he looked at me and said, 'Where's your camouflage Pte. Strawbridge?' "I've got it on my face sir," I replied.

"I can't see it then," he said, and I said, "That's the idea sir."

"Anyway, we got to where we were going and we harboured up for the night, in a triangular position, right slap bang in the middle of the rice paddies. I was on a machine gun looking down two rice bunds. If you can picture a T junction, I was where the two parts of the T meet and therefore I could see down two bunds. We had three machine guns on the patrol but at the time the others were all asleep. I was sitting on the gun and, suddenly, I see a nog standing right beside me looking down at me with his rifle pointed right at me. The bastard had come up on me from behind and I wasn't expecting that. He tried to fire his rifle, but luckily for me it jammed, giving me enough time to pick up my rifle and blow him away. The bugger fell down on Wattsy here who woke up thinking it's raining nogs. Poor Wattsy got a hell of a fright, but then, so did I. You didn't shit yourself though Wattsy, eh? You only thought you did mate."

Haydn cut in saying, "When this nog fell down beside me, I thought we were being overrun. Coming out from a deep sleep to find an enemy soldier only a couple of feet away scared the hell out of me. For a minute there, I didn't know what the hell was going on."

Strawbs went on, " I reckon there were about fifteen of them and they came out of Hoa Long heading for the Warburtons."

"Yeah, bloody Hoa Long has always been a nest of Viet Cong. What happened then Strawbs?" I asked.

"The VC didn't hang around to fight and they took off like lightning. In the morning, an APC came and the dead bloke was loaded on board and we took him to Hoa Long, dumping him in the middle of the street. Of course, straight away the people gathered around to see who it was that we'd got. One woman came and looked at the body, and then she started wailing and carrying on. She was down on her knees and clasping her hands in front of her. It was obvious she knew the bloke, probably her husband, so she was taken in for questioning."

"I tell you what Strawbs, if you don't believe in God after looking down the barrel of a gun that misfires you never will," I said.

"Yeah, the bastard had it pointed right at me and it was one of those weapons where the butt folds out, and the bloody thing misfires, how lucky can you get. The trouble is Stan, it's given me plenty to think about and I wake up almost every night seeing this bloke looking down at me with his rifle pointed right at me."

"I'm just glad you were awake and on the job Strawbs, the bastard would have had time to clear the jam in his weapon and blast a few of us away," commented Haydn.

Strawbs turned to Hadyn and asked, "Was Harry Birrell (their former tent mate) on that Taor, Wattsy?"

"I dunno mate. Harry went home about then. The poor bugger was as deaf as a post. He had crickets screaming in his ears all day long. It was before your time Stan. We were out in the bush on an operation and one day the word gets passed down the line to be quiet there's an enemy camp up ahead. The word is passed by Lyle Orreal to Harry who hears bugger all of it and he yells out loud in reply, how many stamps? Everyone on the patrol nearly died of shock. The poor bugger was sent back home to Australia after that. He was deaf before he left Australia but they sent him here anyway."

"Yeah, anyway getting back to this TAOR patrol, the day started off bad and so did the next day," said Strawbs. "When we got back to the lines after the patrol the Company was looking forward to going down to Vungas in a couple of days, but the following day, Mad Dog Chitham puts me on a ready reaction team and he takes one look at me and sees that I hadn't had a shave and the bastard gives me seven days CB (confined to barracks). That really pissed me off. The next day when the trucks left with all the boys on board I went up to Perksy, the MO, and complained about my piles giving me trouble. Perksy gave me a chit to go to the hospital down at Vungas to get my piles treated and when I got there they injected some sort of acid into my arse. Anyway, after that, instead of going back to the Dat like I was supposed to, being on CB and all, I went to the Badcoe club and got on the piss with the boys. We were all pissed as farts and that night, about midnight, I was as thirsty as buggery so I decided to break into their storeroom and pinch a carton of chocolate milk.

"I'm halfway through the window of the storeroom with my legs hanging out and these two pogos grab me by the legs and pull me back out. Well, I into them, and gave them a few smacks around the head for their trouble, and while I'm doing that, I couldn't help but think that this is as close to the war as you two pricks are gonna get, and this is the only fighting you're ever gonna have to do and you're gonna lose into the bargain. Those pogos down at Vungas are all soft and flabby from too much piss and it was easy to give them a hiding. Anyway, Mick Bell was the Duty Officer and he couldn't get me out of the shit so I was charged. Everybody was pissed though, officers and all. I got twenty eight days on the hill for my trouble."

Haydn was sitting there all this time very quiet with his usual big grin on his face and then he said, "Serves you right Strawbs, you never could behave yourself, you dickhead."

"Shut up Wattsy or I'll give you a clout around the ears," responded Strawbs.

Martin Bink entered the conversation and said, "You're bloody good out in the bush Strawbs but when you get back here on the piss, nobody knows what sort of mischief you're gonna get up to. You're a mad bastard, that's for sure"

"Ah well, you gotta have some fun along the way, that's all I know," replied Strawbs.

The diggers were looking forward to going to the boozer again for a couple of beers before they go bush again tomorrow. The two cans I had tonight were enough to put me on my ear again. After the boozer closed I walked back to the lines and went down to Bob Hannah's tent for a bit of a yarn. We were talking away and Bob mentioned something about Operation Overland. "When was that operation Bob?" I asked.

"Let me think! About the first week in April."

'Can you remember what happened?"

"Yeah! We were in day two of Overland. We'd left the American cavalry secured LZ the previous morning. Patrolling through the area we followed a flowing creek and found a track that crossed the creek. It appeared to have been well used, and fresh tracks indicated very recent use.

"Lt. Langler was asked to ambush the track in an area some seventy metres from the creek. We put the ambush in place and waited. It was very hot and dry and all movement was noisy. The dry leaves and twigs betrayed any movement within the ambush site. It's a strange feeling, but the quietness and lull in sound of any bird life, together with a feel of uneasiness, awakens and strains the senses.

"Suddenly, the claymores made an earth shuddering sound as they went up. The blast shattered the peace, and rung in our ears. It rained debris for a long time. The M60 and small arms fire raked the ambush site for what seemed like minutes, but in reality, was probably only thirty seconds and then it became quiet again, except for a few leaves fluttering from the trees. Dust was still settling and you could hear the sound of rifle magazines being re-filled.

"Lt Langler yelled for a sitrep (situation report) from the killer group. One enemy seen and the ambush initiated. A large tree had fallen across the track obstructing a full view of the killing area and loud moaning could be heard from near the fallen tree. The gunner fired his M60 into the area from where the sounds were coming from, but the moaning continued. L/Cpl Martin Bink was ordered to conduct a sweep of the killing area. Half the section had reached the track and Bink reported a dead enemy, laying on the track beside the dead tree.

"When the clearing patrol returned, L/Cpl Paul Snell and I were ordered to go out and bring the body into the ambush site. We reached the tree where it crossed the track. I noticed the tree was worn where backsides had slid across it over a period of time. The body was that of a very young Viet Cong. He didn't look any more than eighteen, but sometimes it's hard to tell. The two of us grabbed him by the legs and dragged him back to the ambush site. He was wearing grey shorts, a black collarless shirt, Ho Chi Minh sandals and he had a bandolier made from an Australian army mattress blow up section. His rifle was an AK47 and very new. He had on the standard green webbing. Inside the bandolier, we found used tea bags, an Australian ratpac chocolate and a packet of rice. It was obvious that he and his comrades had sniffed through a recent Australian position prior to walking into our ambush. Arab Evans and me buried the VC in a shallow grave within the ambush position itself.

"We remained in this site, and later in the afternoon I was a member of a water party that was sent to the creek to refill water bottles. Tom Cross was in charge. We filled the bottles and the section was ordered to do a recce on the other bank. A couple of us crossed the creek first. Ted Hamilton and I took up fire positions to give cover while other members of the patrol crossed. When we were nearly all across, Tom ordered us to move forward. Ted was leading us into a clearing with low dead grass. He'd moved only about three metres up the track when he gave the enemy signal. We both took cover behind a clump of bamboo. The rest of the section had not yet fully emerged from the creek.

"Ted and I could see one VC moving from our right across to our left. He was alert and moving at patrol pace, twenty metres to our front. We both fired simultaneously. He rose into the air as the rounds smacked into him and then fell down into the grass. Jack English fired his M60 into the contact area and we could hear loud yelling from the enemy patrol. At this point, we broke contact and moved back across the creek, returning to our ambush site. Lt Langler met us with a big grin on his face. It was all in a days work."

"Tom would've been happy as well, Bob."

"Yeah, Tom was good that day, but shit, he can be a hard bugger to work with though. There was one occasion, on a lighter side, when four platoon members were attending the morning pill parade. We were on the road outside the Platoon Commander's hootchie. Crossy was taking the parade and he noticed Arab Evans emerge from his hootchie and slowly making his way up to the parade area. Sgt Cross called out, 'C'mon on black man, we can't wait all day for you.' Arab got to the parade ground and said, 'Sergeant, I resent being called a black man.' Sergeant Cross replied, 'Pte Evans! There is no racial discrimination in this man's army. Cpl Wakefield, chain that black man to a star picket.' It was a piece of sarcastic humour I'll never forget."

I told Bob I'd had a bit of a run in with Tom myself on the last op. We were harboured up and it was mid morning. Tom came across and asked for my section machine gun to be moved to the other side of the perimeter. I didn't ask him why – I naturally thought it would be to cover a track that another section was covering and they'd now gone out on a recce or something like that. Earlier I'd had the blokes clean their rifles and when they'd done that I gave the go ahead for Jim to strip the machine gun and clean it. It was all stripped down when Tom came across.

I said to Tom, "As soon as the gun is assembled Sergeant I'll get Jim to take it across." This annoyed Tom. He said, "When I say now Corporal I mean NOW. Now means now. Do you understand?"

I said, "I understand what *now* means Sergeant. That's not the problem. The problem is, I'm not having my gun moved fifty metres across country when it's all in bits and pieces. Anyway it's no good in that condition, doesn't matter where it is. Jim'll bring it across as soon as he's got it together, and that's what he'll do." Well, he just turned around and walked away. I never heard another thing about it.

Having said that though, I told Bob that Tom does have his good points – I reckon we're the only platoon in the battalion that gets a rum ration. Tom brings around the bottle of Captain Morgan rum every night when we're in the bush. It's bloody good. He doesn't have to carry those bottles in his pack, but he does. "We've got to give him that," I said.

"You're right Stan. Tom's a strange bugger, I don't think he's got over being in a recruit training battalion. He still thinks he's there. But I must admit, I really look forward to him coming around with the bottle of rum. It warms the soul, especially when you've got a wet arse from the rain. Which is all the time."

"Yeah!" I replied. "Some of my blokes don't like rum but I get them to hold their water bottle top out anyway, for a fill up. When Tom's gone, I go and collect and I end up with three or four toddies. Those together with a cigar from the supplementary packs is tops."

2nd August. The troops received fresh ammunition in readiness for the next operation. The TAOR patrol returned and told us about the drama they'd had crossing a swollen river. The heavy rain overnight caused the river to double in size. In the process of trying to get across they lost two M16 rifles and Kevin Lynch nearly drowned. The current was that strong it started to drag Kevin under.

At 1230hrs, the company left Nui Dat and we were dropped off in the suspect area at 1530hrs. We moved three hundred metres from where we were dropped off and harboured up for the night.

The next morning we moved out at 0715 hrs. My section led the way out to rendezvous with an element of six platoon. At this point, company headquarters left four platoon and they went with six platoon. We spent the morning patrolling and checking out enemy footpads. We found two graves with dirt thrown over the bodies. It looked a standard Australian burial of enemy dead. Most of the afternoon was spent in an ambush position on a track which showed no evidence of recent movement, so it seemed a waste of time. Towards evening, we dismantled the ambush and moved north where we found a more promising track to lay in ambush for the night.

We left that ambush position at 0800hrs the next day and marched approximately three thousand metres towards Route 2. Three thousand metres is a long march. When we got there we boarded APCs and returned to Nui Dat. Major Chitham had organized a company BBQ, which we were looking forward to. Bob Russell and the other cooks really worked hard to make the evening a great success. The diggers tolerance to alcohol was largely reduced from being out in the bush for the last five weeks and there was plenty of beer to go around. The men let off a lot of steam and pent-up frustrations and emotions ensured a few brawls. Some fellows were carted out of the boozer unconscious. Once the beer ran out it was called a night.

5th August was an easy day. I wrote four letters home and attended to rationing the men for the next operation. After that, I went visiting the tents belonging to my section and then paid a visit on a couple of tents belonging to Barry Wakefield's section. I walked into a tent and found Terry James, Jack English, Terry Godde, Tex Bruce and Colin Evans, the one we called 'Arab' – he has all the appearances of a middle eastern camel driver. We sat around having a yarn and the subject got onto how we each found ourselves in the army. I quickly related my story about working in a bank for six years, then resigning and signing on in the Regular Army Supplement. It got around to Jack English's turn.

He began: "When it was time for me to register for national service I got the forms and filled them out. I didn't want to go to the slammer for six years for not registering. At the time I registered I was working way out in the bush driving a bulldozer, clearing fence lines and sinking dams on a pastoral property. I was working up in the north west of Western Australia. By the time they sent notification that my birth date was pulled out of a barrel I was out in the Marble Bar area, working on a drilling rig as the driller's offsider. When I got the letter telling me to report for a medical it was already days past the date on which I had to present myself. The letter had taken some weeks to find me and when it did, it was another couple of weeks before I got back to Perth. I wasn't particularly worried because I thought my Perth based employer would have let them know where I was working. The boss didn't do this, and when I reported in to the office, the boss said to me, 'You know the National Service mob have been here looking for you.' 'Didn't you tell them where I was?' I said. He shrugged his shoulders and said, 'No. We thought you might want to dodge them.'

"I thought I'd better front up to the Commonwealth Employment Service and report into the department that handles the paper work for National Service. I was told to sit and wait and on no account was I to leave. A pathetic looking public servant with pimples scurried away and another older bloke never took his eyes off me. A short time later, two solidly built blokes looking like bouncers came out, one said to me, 'So you've given yourself up have you?'

"I explained my situation but they didn't seem interested in excuses. The other bloke said, 'We were about to issue a warrant for your arrest.' They escorted me to the doctor's surgery, asking me questions along the way whether I was for or against the war in Vietnam and whether I was sympathetic towards communism. I said to them I don't give a shit about anything. I don't give a shit if I'm in the army and I don't give a shit if I'm not in it. I also told them that I wasn't even sure where Vietnam was.

"The two heavies escorted me into the doctor's room. It was a dingy bloody joint. One heavy went out of the room and waited outside and the other stayed inside the room. The doctor was about 35 and he looked like a heavy drinker. He told me to strip. He took my height and gave me the standard, I'll hold your balls while you cough test. He had a quick listen to my heart and lungs. No more than two seconds. I remember the stethoscope being cold though.

"The doctor pulled out a form, which had about thirty-five to forty questions on it. You know the type. Are you an asthmatic? Do you get headaches? Do you get dizzy? Do you have difficulty breathing? The doctor was racing ahead putting no alongside each question long before he got to even ask it. I had a bad knee problem, a crook cartilage at the time. When he got to this question I said 'yes' but the bugger still wrote down no. 'That won't be a problem for a fit bloke like you,' he said.

"The whole time I was answering these questions I was standing starkers, except for a bandage around my penis.

He asked me 'Have you ever contracted or been treated for a sexually transmitted disease?' I said no. 'So what's this then?' he asked pointing to the bandage. I told him about the drilling rig accident I'd had. The heavy and the doctor both had a good laugh and that was the end of the medical, it was a bloody farce. The rest you know, and here I am with you blokes."

"Well Jack, I suppose it's better sitting here with us blokes than being in jail," said Tex.

"I'm not so sure mate. How I've got myself stuck with the biggest load of dickheads in the army has got me beat."

6th August. The troops spent the morning getting ready for their two-day spree down at Vung Tau. The TCVs arrived shortly after lunch. The troops boarded in a happy mood. The last five weeks has been particularly hard going physically and now they were looking forward to a couple of days off. The Company arrived at the Badcoe Club at 1ALSG in Vung Tau at 1500hrs. Major Chitham gave the usual make-sure-you-behave speech and then set us loose on the public.

The first thing I did was to have a haircut at the base barber shop. This was followed by a couple of beers at the Badcoe club. After this, I went into town and entering a bar I stumbled across some blokes from six platoon. They were already well on the way to being drunk and it was still broad daylight. A system flushed clean by drinking four pints of water every day for weeks on end has its benefits. The diggers can get drunk for two dollars.

Corporal Ernie Hardgrave was on a table doing a strip tease. Ernie was having a great time and I thought to myself, "Jeez Ernie. Your mother would get a shock if she could only see you now." He was having the time of his life flashing his buttocks to resounding applause. When he'd finished and managed to get his trousers back on, I went over to him and said, "I see you've been trained professionally in the classic art of table top dancing Ernie, the crowd loved it mate."

"I can't say I have Stan. But, shit, it's good fun when you're a long way from home though."

The bus back to the Badcoe Club left town at 2145hrs. On it was the biggest load of drunks I'd ever seen.

7th August. I left the Badcoe Club at 0800hrs to go into town. I called in to the R&C Centre to find Le Hoa. All the girls remembered me from my stay down there eight months earlier. I went onto the roof where there was a good bar and had a few beers there. Later I caught up with Le Hoa. She said, "Satan, I think you no come back. It make me happy you come back. *Uc dai Loi* never come back. But you come back. Le Hoa very happy."

"I told you I would come back Le Hoa but you no believe me."

"Today I finis work, you wait for me OK?"

"OK. I wait. What time you finis work?"

"I finis work same time 4 o'clock."

I went to the American USO for a couple of hours and then visited a few bars until it was time to see Le Hoa. I'd bought some food earlier on in the day, which I knew would be safe to eat. We walked the four hundred metres or so to where she lived. Her sister also worked for the Australians out at the Badcoe Club.

The night was hot and I was probably dehydrated from the beer I'd drunk and the humidity. I woke up hot and bothered. Le Hoa disappeared to buy a drink of Coca Cola for me. I didn't get much sleep at all that night. I wasn't used to dogs barking, indiscriminate shooting and all the noise of a town coming and going. Also, shacked up and unarmed in a strange place, takes time to get used to. When dawn arrived I told le Hoa hoa I had to be back to catch the convoy to Nui Dat. We said our goodbyes and I told her I'll see her next time I was in town.

I caught a Lambretta out to 1ALSG, arriving at 0830hrs to find the diggers had already vacated the rooms. Major Chitham had organized an inter platoon swimming carnival to sober everybody up. I was entered into the backstroke and, after drinking beer for two days, it nearly killed me. It took me an hour to recover from the backstroke and then I entered into a couple of freestyle events. Four Platoon won the competition but we were a sorry looking lot.

Pte. Lyndsay Bryan, known as Fisherman, was drunk from the night before and still drunk when we arrived back at Nui Dat. Lt. Langler had him marched to the compound under close arrest. The compound is a ten by ten metre wire enclosure.

The next day Fisherman was taken from the compound and marched up to Battalion Headquarters where Lt. Colonel Alby Morrison gave him twenty-eight days detention on the hill down at Vung Tau. It was my job to place the guards for the night at the compound so that the prisoner didn't do any harm to himself.

The following morning at 0600hrs I went to the compound to check on the guards and the prisoner. I found the compound gate open and, inside, an empty bottle of whisky, the guards asleep and the prisoner gone. I woke the three guards up and asked them what they'd done with prisoner Fisherman.

One of them said, "He was here a minute ago," to which I replied, "Well, he's not here now is he, and you no hopers are responsible for him. You better all hope nothing bad happens as a result of you letting him escape. Now, the three of you can go and find him or the shit will hit the fan." One of the guards decided to mouth off to me and, after a warning which went unheeded, I charged him with insubordination. The three of them left to look for Fisherman and, fortunately, they found him in the lines and marched him back to the compound.

11th August. Four platoon attended a demonstration put on by the Engineers. The demonstration was on the do's and don'ts when encountering land mines. The diggers enjoyed the lesson and found it very informative and helpful. Land mines are now a big problem for us. In the afternoon we went to the range to test fire our weapons.

12th August. I gathered the section together for a frank and open discussion on a number of points. Being a former baggy arse myself, I know the diggers like to have a whinge. This can be damaging to morale if the substance of the whingeing is based on incorrect assumptions. I was aware they were not all that happy. I always made sure the men knew as much about everything that was going on as what I did. Invariably, at the end of these open discussions, the air is cleared and everyone is placed in a better frame of mind. They were upset at Fisherman getting twenty-eight days on the hill at Vungas and me charging a member for insubordination.

Haydn Watt asked, " Couldn't you turn a blind eye Stan?"

"A blind eye to what Haydn? I replied. "It's not in your best interest as a soldier, mine as an NCO and four platoon as a whole if bad conduct is let go unchecked. All of us have a responsibility to ourselves and everybody else in the platoon. It's discipline that will get us home alive. What respect would you have for me as a Section Commander if I don't conduct myself in a fit and proper manner? You have expectations of me as your Section Commander and you also have a job to do as private soldiers. It's not unreasonable for me to expect you to do it. I have a job as an NCO, you all know what my job is and it's not unreasonable for you to expect me to do mine. Being drunk and mouthing off in the lines is not acceptable. Nor, is being drunk on guard duty and letting prisoners escape. It's as simple as that. The man I charged was given every opportunity to recant and he failed to do so but instead he continued mouthing off. He was given the opportunity to avoid being charged but he didn't take it. Being an NCO, it's in your best interest that I maintain good order. If you want to fight one another over nonsense you have to fight me first. If you beat me you can then sort yourselves out. The man I charged was too drunk to fight me. I'd have much rather preferred he did. I don't need stripes to cover my arse. I'm prepared to take them off any time anyone wants. You will find me fair but you won't find me not doing my job. The Regiment's motto is *Duty First* – you know that. I want you all to be perfectly clear where I'm coming from. Would anybody like to say something?"

"No, we're all OK Stan," Jimmy Martin replied. "We've been worked pretty hard lately and everybody has had to let off some steam. The bloke charged deserves to be in the shit. He's acted like a dickhead."

"OK, if we're all happy, having had this discussion, you can get ready for the boxing tournament this afternoon. Lt. Langler is aware you need to let some steam off as well and there's no better way than to beat the crap out of your opponent. Anybody who wants to beat the crap out of me can try his luck."

"No Stan, not you, you're too big. I'm gonna take on Ted Hamilton, and give him a hiding," said Haydn, laughing with delight at the thought of it.

"What about you Klaus, who are you going to fight? asked Vic.

"I think I'll have a go at Phil Whittaker. He's about my size. I need to fight a small bugger to give myself any chance of winning. It'll be good to land one on him. He's such a serious fellow."

"Well, if any of you are going to fight Langler, give him one for me," remarked Colin.

"I'd like to smack Tom Cross under the ear but the queue will be too long," added Jim. "Bloody Tom has got it in for me. I don't know why though."

"Tom's got it in for everyone Jim. I don't think you're anyone special," said Klaus.

The diggers thanked me for having the meeting and for calling them together for them to have their say.

Both Barry and Allan had the same morale problems with their men and had called meetings also. The three of us were sitting in our tent discussing various issues and how we thought they should be best addressed. We were talking away when Haydn Watt appeared at the entrance. "Hey Barry," said Haydn, "I've got your mickey mouse watch, but I need you to hold out your hand though." Barry was in the habit of lending his watch to those on picket to determine the start and end of picket shifts.

Barry held out his hand and Haydn tipped a fistful of springs, cogs and wheels into it. "I'm sorry about that mate. I pulled it apart to see what sort of movement it had and the innards sprung out all over the place."

Barry's jaw flopped and his eyes nearly fell out of his head. "Shit Watt! I'd like to put my boot up your arse to see what sort of movement I get as well. Why can't you leave things as they are? Why do you have to bloody fiddle all the time?"

"I thought it would be OK. I just used my bayonet to see if the back would come off it so I could have a look inside. The guts sprung out all over the place."

"I'll have to pay for this now you prick."

Allan cut in and said, "If you come up with a plausible excuse, such as an unavoidable accident on the last operation, you won't have to pay."

"Good idea Allan." Barry thought about it for a minute then said, "I know, we'll tell Mad Dog Chitham it got hit with a bit of shrapnel when he ranged in artillery near our position one evening during the last op."

"Yeah, that'll do it. We'll go and tell him now."

Barry and Haydn went up to Major Chitham's office and asked the orderly if they could see him. They marched into Chitham's office, Barry saluted and Haydn came to attention. Chitham asked, "What can I do for you two blokes?"

"We're here to report an accident during the last operation. The accident wrecked my army issue watch sir," said Barry, holding all the bits and pieces out in the palm of his hand so Chitham could see.

Major Chitham looked at the jumble of springs and cogs and said, "And how did this so-called accident happen, Corporal Wakefield?"

"Well sir, I'd lent my watch to Private Watt here so that he'd know the start and finish of his picket. Unfortunately, it was hit with a bit of shrapnel one night when you called in artillery to our position."

"Is that right Private Watt? Is that what happened?"

"Yes sir. That's what happened."

"Well, what's going to happen now, is you two blokes can clear out of my office right now. I've never heard so much spurious nonsense. You must think I came down in this morning's rain. Clear off the both of you before I get angry. My God! What's next from you B Company blokes?"

Barry took a step back saluted and said, "Yes sir." They both turned around and hastily departed the office.

Barry walked back into the tent and Allan asked, "How'd you get on?"

"No bloody good! Mad Dog Chitham wasn't having a bar of it. I could kill Watt. If I wasn't in this man's army, I bloody well would, I'd kill him."

"Perhaps you shoulda thought about it a bit longer Barry and came up with a more plausible excuse," said Allan.

"Yes! You're right mate! I was too hasty. I was so pissed off about it I couldn't think straight."

"I've heard a rumour that Captain Dugdale will be acting OC for an operation coming up. Think about it and give him a go," I said

"I will! But in the meantime, what am I going to do for a watch? I've just gotta have one."

"You can borrow my Seiko. I don't use it, have it as long as you need it. It's a bit shiny out in the bush though, especially when the sun reflects off it but it's a damn good watch and better than nothing. My issue mickey mouse is a good watch and I use that, I won't let Watt get his hands on it though."

"Thanks Stan, that'll get me out of trouble until I sort this mess out and get mine replaced."

"Well fellows I'm going to have a bit of a spell. I've gotta be well rested for my bout later." I said.

The boxing tournament got under way at 1600hrs. Lt. Langler kicked it off. "Who's going to fight me? he asked.

"There's not enough sets of gloves in the army sir, but I'll have a go with you," chided Lyle Orreal.

Lyle and the boss gloved up with the sixteen ounce gloves and squared themselves off for the start of their bout. "Prepare yourself for a thumping sir," warned Lyle. "You're gonna go down in the first round and there's no runnin' away either. You're gotta stand and fight sir. Is that clear?" Lt. Langler, feeling confident he was equal to the task, replied, "As long as you don't mind being carried on a stretcher up to the RAP Orreal, it'll be OK with me."

Bob Hannah

Harry Birrell, John Leahy, and Lyle O'rreal

Barry Wakefield training for the boxing tournament

Above: Ken Earney, Jim Muir, John Cowan and Frank Flockhart

Lawrie Smillie

Jeff Strawbridge

Terry James and Terry Godde cutting grass around their tent.

Ernie Hardgrave

The fight commenced with each studying the other to seek out strengths and weaknesses. Lt. Langler commenced the assault on Lyle with a strong barrage of straight right jabs to Lyle's head. Only one connected but Lyle was temporarily taken aback by the attack. He quickly gathered himself and let fly with a wide angled left hook which slammed into Langler's glove, hastily raised in protection. The force of the blow knocked Langler a metre to his left side but he remained standing. The fight gathered interest as each landed blows in an attempt to get the upper hand. Lt. Langler went into a defensive mode, buying time to get his breath. Lyle, sensing a gap, launched a left hook followed by two right jabs, the second jab connecting with Langler's nose. Langler absorbed the punch well and then with his breath restored went in landing a solid punch on Lyle's chest. The wind hissed out of Lyle and he was visibly shaken. Each fighter landed punch for punch and they fought like men possessed. At the end of the fight Lyle and Lt. Langler waited on the decision of the judges. It was a split decision and both fighters were glad it was all over for them.

Allan Tonkin squared off with Barry Wakefield. At the end of the fight Allan remarked, "Barry pounded the hell out of me, but at least I lasted the distance."

Bob Hannah and Ted Hamilton shaped up to one another. Bob is a gangly sort of bloke with long arms and this gave him a bit of an advantage over Ted. It was a good fight to watch. Ted got a split lip but he also landed some good ones on Bob. They were both struggling in the end to last the distance. Another round would have sorted it out. It also ended in a split decision.

Jack English couldn't remember his fight. He started off well and looked like he was going to win. Feeling a bit confident he dropped his guard and copped a beauty under the chin. He went down like a cold beer in a bushfire and staggered from the ring a bit groggy. Next morning he woke up with a hell of a headache and feeling crook in the guts. He believes he lost.

Kevin Lynch, our radio operator, decided he'd have a go against me. I couldn't stop Lynchy. I don't know what his head is made of but I soon found out that it was no good punching him there. He had a great capacity for absorbing head blows and the ones I landed didn't see to have any effect. That was the only place I could hit him though because he kept his gloves and arms close to his chest and guts, covering them well. Lynchy just kept his head down and bored in. He said after the fight, "I'm not going to be so outrageous as to suggest I won Stan."

Terry James fought Bluey McCabe. It was a good fight. Neither was prepared to lose easily. Bluey bore in like a pit bull terrier and Terry had to step back all the time but he kept throwing punches and managed to land a lot. After a minute or so the tide turned and Terry was punching hard but not gaining much. A right cross caught Terry on the left ear and he went down hard. He came up on his knees, took one look at Bluey and attacked, raining on him a flurry of blows. Bluey tried to fend Terry off by hitting Terry fair in the stomach but Terry was mad and pretended not to feel it. He countered with a straight right, hitting Blue smack in the nose which quietened him down a lot. At the end of the fight the judges gave it a split decision. Bluey believed he'd won and was disappointed in the result. He said, "You blokes couldn't judge a peeing distance contest." On the other hand Jamesy thought he was a clear victor and cut in saying, "You're a lucky bastard Blue, another round and I woulda taken you out." Bluey looked at Terry and just shook his head.

Terry Godde squared off against Barry Thompson. It was a great fight. Terry copped a right hook that sent him into the blokes lining the edge of the ring. The diggers pushed him back and Johnny Leah said, "Get in there and fight Godde you weak bastard, don't let him get away with that."

Terry gave his head a couple of shakes to clear his mind, looked his opponent in the eye and said, "Fuck you Thompson!" And bored back into the fight throwing punches left right and centre. Barry was taken back a bit by the attack and had to back pedal, but Godde puffed himself out and was on the backward step soon after. It ended in a split decision but it was a very entertaining fight.

Klaus Cimdins and Phil Whittaker had a go at one another. Klaus was a bit worried about Phil and his ability to fight. Phil is a serious sort of a bloke and doesn't give much away and Klaus was concerned he might be a bit of a dark horse. There wasn't a lot of technique employed and the fight looked more like a slugfest than anything else. Phil got Klaus a ripper in the guts, which shook him up a bit. Klaus stepped back a couple of paces to get his breath. "Right Whittaker! You're fucked," he said and dived back into the fight, giving Phil a good right to the jaw. Both claimed to win and the platoon couldn't decide whether it was a draw or what.

Graham Pollock, who came into my section as a reinforcement at the beginning of August, thought he'd miss out on a fight as he had no one to match up with. Lt. Langler, who'd recovered from his bout with Lyle, offered to fight him, however Graham, being over six feet tall, had a height advantage and Lt. Langler was hard pressed to get under his reach. The fight was a good one to watch but Lt. Langler ended up with a cut lip – he fought well though and received favourable comment. Consensus of opinion had him lose on points. I actually thought he'd won.

The blokes really enjoyed their bouts and they enjoyed watching and got into the swing of it literally. It was the ideal way to let off some steam and everyone felt much better for it, even though they were physically worn out by their efforts. It went down as a very memorable afternoon . . . and a few beers that evening went down like some of the fighters.

13th August. A hard day's work was put in today. We put up two hundred metres of concertina wire on the perimeter. The perimeter wire extends to five lots of wire deep and three coils high.

In the afternoon we were briefed on the details of the next operation, land clearing. As an adjunct to the land clearing,

B Company is sending two teams to Dat Do to train the Vietnamese regional Forces. Lt. Langler has informed me that one of the teams will be my section and that Sergeant Cross will be in charge of the team.

14th August. The Company left at 0900hrs for their area of operations. Captain Dugdale is commanding B Company as Major Chitham is assigned to District Headquarters for the operation. Captain Dugdale's first task is to secure FSPB Searle. Having established Searle, the company moved out with tanks and APCs to protect the land clearing team whose job it is to clear the "Long Green" area from Dat Do to Hoi My in the south west.

The training teams remained at Nui Dat because we're not required to deploy to Dat Do until the 16th. The morning was spent getting briefed by the Intelligence Officer, the Medical Officer and the OC. The afternoon was spent in getting stores organized for our deployment. Apart from that, there was nothing much else for us to do. The following day was the same.

16th August. We left Nui Dat at 0830hrs for the RF 189 Company compound assigned to us at Dat Do. We arrived to find the compound relatively well set out by Vietnamese standards. We were able to commandeer about a third of the floor area of a galvanized iron shed for our accommodation. The rest housed Vietnamese families. They're separated from us by a flimsy screen, that, if we wanted to, we could look over it and watch them having sex. The shed enabled us to put our stretchers down each side of the wall, leaving a passageway a metre wide in the centre of the shed. The floor was concrete and there was a six-inch gap between the floor, and bottom of the walls. The walls stopped well short of the roof to allow air to circulate in and around. We set about putting up our shower and toilet facilities. This activity interested the Vietnamese locals. The inhabitants of the compound are the RF soldiers, their wives and children. Each family is allocated a small space of about two metres by three metres in which to live. There is just enough room for the family to sleep, and nothing more. Each family is separated from the next by a two metre high, cloth material screen. The living conditions are unimaginable by Australian standards.

The Company Commander is Lt. Bin. Originally, he lived in North Vietnam but came South when the country was partitioned between North and South. Lt. Bin is only a short man but is quite stocky by Vietnamese standards. In the evening we had a few drinks with him before settling down for the night.

17th August. Being Sunday, it's a day off for the soldiers in the compound. We mainly concentrated on getting ourselves comfortable and putting our supplies stored in an accessible and tidy fashion. We don't have a lot of room and we need to be tidy as we can possibly be. I was invited by a Vietnamese Sergeant and his wife to have lunch with them. I had to accept because not to would be considered bad manners and we didn't want to get off to a bad start. Under normal circumstances, I can eat pretty well and there's not much in the way of western food I don't like, but Vietnamese food is another story.

On my plate was a skinned frog with vile fish sauce called Nuoc-Nam poured over it. There was also some rice and vegetables. One of the vegetables was sliced bamboo. The smell made my stomach rise to my throat. Swallowing hard, I pushed it down again so as not to be sick. There's got to be a way out of this predicament, I thought to myself. I started to eat the rice and vegetables, taking a little of the frog from time to time. Fortunately, I brought to the meal a few cans of beer and this helped to wash down anything sticking in my throat, which was everything.

After a period of time had elapsed, which I though polite and acceptable, I took a packet of cigarettes from my pocket. Removing about ten from the packet, I threw them into the corner of the room. My hosts leapt from their chairs at the table to gather the cigarettes, sending half a dozen chickens pecking crumbs from around our feet scattering in the process. By the time the confusion was all settled, my plate was clean. My pocket had eaten the frog. The time spent with the Sergeant and his wife was enjoyable though.

18th August. The first day of training for one of the RF Platoons. Their cooperation is good and they seem willing, if not eager, to learn. They play around a lot amongst themselves. One can liken it to teaching thirteen and fourteen year olds back home. It seems strange to teach such serious matters as the art of warfare in an environment where every man woman and child is affected by the war and they're like kids. They are friendly towards us, which makes our job much easier. They're aware that the average Australian soldier is far more capable and more highly trained than most of their senior officers.

In the evening, I was invited by another sergeant and his wife to dine with them. I made sure I had plenty of cigarettes in my pocket. This meal, however, was far more palatable than yesterday. The meal consisted of rice, fish, tomatoes, lettuce, soup and other vegetables unknown to me. We have to be very careful from a hygiene point of view when eating food prepared by the Vietnamese.

19th August. Training of the RF is going ahead very well. Some of them have worked with Australians before and have no difficulty in understanding what we mean. They're a friendly lot but look forward to knocking off work. They're not used to putting in a whole day's work. They also get very tired after the midday meal. It's normal for them to have a sleep after lunch. They can't understand how we get straight back into work.

20th August. We have an interpreter with us called Quan. He was called away today to other duties and consequently training came to a standstill. The fighting bays around the compound need rebuilding and we got the Vietnamese to start work on these for the day.

In the afternoon, we decided to change the drum we had as a pan in our toilet thunderbox. When we arrived and set up our toilet we half filled the drum with diesel. The drum was now full and Sgt Cross asked one of the diggers to take it twenty metres away and throw a match into it. The Vietnamese always kept an eye out for what we were doing. Our presence fascinated them to some degree. They weren't aware there was diesel in the drum. They thought it was simply a drum of white man's shit. When the lighted match was thrown into the drum and the white man's shit burst into flame, word spread quickly around the compound. In next to no time there was an audience of forty or more. They stood there for two hours looking at the burning drum, wondering what the Uc Dai Lois eat to make their shit burn.

21st August. This morning we trained the Viets in ambush procedure and tactics. They don't like our method, believing we position the claymore mines too close to them. The Viet NCOs have absolutely no control of the men under them. They much prefer to be friends, than to actually lead them. They get by on some sort of consensus basis. As a consequence, there is no system that resembles a chain of command. Lacking method, everything takes a lot longer for them to complete than one would expect. We've told them that we'll be taking them out to actually put in an ambush after dark tonight. They made their feelings be known. They tell us that they don't like to do this. It's too cold and wet. Furthermore, why go out of our way. If the VC attack us in our compound we'll fight, but we don't go out looking for them after dark.

Sergeant Cross is adamant that they'll be going out on an ambush tonight and he informs them that night is the best time to get the VC.

Daytime training to them is a bit of fun and falls within their comfort zone, but night work is disagreeable

The Viets ended up agreeing to go because their Company Commander, Lt. Bin, tells them the Australians are in charge of training. He doesn't like the idea himself because he wants to keep his men happy.

In the Company there are about a dozen ethnic Chinese. It's very apparent the Chinese are more intelligent. They spend a lot of time talking with us, improving their English. Being an ethnic minority group, the Vietnamese give them the stick and they have to do all the dirty work. Our observation is that the Chinese are more reliable and trustworthy and we've made up our minds that when we leave the compound we'll always have a number of Chinese with us for our own protection. It's known that the Vietnamese in the past have shot their American advisers and simply ran away from the battle if the going gets a bit rough. We don't want to be placed in such a situation, and generally only six of us at the most go out with the Vietnamese. We always leave a couple of diggers back at the compound because if we didn't we'd have no gear left when we returned. Everything would be pilfered. We've already had situations where grubby little hands come under the gap between the floor and wall of the shed we're billeted in. We see the hands feeling around for anything they can get hold of. Rations are well sought-after items. Furthermore, if the kids are not successful in pilfering from us they get a hiding from their parents who insist they do better next time.

We left the compound at 2000 hrs, to go to the predetermined ambush site, which is a wide road in the village but near the outskirts of Dat Do. We have to organize them as they lack any sort of appreciation of the big picture and of what's required. We're careful to ensure they position the claymores and then unwind the electrical leads on their way back to their gun position and not the other way around. To reverse this procedure can lead to an electrical charge developing in the lead. A strong radio signal can do this, detonating the claymore while you've still got it in your hands. We did not expect to achieve any results by this ambush. We'd at least be able to assess the deficiencies, concentrating on them in further training. The noise they make amongst themselves is staggering. Everybody for two hundred metres around would have known we were there. The following morning they're all anxious to go back to the compound. They're standing around shivering and generally are very uncomfortable. We consider the temperature mild by comparison.

After we'd all packed up we went back to the compound. Sgt Cross decided to have a debriefing on how the Viets went. It's obvious to us they have a lot to learn. We decide the only way we're going to get results is to concentrate on the squad leaders. The rest of the day is spent with me and two other Australians instructing them. We impress upon them the need to be quiet and for stealth. We also inform them they are to take absolute charge. Their men are to set up the ambush under their direction. They're not to involve themselves in the work. Decisions at the ambush site are not to be made by an organizing committee. We impress upon them the need for them to supervise, maintain control and to keep the whole process in their hands. In order for them to do this they have to know what the process is. That is, the direction from which to arrive at the ambush site, the best place to put in the ambush once at the site, where to site the machine gun, rear protection, the number of claymores required and where to position them and where to position the men. Other details such as ensuring the hand held electrical device has enough charge and that the detonators and detonating cord are in good order are also dealt with.

The other diggers had the Vietnamese soldiers doing the same thing but more from the mechanical function of putting in the ambush point of view.

Late in the afternoon we told them they'd be going out again tonight to practise what they'd learnt today. They were also told that the Australians would remain in the background and that if they do it well we will give them tomorrow night off.

We left the compound at 2030 hrs, and went to another area to put in the ambush. There was still a lot of carry-on and laughing but it was a substantial improvement on the night before. We were not confident that we'd ever achieve a good standard. A standard consistent with the Australians is not deemed possible. In the month we have with them we can only hope to achieve a reasonable standard.

23rd August. It is payday for the Vietnamese, and a day off. The day off is given because the RF go on a drinking spree. The end result of this is they're less than useless and it makes good sense to treat it as one of their days off. If they've got the day off there's no work for us either. The average soldier is paid thirty dollars a month and this is soon to rise to forty dollars. When I first arrived in Vietnam over twelve months ago it was only twenty dollars a month.

Lt. Bin invited us Australians to a party this evening. There were eight of us and he matched our number with his NCOs.

It was a good party. We made a contribution by bringing along some beer. They like our beer but it puts them on their ear pretty quickly. On the other hand, they have a higher tolerance of rice whisky than what we have. We weren't game to ask what meat we were eating. Most of us were sure it was dog because it had a flavour unlike beef. We thought it best to remain ignorant and hopefully enjoy it.

The party finished around midnight and we called it a day. Sergeant Cross thanked Lt. Bin for his hospitality and informs him that us Aussies will host the next party in a couple of weeks.

24th August. Today we concentrated on training the RF in fire and movement. We went to an open area only a hundred metres from the compound in which to do the training. We started off by explaining why fire and movement is necessary. Sergeant Cross then told them his Australian soldiers would give a demonstration. I took my men to the far end of the paddock and had them lie on the ground spread out, but in two groups. When Sgt. Cross blew his whistle to commence, I had the first group stand up and run fifteen metres keeping in line and dropping to the ground and pretending to fire their weapons when they hit the ground. The second group then stood up and ran fifteen metres to a position in advance of the first group dropping to the ground and firing. The first group repeated the process, followed by the second group and so on, until we reached the end of the paddock. It was an excellent demonstration. Extremely well coordinated and carried out. The Vietnamese were impressed.

It was now turn for the Vietnamese to have a go. Sgt. Cross again explained to them what was required and handed the exercise over to the squad leaders for them to carry it out. It took ever so long to organize themselves into groups. Eventually they got there and Sgt. Cross blew the whistle to commence the exercise. They know what to do in theory but to carry it out is entirely a different matter.

Sgt. Cross looks across to me and we both shake our heads in amazement. I said, "That looked like a charge out of a Genghis Khan film Sergeant."

"They're a hopeless lot," he replied. "It must be a cultural thing. It's more of a game to them than anything else."

We ran through it a number of times but their concentration started to wane, so Sergeant Cross told them to go back to the compound, and that we're all going on an ambush tonight and again tomorrow.

26th August. Four children playing near the compound were killed by an M16 mine and assault Pioneers from 9RAR Support Company were called in to assist clear the area to get the children's bodies out. The Vietnamese were concerned we were taking too long to bring the children out but it is common for other mines to be laid to explode on the people going to assist. The area has to be fully cleared first. We believe the mines were laid to get us.

Dat Do is a large town. There are two main roads in and out of the town. One road runs east west and the other north south. Our compound is situated at the southern end of Dat Do, on the road leading south to a village called Phuoc Loi and then the road goes to the coast. Heading south from the compound there's five hundred metres before the township actually gives way to the rice paddies. In this five hundred metres are situated a number of better class homes on large blocks. They have good domestic gardens and a number of fruit trees around their homes. The eastern, northern and north-eastern perimeter of the town is protected by multiple coils of concertina wire and a chain of manned bunkers.

Shortly after we first arrived at our compound in Dat Do we were surprised by a rifle shot. We didn't take too much notice at the time but every now and again a rifle was fired. In the end our curiosity got the better of us. Sergeant Cross asked Lt. Bin what the rifle firing was all about. Lt. Bin informed him that the sentries out in the perimeter bunkers don't have their radios on all the time to conserve batteries. "When we want to talk to them over the radio we fire a shot. They know to turn their radio on when they hear the rifle shot." We didn't offer a battery. We knew they would take it and still use their traditional method of firing the rifle.

27th August. It's Old Souls' Day today and a national holiday. The people in the villages work in their cemeteries tidying up graves and repainting some.

We'd arranged for another party for which we're going to supply all the beer and three days ago we'd sent back a note with money to our boozer by the re-supply vehicle. We'd put in five dollars each to buy the beer. The note asked them to obtain American water containers and to fill the water containers with the cans of beer. These containers have a very large screw top. A man holding a beer can is able to easily fit his hand through the opening. A nominal amount of beer was one thing but the amount we required needed a clandestine approach.

The long-wheeled base Land Rover pulls into our compound. Sitting on top of what looks to be our water are three officers on their way elsewhere. They'd taken advantage of the opportunity to get a ride on our re-supply vehicle. We unloaded the containers and quickly stacked them inside our shed. One of the officers said, "You blokes must go through a lot of water."

"Yes sir we do. We use a lot cleaning things – we don't want to catch the plague down here living with this lot."

"That's good, soldier, very commendable."

The party was a success but we didn't have enough control over the beer. The Vietnamese hanger-ons managed to get away with half of it.

The next few days were put in doing some routine patrolling. We were trying to teach the Vietnamese how to use a compass, protractor and map. They've a basic idea but they know that it's a skill they'll never have to use. They see themselves as base defence and nothing more. On the last day of training we ended up a few miles away from the compound. The day was hot and we'd been working out in the sun. There was no shade at all. Sergeant Cross arranged for a South Vietnamese army vehicle to come and pick us up. Once the Aussies boarded all the seats were taken. This left thirty-one South Vietnamese RF troops to pile on wherever they could. On the bonnet of the truck sat six of them. The driver had to stand on the side running board to see. He steered while another man in the vehicle worked the gears and clutch. There were men on the mudguards, more on the cabin roof, others hanging off the sides and back of the vehicle. You'd think it was impossible to fit thirty-eight people onto a vehicle that had a carrying capacity of eight. They did it though.

1st September. It's a rest day for the Vietnamese. Just as well too. All the Aussies including me have diarrhoea. We're in a terrible state. There is only one thunderbox between the eight of us and at the moment we need eight of them. We come to agreement that each man can only sit on the toilet for thirty seconds and then he has to go to the back of the queue. There are seven standing in the queue all day. We knew that it would have been unlikely to *not* get diarrhoea. Mixing with the grubby little kids who were always around us was a dead certainty to give it to us. The Vietnamese are yet to discover hygiene. On doing a walking tour of the compound a visit to the pit they use as a toilet is not on a list of 'Must Sees." Half the time they don't even get to the pit . . . near enough is good enough. I stumbled on it inadvertently on my second day here. I warned the others as to its whereabouts. Sergeant Cross arranged for some milk of magnesia to come down on the next re-supply.

2nd September. We start training a new platoon today. We've decided to do the training in the compound to be near our toilet. We all have very sore anuses aggravated by the diesel in the drum splashing on our anus. We've decided to put a lot less diesel in the drum for the next few days.

After the day's training was over I took the Vietnamese out on an ambush. I took three other Australians with me. Fortunately there was a sprinkling of Chinese in this group as well. The ambush was purely for training.

3rd September. The army's public relations unit paid us a visit today. They took some photographs of the diggers training the Vietnamese. They told us some of the pictures taken might be submitted to newspapers back home. Apart from that, training proceeded as usual.

4th September. The day started off on routine basis of training but the night was a different matter. At 2300hrs the VC launched an attack on our neighbouring compound, 613 RF Company. There's a training team of Australians from B Coy 9RAR there as well. The attack went on until 0500 hrs. The two 82mm mortars in our compound fired all night in support of the other compound. At the same time, the VC attacked some of the bunkers in the north-eastern section of the town perimeter defence. One of the weapons they used was a flame-thrower and at daylight we found one bunker burnt to a cinder. One of the defenders was found dead, still in a firing position with the weapon half melted in his hands. The Vietnamese RF lost five men killed. Many others were wounded in the attack including three Aussies. The attacking force was countered by support elements of B Company, who also fired their mortars.

Major Ted Chitham, located at district headquarters in Dat Do, orchestrated the defence and called in "Spooky" to destroy the attacking force. Spooky is a DC3 aircraft with gun platforms on it. The mini guns (or Gatling guns) put down a hail of machine gun fire that literally covers almost every six square inches of the targeted zone. Sometimes, out on operations, when we dug our shell scrapes, a shallow body length pit from which to fire from, we also dug another little hole at arms length in front of the pit. In this hole we put a ration can with cooking fuel in it. If Spooky was required at night we'd light the fuel and the aircraft crew, having spotted the ring of fire, know exactly the parameters of our position. Generally speaking, at night he was called "Spooky" and in daylight hours, "Puff the Magic Dragon."

Training has been postponed this morning due to last night's attack. We went ahead with training in the afternoon though.

7th September. Sunday, a rest day for the Vietnamese.

8th September. I took a patrol of Vietnamese out today to more or less have a wander around the southern part of Dat Do. The homes are well spaced and it's definitely the better part of town. We came across a girl working a loom under a skillion roof next to the fence between the roadside and her home. She was an extremely attractive young woman with a flawless complexion. I stood watching her work the loom and spoke to her using one of the Chinese as an interpreter. I spent about fifteen minutes talking to the girl and I could have spent a lot more time, but unfortunately I had to move on.

9th September. It was a strange day today. I took the Viets on a training exercise using a compass. When we got back to the compound a couple of hours later they were given twenty dollars back pay in relation to the pay rise from thirty dollars a month to forty. Whilst it wasn't a normal payday, and therefore a day off, they all decided to abandon their posts and take the day off to get drunk anyway. The RF Company Commander, Lt. Bin, punished the Platoon Sergeant by giving him a physical beating for letting the men abscond. The Platoon Sergeant just had to cop it sweet. He was punched in the head and kicked around quite severely. It wasn't severe enough though to stop him from then going and giving the squad leaders a thorough hiding. The whole beating went down the line. The squad leaders then gave the ordinary soldiers a physical beating. We just watched all this in amazement. It was very entertaining though.

It reminded me of a time last year when some of us from 3 RAR went to the Australian made village of Ap Sui Nhai. A South Vietnamese soldier who'd stabbed his wife for having an affair was put into a bamboo cage. When we came across him he was holding two grenades with the pins pulled from each. The bamboo cage was only about a metre square. If he went to sleep, that was the end of him. I never heard the end result.

Notwithstanding the day's strange activities, we took our training platoon out on a night ambush. The bunkers on the perimeter came under attack again. We were caught up in the firing line and had to go to ground for cover. Bullets zipped over our heads and it wasn't safe to move. Stray rounds ploughed into the dirt within feet of me and I was amazed I wasn't hit by any of them.

10th September. It has poured rain all day today. We trained the Vietnamese in weapon handling but did no training in the evening.

11th September. Another day spent training and there was nothing unusual about the day at all. The fun started at 2300hrs, when the VC launched an attack against our compound. The attack was restricted to rocket propelled grenades being fired into the compound. We took what cover was available and the men manning the perimeter weapon bays returned rifle fire. The attack was short-lived and no real damage was sustained. A few Vietnamese were wounded by shrapnel but there were no life threatening wounds.

12th September. We conducted a normal day of training and then we put in another ambush during the evening. The Vietnamese don't like working at night and there's a bit of disharmony as a result of it. Lt. Bin asks for a pay off, in other words, to get his cooperation, we have to bribe him. One day it's a stretcher, the next it's a lantern, the next a box of C-rations.

We find this extremely disappointing. Here are we Australians, over here in Vietnam, trying our hardest to assist them remain free and out of communist control and it's hard to deal with the fact that, in order for them to co-operate with us and assist stave off a communist victory in their own country, we have to bribe them. This is a turning point in the war for me. Our professionalism as Australian soldiers reflected in our work ethic is worth more than their will to keep their country free. It's not good for any of us.

13th September. It's Sunday and therefore another day off for the Vietnamese. We find this business of having Sunday off quite unusual – something we have got out of the habit of doing. Sunday for the Aussies is just another day in which to fight the war. We don't plan our activities around Sundays. I spent the day checking existing claymores and putting in a few more in front of the compound. I also put in place some flares and connected them with detonator cord.

14th September. We commenced a two-day operation around the outskirts of the village. At 1900hrs we sighted some

VC and called in the Vietnamese mortars from our compound. Sergeant Cross and myself were laying on the side of a rice paddy bund waiting for the mortar to explode what we thought would be a couple of hundred metres in front of us. We heard the whistle of the mortar coming in and then the whistling stopped short of us. We looked at one another in surprise, knowing it was going to be a drop-short and we were in for it. Instead of exploding in front of us where it was supposed to, it exploded only fifty metres behind us. The Vietnamese got all excited and were worried we'd be calling more in. We were lucky that, being the wet season, the effect of the mortar was mitigated by the water and mud in the rice paddy. We didn't bother about calling in more. We'd observed the mortar bays in the compound and they appeared to be left over from the days of the French. The Vietnamese didn't apply science when firing them. The circular bays were about a metre deep and two metres in diameter. The floors of the bays were concrete and the walls were brick. The only directional markings they had were the four points of the compass – north, south, east and west – marked off around the wall of the bay. Everything else was guesswork. Sergeant Cross deemed the friendly mortars to be more of a risk to us than the escaping enemy and we let the matter pass.

15th September. We returned to Nui Dat today, arriving at 1630 hrs. All the men on the training team are quite tired. We're going to have a couple of beers and after the evening meal we're going to call it a day.

16th September. Most of the day was spent in personal administration and tidying up our tent. I had two injections, one for cholera and one for plague. After living with the Vietnamese for a month I wasn't quite sure whether the injections were coincidental or as a result of us being exposed to the squalor of the Vietnamese compound. Either way, I was glad to have the injections.

17th September. We went to work today around the platoon lines. The grass around the tents has grown quite substantially and it's necessary to cut it back. We're all hard at it with slashers. The grass outside Terry James's tent is extremely high and I took a photograph of him and Terry Godde cutting it down

18th September. Another attack of diarrhoea struck me and the other blokes who were at the compound in Dat Do. We're thankful that we're back at Nui Dat and can get quick treatment from Capt. Bruce Perks, the MO.

19th September. We went to a concert at Luscombe airfield this morning and were entertained by a group from South Australia. They put on a really good show. The heavens opened up and a downpour of rain reduced visibility to ten metres. We couldn't see the stage and the entertainers couldn't see the audience. The rain passed in ten minutes and the entertainers could not believe we'd all just sat there through the rain. Nobody moved at all. I think it was the highlight of their trip. They were absolutely amazed we didn't run to get out of the rain.

A little after 1330 hrs, the TCVs called to pick us up to take us to Vung Tau for two days out on the town. I went to see Le Hoa a couple of times. The diggers are fairly subdued this trip. There wasn't any trouble at all. I think the trouble from last time has quietened them down a bit. We left Vung Tau at 0930 hrs on the 21st of September to return to Nui Dat.

22nd September. Today I took fourteen men out on a TAOR patrol. The only difficulties we had were crossing some streams turned into swollen rivers from the daily monsoonal downpours. Our toggle ropes connected together came in handy reducing the risks. The first man crossed with the rope tied around his waist. Once he was safely across he was able to tie the rope off on his side. The last man across had his end of the rope tied around his waist. I didn't want to come back minus any men or rifles as happened on the previous patrol when two M16 rifles were lost in a river. These rivers can turn from moderate to dangerous in a matter of minutes. Sometimes you can get one or two men across without a problem, but then the river can rise a metre in minutes, making crossing dangerous.

23rd September. Four platoon mounted company duties today. For those not assigned specific tasks like working in the officers' mess, sergeants' mess or the ORs' mess there is other work of a general nature to do around the company lines. For example, drainage for the ablution blocks needs attending to from time to time.

On the 27th September, B Company went on a show of strength up Route 15 towards Bien Hoa Province. The whole company was mounted on APCs and supported by tanks. It's good to let the local people view this type of force from time to time – hopefully it will help keep them on the government side.

30th September. At 0800hrs, we flew out of Nui Dat on Operation Jack into an area named Apache, in AO Stuart. AO Stuart is in the southern part of Bien Hoa Province. Bien Hoa stands for 'land of peaceful frontiers' which it might have been once upon a time but it no longer qualifies for such a nice name now.

We got there to find a desolate place, previously defoliated. We moved only five hundred metres from the landing zone before we harboured up for the night. The next morning we returned to Apache to pick up some American Engineers we have to escort for three and a half kilometres to a river they wish to check out for a possible bridge site. The bridge will be required to move heavy equipment used by the land clearing teams across the river.

The next day we marched back to Apache and by the time we got there the diggers were very tired. Unfortunately, we still had to go another fifteen hundred metres to a track we're going to ambush for the night.

Next morning we packed up the ambush and marched back to Apache. We arrived there at 0800 hrs and boarded choppers to fly to an area five kilometres east, along the Firestone trail. A re-supply was received at this point, before marching eight hundred metres north to a river. We had our midday meal there and then crossed the river and went a further fifteen hundred metres to a night position. By this time my shirt and trousers were badly torn and I had sore feet. My pack felt it was getting heavier by the minute. The day's march covered four kilometres. This is an unusually hard day. Three thousand metres is generally considered a good day's work in jungle and thick scrub. The following day we were joined by company head quarters and Five Platoon. We didn't move for the day and were thankful for the rest.

The next day we marched to a feature where we met up with the forward elements of the land clearing team. We remained there for the night. The platoon rejoined the rest of the Company the following day and received a re-supply. At 1415 hrs we left that position and marched two thousand metres northwest, to harbour up. There were a lot of monkeys in the trees and it was interesting to watch them jumping from limb to limb. Sometimes they miscalculated the length of the jump and had to quickly move to plan B. While I was watching the small monkeys a very large monkey, which looked like a Gibbon, came swinging through the trees. I thought it must be a Gibbon because it was the size of an Orang-utan. He nonchalantly swung through the trees above our heads and continued on his way. The other monkeys hung around all night and never gave us a moment's peace in which to get some sleep.

We broke harbour at 0700 hrs, and marched to a former landing zone to spend the night. The following morning we marched a thousand metres northwest, looking for a clearing positioned on the map. The clearing wasn't where we thought it would be and we had to march nearly double the distance to find it, and the men were quite thirsty by this time. I've got two new reinforcements in my section, one is Bluey Bert and the other Graham Pollock. We're having a rest and something to eat in the shade of some bamboo.

Bluey looks across to Pollock and says, "Graham me old mate, I'm right out of water – can you spare me a drink." Graham, reaching for his water bottle, handed it over and said, "Here ya are Blue, take a small swig out of this, but not too much though, that's all I've got."

Bluey took the bottle and unscrewed the cap, then tilting his head right back he raised the bottle to an inch above his now wide open mouth. The cool clear water poured straight down his throat in one continuous stream, glug, glug, glug and the lot was gone in a blink.

"You bastard Blue! You bloody bastard! I said you could have a small swig to keep you going but you've drunk the lot, you prick!" Bluey, wiping his mouth and with a big grin on his face, said. "I just couldn't help myself Pollock. Once the cool water was trickling down my throat, I didn't have the strength to pull the bottle away."

"You're nothing but a bastard Blue! Now I don't have a drop myself, ya prick."

I was listening to all this, and at the same time watching a couple of scrub fowls pecking around amongst the dry bamboo leaves on the ground. They didn't seem to mind me sitting only a couple of metres away. They're colourful little things, about the size of a bantam. I made sure not to move, as I knew they'd dart away in a flash. It was a good little spot to have a rest. Apart from the scrub fowls there were also red squirrels running around on the ground, then darting up the bamboo and jumping down to the ground again. Squirrels are quite a common sight.

Turning to Pollock, I said, "Well Graham, you know what to do next time mate. A bottle of water, or part thereof, is ten bucks to arseholes like Blue. It's cash up front, or die of thirst. No dough, no drink."

"I've bloody well learnt a good lesson today Stan, some buggers just don't appreciate a favour."

It rained all night and it was impossible to keep the water from running into our hootchies. We used entrenching tools to dig gutters to take the water away but the rain was too heavy and we were camped on some slightly sloping real estate. The gutters overflowed and in poured the water. It was a miserable night to say the least.

9th October. We received a re-supply and the company moved to deploy around a suspected enemy bunker system. We couldn't find the system and a number of patrols were sent out looking for sign. Lt. Langler asked me to take my section out on quite an extensive patrol looking for tracks used by the VC. The area we were asked to cover required a journey of four legs. Most patrols were contained within three legs. Each leg on this particular patrol was about a thousand metres. After we'd gone a hundred metres from the company, we broke out of the jungle onto a large flat plain. The plain was featureless. There were no hills or mountains from which to get bearings. The grass on the plain was up to our knees and was punctuated by clumps of bamboo scattered randomly across the plain. Each clump looked like the next. There was nothing to distinguish one part of the plain from another. We patrolled along the predetermined legs, on their respective compass bearings, stopping every hour for a smoke or a brew. We'd left the company position at 1100hrs and were looking for tracks that cut across the plain and also tracks on the edge where the plain gave way to jungle. If we found a track it might suggest a bunker system nearby.

We were making very good time. The only hold up was wading through the long grass. The grass was wet from the rain early this morning. We were half way along the third leg when Vic Patrick, the forward scout, stopped and beckoned for me to come alongside him. I walked up and Vic, pointing to an object on the grass, said, "What do you make of that Stan? That large egg over there."

"Jeez, it is a large egg. I've never seen one as big as that before. It's much bigger than any emu egg I've seen."

I signalled the other five blokes to come and have a look as well.

"Shit! What sort of an egg is that, there's no bloody emus or cassowaries in Vietnam, are there?" asked Henderson. "Not that I'm aware of," chipped in Peter Wynd.

"What about ostriches? Are there any ostriches?" asked Vic Patrick. "No. Only in South Africa," I replied.

"What about a snake?" asked Wynd. "Could it be one of those great big pythons? You know, the ones that grow twenty feet long. Big, like a power pole."

"Fuck Peter! Snakes don't lay eggs," responded Vic.

"Yeah some do. I think those big pythons do," replied Wynd.

At this point in the conversation everybody had a look over their shoulder and sideways as if half expecting a big python to wrap itself around them. "I think Peter's right. There's definitely no bird that lays an egg this big in Vietnam," I said.

"What about we take it back with us and have scrambled egg for dinner tonight," suggested John Arnold.

"Bullshit we will!" said Peter. "The mother will follow our trail and swallow one of us up while we're asleep tonight. Anyway, there'll be a baby snake inside. You can't scramble snake eggs."

"Yeah. We'll leave it alone. The mother is probably not too far away. Let sleeping dogs lie I say. C'mon Vic, push off mate and we'll follow."

Vic Patrick headed in the direction we were going and the rest fell into their spot in the line as we left.

There were only about six hundred metres to the end of the third leg. We got there in half an hour and pulled up under some bamboo for a rest and a smoke.

After fifteen minutes I said, "C'mon fellows, saddle up, we're on our way again." When everybody had got to their feet and put their packs on, I said to Vic, "Right Vic. Are you ready to lead out?" "Yeah, I'm right to go."

Pointing to indicate the direction I said, "Right, head out mate."

He looked at me with confusion on his face and said, "We're going home aren't we Stan?" "Yes, this is the last leg."

"Well if we're going home, we gotta go that way," he said, pointing in a totally different direction.

"No! It's the way I indicated. I've been following the map and compass."

Vic was quite sure I was wrong and he said to the other blokes, "Any of you blokes got any idea the way we gotta go to get home?"

Four of them sided with Vic's sense of direction and two didn't have any idea. This made me a little worried and I said, "Righto! Let's have a look at the map and our bearings again. It won't hurt to spend a few minutes checking."

I spread the map out on the ground. The four legs we had to march on were ruled and marked in red ink on the map. The bearings were written down in my notebook, which I'd taken out and put down on the map. The relative page was open showing the bearings. Taking my protractor from my pocket, I positioned it on the map to get the first bearing and asked, "Well Vic. What does it say? Does it agree with the first leg written down?"

"Yes it's OK," he replied.

"Now for the second." I repositioned the protractor and said, "What does this one say Vic? Does it agree with the second leg?"

"Yes, it agrees Stan."

Repositioning the protractor I asked again, "Does the third leg agree Vic?" It did.

"OK. Now for the last leg." I said repositioning the protractor. Vic beat me to it this time. "It agrees with what's written down as well Stan."

"OK then, there's only one thing left to do. I took the compass out of its pouch on my belt. During our smoko, I'd preset the compass for the last leg and, placing it down on the map, I waited until the compass card settled and then said, "You tell me which way it's pointing Vic and that's the way we'll go."

Vic stood up and pointed to the direction in which I'd indicated to him five minutes earlier.

"I'm heading off in that direction," I said. "You blokes can be guided by your fucked-up sense of direction but I'm sticking with the compass."

"I'm coming with you Stan, these other dickheads can go where they like," said John Arnold.

"With a big grin on my face I asked, "Is anybody else coming with me and John? Hold up your hands if you're coming with us." The other five held up their hands.

It was nice to pretend for a minute that we were a democratic patrol and that the diggers had a choice. We all knew there were no individual choices. I was the patrol leader and that was that. The responsibility for the patrol was mine but it was a little bit of fun anyway. Furthermore, it was good to involve them in the exercise. Compass protractor and map is interesting when the exercise has a practical application such as the one we just went through. It was also a good reminder to the rest of the patrol that a featureless plain, like this one, has its own traps, when reliance for direction is based on one's senses.

Vic led off and another hour elapsed before we came across the track we'd made when we originally came out from the jungle onto the plain. We then simply followed our track back into the company position.

10th October. Four VC were killed today on the edge of a bunker system. The system was the one we were looking for yesterday. It was late in the afternoon when the company came across it. The VC look quite young and they appear to be North Vietnamese regulars. It's raining lightly and the blood draining from them is mixing in with the water on the ground, making the blood easier to smell. To me they always look like wax dummies soon after they're shot and have bled a bit. All colour goes from their face.

The company has moved into the bunker system and taken it over. The system is typical of most others. They have their fire lighting areas walled up so that light from the fire is contained. The bunkers are well camouflaged and the system is in dense jungle as usual. Sunlight finds it hard to penetrate through the canopy and the wet ground has absorbed the pungent odour of the inhabitants and we feel dirty just being here. Even though we're filthy in our own sweat and dirt, it's our own friendly dirt which we're used to and it seems clean by comparison.

By the time the company had spread itself out for the night it was getting on dark. My section found itself harboured next to the dead VC and only metres from their shit pit. The smell is unbearable. All through the night it rained heavy. I've pitched my hootchie to protect myself from the rain and I'm lying under it in my silk, listening to the rain falling onto my hootchie. Large drips from the trees fall, making a heavier amplified sound as they hit the plastic. I've pitched my hootchie the closest to the dead bodies in consideration of me being the Section Commander. On my own, and in my hootchie in an enemy camp with dead bodies only metres away and rain coming down, doesn't particularly make me feel comfortable. If you're not on picket the pitch dark and the heavy rain makes you stay in your hootchie and despite the fact there's about another ninety blokes or so in the camp you're still lonely on your own when it's raining like this and you have no-one to talk to.

I'm wondering what the hell I'm doing here so far from home and I feel a little detached from my real self. My imagination is running a little wild and I'm thinking to myself. "What if the VC put in a probe to recover their dead? I won't be able to hear them because of the rain on my hootchie. They'll surely stumble over my hootchie, and here I'll be, stuck in my silk, like a trussed up pig," but the night is wild with thunder, lightning and rain and only a superhuman could do what my imagination is running away with. My common sense tells me nobody can creep up in this, or even more to the point, would want to creep up. Knowing this, though, was little help in getting to sleep. At some stage through the night I managed to get to sleep but I was glad when daylight broke.

After we'd breakfasted, we set about destroying the camp. Trees were ring-barked and items that would burn were thrown onto a fire. A couple of American helicopter gun ships saw the smoke and came for a look. At this point we became worried. Americans in the course of their history have developed a reputation, earned or unearned, for shooting up their allies by mistake. The gun ships are hovering just above the jungle canopy so they can get a good look. I can plainly see a door gunner standing up and leaning out for a better look. I quickly look around for a VC bunker to jump into if he starts firing. In the meantime, all the diggers are waving their bush hats and giving the thumbs up sign. Once the Americans are satisfied we were Australians they departed the scene. Bien Hoa Province is American responsibility, and normally their area of operations, even though we conduct a lot of operations here as well. However, there are always American choppers around about up here.

After the bunker system was earmarked for an air strike, we moved out. In the afternoon we came upon a river that was swollen from last night's heavy rain. There was no hope of crossing it before next morning. The following morning the river had subsided enough for us to cross.

Once across, we marched to an old re-supply area where choppers flew in to re-supply us. Having been re-supplied, we boarded APCs and were taken three and a half kilometres to the Song Ca River, just north of the border between Phuoc Tuy and Long Khan provinces. The Company had a swim in the river and at 1200hrs commenced to move two and a half kilometres to the south-east. After a short rest in this position, four platoon broke away from the Company and went another five hundred metres to harbour up. The following day we checked out an entire grid square but failed to find anything of significance.

15th October. Four platoon is to rendezvous for a re-supply 3½ kilometres away from our current position. The march is hard and hot. Little shade is available. My gunner, Jimmy Martin, went down with heat exhaustion only 500 metres from the finish. We got him into a little bit of shade and poured what water we had over him from our water bottles to get his body temperature down. While we were waiting for Jim to recover, we took off our packs and had a rest. Graham Pollock and Bluey Bert are nearby. Graham yells over to Bluey, "Hey Bluey! Have you got any water mate? I need a drink. I poured all what I had over Jim to cool him down."

Bluey looks across to Graham and says, "Pollock, old chap! There's one thing ya gotta learn in this man's army, and that is you have to look after number one. Sorry mate."

Graham, put out because only a few days ago he gave Bluey a drink, even though he was short of water himself, and Bluey had drunk the lot on him, says, "Bluey, there's one thing I have learnt in this man's army you're by far the biggest prick in it!" "C'mon Pollock don't be like that mate," Bluey replies.

Graham, looking across to me, says, "That Bluey! He's such an arsehole!"

After half an hour Jim recovered sufficiently to move on. However, I didn't want him carrying the machine gun so I gave it to his number two, Haydn Watt, to carry for the rest of the day.

We made the rendezvous in time. The reason why we had to make sure we arrived in time was to vote in the federal elections. Not long after we arrived the re-supply choppers came in carrying ballot boxes as well. All the diggers were given voting papers to complete and place in the boxes. After I'd voted I lay back against a tree and thought to myself, what a great country Australia is, democracy at its best. Here we are, fighting in a war out in the jungle somewhere in a foreign land, and the system gives us the opportunity to vote. We haven't got the faintest idea what we're voting for and we don't have a clue as to the issues, though we suspect the war is the main issue. God only knows who our local electorate contestants are, but this is what we're fighting for. All we can do in our ignorance of the issues, is to vote in terms of the party card of our choice.

After we'd all voted, and had been re-supplied, four platoon went another one thousand metres to a night harbour position. We left the harbour at 0800hrs, and marched south for 2½ kilometres to a river. The troops were very hot and tired so sentries were posted and we all jumped in for a swim. It's good to have the opportunity to have a wash and get rid of our sweat and grime. A few of us washed our clothes as well. Putting on wet shirts and trousers is the least of our problems – at least they're relatively clean and don't stink as much.

After we'd rested and had a brew, we pushed on for another five hundred metres. Barry Wakefield took out a small party from his section on a water detail. They heard enemy voices. Subsequently, we remained as a blocking force and five platoon swept through the area, driving enemy out of a bunker system. Five platoon seems to be having all the luck. Only a few days ago, Lt. Peter Cosgrove and his platoon assaulted an enemy manned bunker system, killing a number of VC.

Once five platoon had completed their sweep and secured the system Company Headquarters and six platoon joined them. We followed into the camp the next morning and not long after we got there we went on a clearing patrol about four hundred metres out from the camp. Two VC, entering the camp unaware we'd taken it over, were shot dead.

18th October. Four platoon moved to a bridge crossing the river not far away from the bunker system. We put in a very good and well set up ambush but, unfortunately, it was not sprung. Back at the bunker system, engineers arrived and placed eight hundred pounds of explosives to destroy the camp. Once they'd completed their work we moved to a safe distance and then the camp was destroyed. Five and six platoons marched south and four platoon along with Company Headquarters moved back into the camp to set up an ambush for the night. No enemy came back into the camp during the night however, and at daybreak we packed up and moved south for fifteen hundred metres, harbouring up for the night on the bank of a river.

Allan Tonkin's one section and my three section went on a 3000 metre patrol. We didn't find anything to suggest enemy had recently been in the area. When we returned to the main body, along with Company Headquarters, we moved two kilometres to join up with six platoon who were occupying a bunker system. We arrived at the system and shortly after an ambush that was set up on the edge of the system was sprung. Three VC were killed in action as a result.

The next day the Company moved south to the Firestone trail where we were re-supplied. Four platoon remained on the trail and set up an ambush for the night.

23rd October. Four platoon moved north along the Firestone trail and into a position we're going to ambush for three days. My section has a very uncomfortable position in amongst a lot of rocks with sharp edges sticking into us. All the same, it's a very good position tactically.

Six platoon in an ambush position on the trail killed a VC the next day. We also saw a number of VC but they were too far away to engage and, unfortunately, they didn't come our way.

25th October. B Company received a re-supply on the Firestone trail and then headed south to find ambush sites. Four platoon went 2½ kilometres but we couldn't find a decent track to task on. The next day we went north and put in an ambush on a prospective track. It rained all night making us uncomfortable and minimizing our chances of success as well.

26th October. We packed up and left the ambush position at 0645hrs, earlier than normal because we have a very big day's march ahead of us. Along the way I ran out of water and became thirsty. Fortunately, before the day's end, we came upon a river from which we were able to refill our water bottles. By the end of the day we'd marched five kilometres and by normal standards this is a lot of leg work. We put in an ambush a short distance from the river on an ox cart track. The following morning APCs came to pick us up to take us back to the rest of the Company to be re-supplied and we remained with the Company for the day in order to rest up a little.

29th October. We boarded APCs and went up the Firestone trail to a culvert, which is to be our three-day ambush position. All three platoons went into ambush positions spaced out a short distance along the trail. We saw ten VC carrying branches as camouflage above their heads coming our way. When the VC hear aircraft overhead, they go to ground and hold the branches over themselves, making it virtually impossible to spot them.

We were in a much better position to engage them than the other platoons but unfortunately six platoon couldn't resist the temptation to have a go and scared them off. We would've had good results had the VC been allowed to come through to us.

5RAR are shortly to take over from us in the AO and on the 30th of October we moved along the trail to where a new fire support base was to be established for them. We patrolled around the area to secure it. We were informed an American general was paying the unit a visit and he wanted to talk to the diggers around the perimeter. We were given boot polish and brushes and told to clean our boots. The general came around some time later with an entourage of American and Australian officers in tow. We looked quite odd with clean boots and filthy clothes. As he approached our individual positions, we got to our feet and came to attention. When it was my turn, he asked in his American accent, "How are you doing today soldier?"

"Very well thank you sir." I replied, and he moved on to the next digger, Haydn Watt.

Haydn was already standing, having done so when he saw the general approaching me. The general asked, "And your name soldier?"

"Watt sir," replied Haydn.

"Your name soldier – I asked you your name."

"That is my name sir, Private Hadyn Watt sir."

"I see, I beg your pardon, soldier. How are you doing today private Watt?"

"I'm fine, thank you sir."

Haydn was standing before the general with his polished boots, but his shirt and trousers looked as though he'd been dragged through the pig-pen and back again. We'd been out in the bush a month by now and we all looked a shower of shit standing there stinking in our filthy clothes.

The general looked him up and down and asked, "How often do you men get a clean set of clothes?"

Haydn always had a cheeky sort of grin enhanced by his moustache. He couldn't suppress one now spreading across his face, and replied, "Well sir, I can't ever recall getting clean clothes out in the bush. We don't expect clean clothes in the bush sir."

"How long then soldier have you been out on this operation?"

"About a month sir."

"Goddam! A month without clean clothes! Goddam!" Turning to one of his American officers, he said, "Did you hear that Captain? I like these Aussies. A whole month the man said. Our guys are a bunch of pussies, Captain!"

"Yes sir. I did sir, a month sir. Our guys are pussies sir."

"Goddam!" he said again and then moved on to the next digger.

31st. October. We remained harboured up in defensive positions around the fire support base while it was being established. It seemed a long day and I didn't sleep that well during the night.

The next morning B Company flew out of the Firestone trail by chopper and we were back at Nui Dat by 1000 hrs. We'd been out a month and stank a lot. Once we'd cleaned our weapons, it was good to have a shower and put on clean clothes. The first beer in over a month was terrific.

The next day we had to ourselves. It enabled us to get our gear clean and generally do whatever we wanted to do. Once I was pretty well squared away I paid a visit to an old school friend, Barry McDermott, who was a cook around in D Company.

3rd November. My birthday. I was looking forward to having a few celebratory beers with my mates. Unfortunately, the men's tolerance to beer has disappeared as a consequence of them drinking only water for the last month. A number of them overdid it last night at the boozer and Captain Dugdale has closed the boozer for 24- hours in punishment. My mother has sent me a nice birthday cake and, unable to go to the boozer, Allan, Barry and myself decided it was a good idea to remain in our tent and eat the cake. We did, and we thoroughly enjoyed it.

4th November. Lt. Langler asked me to put my section to work on sandbagging the corners of his tent. The diggers did a good job and were finished by lunch-time. I let them have the afternoon off to enjoy the Melbourne Cup. We had a sweep going but unfortunately, the horse I drew had a propensity for looking at the arses of horses in front.

5th November. We were informed that Lance Corporal Bink was killed by a land mine today. Binky, as we called him, had served in four platoon for about eight months. On learning this, I thought back to the occasions when he was acting section commander while Allan Tonkin was away on R & R leave or R & C leave. Binky had a bad habit of wanting to put his machine gun group in a spot I'd picked out for my machine gun group. As I outranked Binky, he always had to tell his gunners, Tex Bruce and Laurie Smillie, to pick up their gun and move it to another spot. Tired and hot gunners hate to be asked to pick up the gun again to move once they've put it down. Once Binky's group had moved I'd then have my gunner, Jimmy Martin, put his gun down in the same spot. Tex and Laurie never went crook at me, they always abused Binky for getting it wrong in the first place. I was saddened by the news of Binky's death and reflected upon my behaviour towards him in telling him to shift his gun group all the time.

Lt. Langler has been making us do an early morning run and my muscles are stiff and sore as a result. The diggers are fit to carry a heavy pack all day but most of us have got out of being fit to run. You never run with a heavy pack on your back if you can help it.

7th November. At 0815, four platoon flew out by chopper to the Short Green. When we got there my section boarded an APC to provide infantry protection for the Engineers on land clearing. Helicopter gunships rocketed and strafed the area prior to us moving in. The next day all my section had to do was remain in the temporary camp set up for the task. It was extremely hot as it always is down there. The place is all sand, which reflects the heat. It's one of the most uncomfortable days I've ever spent in Vietnam and that's really saying something – there are lots of contenders for the honour.

In the middle of the night, Tex Bruce, having a dream, sat bolt upright and yelled out, "You silly bugger! You've left the gate open and now all the sheep have got out." Tex went back to sleep straight away, meanwhile every other bloke in the platoon, woken by the yelling, is standing to, with their rifle in their hands, peering out into the blackness of the night expecting an attack. We naturally thought it was the enemy yelling to one another. Nobody on our side yells out during the night so it has to be the enemy. We stood to for half an hour while Tex was sound asleep rounding his sheep up.

9th November. We left the Long Green at 0815hrs and flew back to Nui Dat. We had a couple of hours to get ourselves organized because B Company is leaving at 1115hrs on a three-day operation.

After arriving at the drop off area, four platoon went north for a distance of about thirteen hundred metres to harbour up and by that time we all had dozens of leeches on our bodies.

The next day, we moved east and came across a bunker system. Explosives were dropped in with Engineers and the system was blown. We went further east before harbouring up for the night.

11th November. Armistice Day, but we're going to soldier on, so we broke harbour at first light and met up with Company Headquarters later in the morning. In the afternoon we were working close to five platoon. At some stage in the afternoon the forward scout of the lead section of five platoon was crossing a creek and a VC, moving to get a better position from which to shoot at them, was spotted by the Section Commander. The Section Commander opened up with his M16, scaring the VC away. By the number of packs they left behind, it was estimated there were nine of them. It appears they'd stopped for a bit of a spell but unfortunately for them, five platoon came along and spoilt their party.

The next day we returned to Nui Dat, arriving there at 0900hrs. I took advantage of a bit of spare time to go down to Pearsons Pogo Palace for a haircut. Its correct name is Pearsons Community Centre, named after a former Task Force Commander, Brigadier Pearson. Notwithstanding that, it will always be referred to as Pearson's Pogo Palace . . . the pogos are the only ones who will generally be able to use the facilities there. The warriors will always be out in the bush on operations and won't have much opportunity. If they're lucky though, they'll be able to snatch a haircut like me from time to time.

13th November. Allan Tonkin, Barry Wakefield and I were on the ball early today to make sure our men turned themselves out looking reasonably well dressed for the Battalion's Second Anniversary Parade. Formal parades have been a rarity, even at platoon level, let alone Company or Battalion level. At 1000 hrs, Sergeant Cross called us on parade and he ran us through a few drills. Lt. Langler arrived on the scene and Sgt. Cross handed the platoon over to him. We marched all spick and span to the Company parade ground to be joined by Company Headquarters and Five and Six Platoons.

B Company then marched to Kapyong helicopter strip to meet up with the rest of the battalion for the parade. Such an event reinforced the cohesiveness of the Battalion. Brigadier 'Black' Jack Weir took the salute. Finally, with a Military band playing, we marched back to our company lines.

After lunch, Lt. Langler called me to his tent to inform me that in the morning I'd be marching out to D & E Platoon, Headquarter Company, 1ATF. I'd heard of D & E Platoon but didn't have the slightest idea of what they did, but imagined it to be an easier life than with a battalion. I later found this not to be so.

I spent the rest of the day packing my gear.

Chapter 6

D & E Platoon, under Cosgrove

✦

On the morning of the 14th November I said my goodbyes to the platoon and, along with a number of others from 9RAR, was trucked over to HQ Company. When we got there, no tents were available and we dossed down anywhere we could find for the night.

The following morning, we erected two tents and started to sandbag up one of them. We finished the first tent that day which allowed some of the fellows to move in. The men seem quite happy with themselves as pressure of being in a battalion doesn't seem evident, even though none of us has any idea what D & E Platoon is all about. At this stage we haven't seen much of the Platoon Commander, 2nd Lt. Russ Henderson, or Sergeant Rick Jeffrey. After they'd introduced themselves and welcomed us, we were simply instructed to get tents up and organize ourselves into them. We were then left alone to do it.

The next day, we had the second tent sandbagged by lunchtime. In the absence of any other orders or direction from Sgt. Jeffrey, I knocked the men off. They'd worked well sandbagging the two tents. After I'd tidied myself up I pulled out my captured AK 47 and asked if anybody wanted to buy it. The weapon was in good shape and I ended up selling it for $21.

The following day, all the men who'd arrived from 9RAR, except for one, volunteered to go into D & E Platoon. A few had come from B Coy., Jim Muir, Ken Redding and Colin Moyle came from five platoon, Bluey, Bert and myself from four platoon and then there were Bluey Lewis from D company and men from the other two companies of 9RAR. The men were sorted into their respective sections and I was given the job as Section Commander of Three Section. The other two Section Commanders were Des Weller, One Section, and Bob Pollard Two Section.

Lt Russ Henderson and Platoon Sergeant Sgt. Rick Jeffrey and a number of the men have already been with D & E Platoon a long time. Lt. Henderson, through Sgt. Jeffrey, informed us that we would be going out tomorrow for at least a six-day operation and to get ourselves sorted with rations and ammunition. After that, we used the rest of the day writing letters and attending to personal matters.

On the 18th November at 1415hrs the platoon left Nui Dat aboard a troop of APCs, along Route 2, until the lead track was knocked out by a mine, just north of the village of Ngai Giao. Fortunately, nobody was seriously hurt and the damaged vehicle was taken back to Nui Dat. We subsequently harboured up for the night a few hundred metres east of Route 2.

Next day, we continued our way up Route 2 with minesweepers clearing the way. Later in the day, we cut across country east of Route 2, until we entered a rubber plantation. At the same time as we entered the plantation two VC were seen running down a track and into the jungle on the western side of the rubber plantation. The infantry dismounted from the carriers and Lt. Henderson ordered the platoon to check out the track. Dusk was setting in and it was also starting to rain again. Corporal Des Weller's section led the way into the jungle with his forward scout, Jim Fraser out in front. Following was Platoon Headquarters and then the other two sections.

We'd only gone into the jungle about a hundred metres when rifle fire was exchanged. Lt. Henderson, having his rifle shot from his hands in the exchange, took into account the rapidly failing light and heavier rain and ordered a withdrawal back into the Courtney rubber plantation where we harboured up for the night.

Jim Fraser went up to Lt. Henderson, and said, "You know boss, there were two of the buggers. I saw them silhouetted against the fading light. I reckon I got one of 'em though, but I can't be sure. There was also firing coming in at us from two o'clock and ten o'clock. I reckon there's a bunker system nearby."

"Don't worry Jim, we'll sort it all out in the morning. We can't do anything tonight. If you got him, chances are he'll still be there tomorrow. If there was only one other on the track, he'll have shot through."

First thing the following morning, Lt. Henderson told me to take my section down the track again to the point of contact and have a look around. The platoon had only been together about three days and a lot of us had not worked with one another before but everybody in the platoon was well experienced and the men had no problem settling in and working well together.

Lt. Henderson is well experienced and is due to go home shortly, as is Sgt. Rick Jeffrey who has done a previous tour with 1RAR. Cpl. Des Weller is also on his second tour. On his first tour Des joined 6RAR as a reinforcement after the battle of Long Tan and then, when 6RAR went home, he joined 2RAR until his time was up. Including myself, also on my second tour, I doubt there'd be another Australian Infantry Platoon in Vietnam with this amount of experience.

I requested the forward scout for Three Section to head off. I've only known him a week and I'm not sure at this stage whether he's experienced enough for the job. He's carrying an automatic SLR, which I find strange. It's a heavy weapon to carry compared to the more favoured M16. As we passed from the rubber into the jungle I went up to him and told him that upon return to Nui Dat I'd be much happier if he exchanged it for an M16. I felt the automatic SLR is most likely to pull up and off to the right and not be able to bring a number of rounds accurately to the target. The scout had spent time as a tracker with the dogs, but I doubted his credentials as a forward scout. Anyway, time will tell, I thought.

I instructed him to lead off again and to exercise caution. Once we got down the track to within forty metres from the contact point I lay on my stomach and had a look forward under the undergrowth. I stood up and signalled for Montesalvo to stop. I made my way to him and said, "There's a body on the track some forty metres ahead."

"How do you know?' Montesalvo asked.

"It pays to get down on your guts now and then and to have a look under the foliage, you will be surprised how much you can see, particularly in this rainforest type of jungle."

We made our way to the body and secured the area by pushing a little further down the track and out to the flanks and placing sentries. Looking at the body before we moved it, it was obvious the force of the rounds had lifted him into the air. It was also obvious that he would have been dead before he hit the ground. He finished up in a sitting position, as one would be in doing the splits. His head was resting on the knee of his outstretched right leg. His left leg protruded straight behind him

I said to the forward scout, "Have a good look at where Jim's rounds have hit him. The poor bugger's been hit with a solid burst of rounds, striking him in the right thigh and up his whole right side as far as his chest. I reckon at least eight rounds have hit him. I very much doubt if your weapon, kicking like hell, could do the same."

"I think you're right," the scout replied. "I'll get rid of it when we get back."

I put a toggle rope on the body and ordered everybody down while I gave a good pull. This was just in case the body had been booby trapped during the night. After waiting a few seconds, I gave the all clear and we checked the body out for papers. He was carrying what we commonly call an AK50 which, in essence, is an AK47 with a folding bayonet attached. One of the men checked his top pocket, which was secured by a safety pin. He came up with a small clear plastic bag with money in it and, giving it to me, he said, "A top up to platoon funds Corporal."

I didn't open the bag, but shoved it in my own top pocket.

We left the body for collection by his comrades and took his weapon back to our Platoon base. We didn't push down the track again for a more substantial look and the next day we were back on the carriers, heading west across Route 2 until we came upon an illegal village. This is a village outside government zones specified for the location of a village and therefore, without doubt, a communist village. We approached the village on the high ground, giving us a better view of the lay of the village. Suddenly a VC, dressed only in shorts, took off across our front to our right. He was running across a hundred metres of open space, heading towards the jungle. The grass was up to his waist and he ran like a Springbok, taking giant leaps to clear the grass. A few of us saw him at the same time. The Crew Commander of the carrier, opened up with his twin 30 calibre guns, but the VC made it into the jungle before anybody could get a good shot at him. None of the infantry sitting on top of the carrier could bring their weapons around in time to take good aim before firing.

We went through the village, finding only women and children. The houses were well spaced out. There was not one male over ten years of age in the whole place. No doubt they were off with their VC units somewhere. We left the village later in the day and set off more or less southwest to put in an ambush.

Failing light forced Lt. Henderson to task on the only track we could find. It was an old centurion tank track, about six inches deep, which had been turned into a footpad but it looked as though it hadn't been used for a long time. Sergeant Rick Jeffrey came up to me and said, "Well Stan, Buddha was the last bloke to use this track but we've none other, there's no time before it gets dark to look for a better one and the boss says it will have to do. You are to put in an ambush at this end of the track and you'll have Des Weller's gun group, that's Greg Kennett and Demo as well as your section. The rest of us, along with Bob Pollard's section, including the carriers, will be setting up ambushes to your rear to catch anybody heading toward the village. They're more likely to be going in than out, seeing that we've already gone through the place today. Anybody in there is not going to come our way. They know we'll be down around here somewhere for sure. So in actual fact your ambush will be in the rear."

Seeing the track hadn't been used for ages, I decided to take my boots off for the night and give my feet a rest.

I carried six of the sections claymore mines and Brian Grace carried the other two. I carried them to ensure the ends of the detonating cords were kept dry. If the ends get wet the white powder like explosive substance in the cords end, turns a green, yellow colour. This had to be cut off or otherwise there is a good chance the mines won't blow. Furthermore, I like to keep good control over the process of putting them out. I normally have one other to assist me, generally the man who carries the other two mines. The track looking out from our position goes north about twenty metres, then sharp west about forty metres then northeast. The killing ground is the sixty metres of the north and western segments of the track.

I positioned the machine gun half a metre in, on the left side of the track and looking up the track to that part of the killing ground running north. There are about ten of us in the ambush. I spread the men out in a straight line to the left of the M60 facing up the track. The other M60 carried by Greg Kennett is positioned on the western end of the line, giving him and demo an arc of fire more than 180 degrees. The first claymore mine is sited close to the machine gun at the track, but angled in such a way to ensure the back blast from the mine won't be a problem.

The claymores are sited so that each mine's fan shaped directional lethal zone overlaps the mine in front of it, and so on, for the whole eight claymores which are each spaced about four metres apart. Placing the machine gun almost on the track acts as a good deterrent to the picket from nodding off during the night. Nobody wants the enemy walking over the top of them in the middle of the night and this keeps them awake. Once the ambush was set up, and the order of picket made known to the men, there was nothing left to do other than have something to eat before it got dark. We then settled down for the night.

At 0100hrs I woke to a hell of a bang from the bank of exploded claymores. My position is only two metres behind the M60 machine gun facing up the track. On the gun and firing is Greg Kennett.

"Shit! Where's my boots?" I yelled, more to myself than anyone else. Another person's boots are not important to anyone else when an ambush is sprung. I didn't worry about my boots and quickly grabbed my rifle and put a few bursts straight up the track for good measure.

Greg continued firing up the track and in a few moments everybody else in the line was firing into the killing ground as well. The amount of firepower that went into sixty metres of track was horrendous. The portion of the killing ground running west was not visible, even in daylight, because of the twenty metres or so of waist high scrub between the men and the track. The scrub, however, presented no barrier to our fusillade. After about fifteen seconds of firing I called out the order to cease fire. When everybody stopped firing, we heard the enemy cocking their weapons. We opened up again with solid bursts of fire. Very little further noise was heard. The wounded enemy in front didn't want to invite any more of what we were capable of delivering

Pte. Demestichas, known as 'Demo', was manning the machine gun on the western flank. On hearing one VC call out for help, which sounds like the word " more" in English, he yelled out, "I'll give you more, you bugger" and let another burst of rounds fly from his M60.

Both Lt. Henderson and Sgt Jeffrey were quickly on the scene to find out what was happening.

"Stan, can you tell me what's happened?" Lt. Henderson asked.

"Yes boss, Greg Kennett is on the gun and he heard the enemy coming and let them have it. He believes the first one is just up the track a bit, but it's that bloody dark you can't see a thing."

"OK, just make sure everybody keeps his head down and hold things as they are until dawn."

"If you need more ammo there's plenty on the carriers," Sgt. Jeffrey said.

"We're right for the moment Sarge, it looks as though we've got them buggered out there. I don't expect any more shooting."

"Keep your ears and eyes open anyway," Lt. Henderson said.

"We're all under control here sir, I don't think anybody will get much sleep now though."

There was now no noise, apart from a few groans now and then coming from the killing ground and, as expected, the rest of the night was calm. It was a dark night. There was no moonlight. The sky was full of clouds and we couldn't see a thing in front of us.

At dawn, Sgt. Jeffrey came up to me and said, "Stan, the boss wants us to attend to the battlefield clearance. You lead your section out and we'll see what we've got. I'll keep you in eye contact."

From where we stood at the M60 position we could see to the bend in the track and one dead VC. But there also seemed to be a pack on the ground in front of the dead VC. Someone must have been carrying it, but surely there was no way he could have got away, the claymores were right on him.

Sergeant Jeffrey said, "Maybe the bugger got himself around the corner somehow, don't ask me how though, the claymores would have chopped him off at the waist, we'll soon find out though I guess."

Des Weller's task was to have some of his section secure the forward position beyond the killing ground. He told Bluey Costello, "C'mon Blue, we gotta get out there, hurry up." He kept putting pressure on Blue to such an extent that more or less suggested to Blue that he should throw caution to the wind and just get himself out there. Blue was a bit concerned because he knew that at the very least there were a number of dead and wounded in the killing ground. He turned around to Des and said, "Seeing you're in such a bloody hurry, you take the gun out and I'll follow you." Des backed off and let Bluey proceed as he wished.

I wasn't fully aware that Lt Henderson or Sergeant Jeffrey had arranged for Des's number one section to secure the forward area and I thought some of my section would be doing it. I walked a few paces across to the forward scout and said, "Look, be careful here. I want you to cautiously make your way out. Don't pay too much attention to the results of the ambush.

Keep a look out beyond the killing ground and make your way to thirty metres past the ambush site. I'll be close behind you and me and the others will keep an eye on the enemy to make sure they're all dead. Off you go!"

On the way out to determine the results of the ambush there was myself, Bill Gorman, Darkie Dickson, Demo, Greg Kennett and Fred Woodhouse. As I passed through the killing ground, I signalled to Sgt. Jeffrey, by putting six fingers up, corresponding with the number of dead VC.

After the forward position and flanks were secured, I returned to assist Sgt. Jeffrey with the battlefield clearance. I went to the fifth VC in the line. He was in the foetal position, with his pistol in his hand. I rolled him over and he came over onto his back still in the foetal position with his eyes half open. His arms and legs moved up and down a little as though they were on springs and I thought he was going to spring up on me with all fours. It scared the hell out of me for a split second, even though I'd relieved him of his pistol. I thought he was still alive. The only wound I could see on him was a small hole in his forehead. A ball from one of the mines hit him fair between the eyes.

Demo poked the muzzle of his rifle into one of the enemy to make sure he was dead. This act made the dead man's arm fling out, hitting Darkie Dickson on the leg. Darkie jumped two feet straight up into the air and the aboriginal in him disappeared to be replaced by a ghostly shade of white. "Shit Demo you bastard – you scared the crap out of me!" he exclaimed.

The enemy dead were very well dressed in North Vietnamese Army clothing. Four of them carried TT-33 Tokarev pistols and the other two carried AK50 assault rifles. The large amounts of documents and money, together with their good clothing and weaponry, made it obvious that, in the main, they were high ranking officers in the North Vietnamese Army.

Sgt. Jeffrey came up to me and said, "You can see it was the claymores that got 'em Stan – they're all lying down in the tank track. It's just deep enough to give these skinny buggers a natural shell scrape."

"You're right. The bloke I checked out had no gunfire wounds on him at all as far as I could see, there was only one wound on him, smack between the eyes, and that's what did the job."

Once the battlefield clearance was completed, we had a stack of documents more than two feet high. There was also a large amount of money but most of this seemed to have been quickly spirited off from what I could see. The pistol I captured found its way into one of my pockets where I completely forgot all about it. I went up to Sgt. Jeffrey and asked what was happening now. "Are we leaving them here or what?"

"No, I think we're taking them to that village nearby, the one we went through yesterday, and we'll let them take care of the bodies."

A little while later the six bodies were put onto the trim vanes of a section of APCs, two bodies per carrier and, with my section and Des Weller's section aboard, we pulled out heading for the illegal village from where we thought they'd come from.

It only took the carriers five minutes to get to the village and we went into it a little distance, passing a few houses on the way. One woman hurried out, looked me in the eye and spat on the ground. I thought to myself, "A bloody VC for sure." The woman hurriedly followed us, as if she was already aware of the calamity. No doubt everyone in the village would have heard the gunfire last night. The villagers had obviously heard us coming and a number of them were making for the spot they anticipated us to arrive at.

When the carriers pulled up they went into a fishtail position. The crew commanders disembarked to drop the trim vanes and the six bodies fell to the ground. A number of the villagers were making haste towards us, concerned at what we'd just dumped in their midst. They shunted their kids away and seemed to be telling them to clear off. A couple of the kids received a good smack around the ear from their parents to hasten their departure.

Des Weller and Brian "Blue" Costello (rear)

John Martin followed by Brian Costello

Bill Godde on patrol

Ken Redding alias "Dubbo"

Jim Muir

Warren Handley

Brian "Blue" Costello

Max "Blue" Lantry

The villagers were pointing and talking excitedly amongst themselves in Vietnamese, which we couldn't understand, but under the circumstances, we had a fair idea.

We remained on board the carriers and were only in the village for a minute or less. When the trim vanes were repositioned, the drivers spun around and we returned to the ambush site by the way we came. By the time we got back, the brass from Nui Dat had arrived by chopper. I believe it was Brigadier Field and other senior officers as well as Intelligence Corps officers.

D & E Platoons' input into the days events at the ambush site were over and it was now up to the Intelligence Corps to sort out all the documents and glean from them what they can. There was no doubt in our minds, though, this was no ordinary group of VC foot soldiers. We did however, do a little routine patrolling for the balance of the day aboard the APCs.

During the afternoon, when riding on the carriers, Pte. Brian Grace called out to me from the other side of the carrier, "Hey Stan, how much money was that VC carrying, you know, the one Jimmy Fraser shot two days ago on the other side of Route Two. He had it in a plastic bag".

"Shit Gracey! I'd forgotten all about that. Just hang on and we'll see."

I opened up my top left hand shirt pocket, withdrew the plastic bag and opened it. Immediately I gagged and retched. The smell of the dead body had permeated through the plastic and into the money, making me almost fall off the APC. I quickly put the money back in the bag, having only got it half out in the first place, and shoved it back into my pocket.

"Christ, Stan are you OK mate, your face turned green all of a sudden, I thought you were going to be sick."

"Gracey, I came damn near to it, from what I saw it only looks about thirty bucks worth of piastre but it smells like the dead. We won't be able to put it over the bar like this. We'll have to work something out though. We can't let thirty bucks go to waste. I can't smell it in my pocket so it can stay there until we get back to the Dat. Jeez! It stinks though."

We returned to Nui Dat the next day, arriving back there in the early hours of the afternoon. We cleaned our weapons and tidied ourselves up a bit, and that was about it for the day. I found some old mess tins and put a whole tin of fungicidal foot powder in them, then I put the stinking money in and gave it all a good shake.

Pte. Allan Kilpatrick, watching me do this, said, "That should do the trick Stan".

"Yeah, I'll put it in my trunk and bring it out and give it a bloody good shake every now and then, but I reckon it'll take a few weeks, it stinks to high heaven though. There's no way you can give it a good smell without being sick."

I got the pistol I'd captured and had a good look at it for the first time. It was a brand spanking new Tokarev, a Russian made 7.62 mm military pistol. Just about every other communist country is manufacturing them as well. The magazine holds seven rounds and with one round in the chamber that gives it a capacity of eight rounds. It looks as though it has hardly been fired. The blue-black gun metal has not worn in the slightest. A five-point star on the pistol grip helped identify it as a Tokarev. To stop it rusting, I poured copious quantities of spunk oil down the barrel and then heavily oiled a piece of cloth and wrapped the pistol up in it and put it in my trunk.

At dusk, Lt. Henderson and Sgt. Jeffrey came across to the lines and gathered us together to impart a bit of information. "We've caused quite a stir from that ambush," Lt. Henderson said. "But all things aside, like the disappearance of thousands of dollars worth of captured enemy money and so on, we've done very well."

"Any idea who we got boss?" I asked

"Yes, that's what I've come to tell you. According to Intelligence, we got the Chief of Staff of the Bha Long Province, which is a VC amalgamation of Phuoc Tuy, Long Khan and

Bien Hoa Provinces. He was the big catch. Also, we got a Political Commissar and a Colonel from their sapper unit, I think the D 65 Engineer Battalion. You've all done a good job and nobody can take that away from us."

"What's this business about missing money sir? It was all handed in," commented Pte. Woodhouse, with a broad grin on his face.

"Well, the Intelligence are of the view you blokes have got most of it, and that only a small amount was handed in."

"Looking at them boss, it's hard to imagine that such an honest looking bunch of men would pinch any money," Sgt. Jeffrey said.

"Yeah right! It must be all some big mistake, anyway. I'll leave you all to it, just don't spend up big at the boozer with Vietnamese money. I'm going for a shower.

"Oh, just before I go, there's one more thing. They didn't come from that illegal village, but a place called Ap Cam My, which is up northwest of the illegal village. Apparently they had rested up there for three days before moving on and into our ambush. Anyway, there's a bit of a rumour going around that we may have to go and dig them up to have their photographs taken."

"Shit boss! Where're we going to get volunteers for that job – you're going to have to pull rank," I said.

"No problem! Corporal Sutherland. No problem at all!" Henderson replied.

When everybody started to dwindle away to their tents, I said to Greg Kennett just as he was starting to leave, "Greg, hang on a minute mate – I want to ask you something."

"You wanta recommend me to Henderson for promotion . . . is that what's this all about?"

"No mate! Nothing like that! What I want to ask you is something about that ambush the other day. You were on the gun when they came along and what I want to know is when did you first hear them? How far away were they when you heard them coming?"

"It's strange that you ask Stan because I've been thinking about that a lot over the last couple of days. I can't really explain it. My shift on the gun started about fifteen minutes or so earlier and I was sitting up behind the gun and the clackers for the claymores were set out in front of me. As you know it was dark as pitch. I couldn't see a bloody thing up along the track. Suddenly, for no apparent reason or anything tangible that I could discern, I thought it a good idea to lay down behind the gun and pick up one of the clackers. I did this and just as well I did because a couple of minutes later there they are. The first man from what I could hear was not too far up the track in front of me. That's when I thought I'd better let them have it."

"And you didn't hear anything? Nothing at all to suggest they were coming?"

"Nothing Stan. There was nothing that I heard or saw that suggested I should get myself ready. I just did. It's quite strange."

I said to him, "I've been in this country long enough to ponder a few things myself. I know one bloke from 3RAR who at the time of the Battle of Balmoral had a lucky escape. Six platoon was patrolling and they found an enemy camp. The VC let them come well into the camp before hitting them with a directional mine. Well, this bloke's bush hat fell like confetti to his feet and he didn't get a scratch. Then there is Strawbs, a few months back from four platoon 9RAR who, on a TAOR patrol in the middle of the night, had a VC less than three feet away point his rifle right at him at point blank range and squeeze the trigger. Strawbs heard the click but the round failed to fire. Strawbs realized the rifle had misfired and jammed, allowing him to quickly grab his rifle and let him have it. As for me, I had a lucky escape with a grenade set as a booby trap last tour. I didn't really fully appreciate how lucky I was as well as this other bloke, Tobin, at the time. It's only thinking about it from time to time since that makes me believe there has to be a God out there looking after some of us Greg, that's all I can say mate."

"I think you're right Stan. I've been thinking about this a lot and asking myself, why did I get myself ready, what was it that made me do that. And the only answer I can come up with is divine intervention, but I've never been overly religious. It's amazing, giving me something to think about that's for sure."

Later that evening, I went round to B Coy 9RAR to look up some mates. As I approached the Company lines there was a barricade across the road. The Company was sealed off. An NCO I hadn't seen before was on the gate.

"You can't come in here mate. A crime's been committed and the Company is sealed off. Nobody is allowed in or out," he said.

"Shit, I've just walked all the way around from HQ Company to see a couple of mates. I was a B Company man up until the fourteenth of this month," I replied.

"Well, who do you want to see in particular?"

"Corporals Wakefield and Tonkin from Four Platoon."

"Just wait here, I'll get in touch with the command post by radio and they can get a message asking them to come up to the gate, but you're not allowed in."

He did this and about five minutes later Barry and Tonk turned up. They told me that the Platoon Commander of six platoon had been murdered while he slept in the early hours of the morning.

"Jeez!" is all I could say.

"Yeah!' They allege he was killed by a hand grenade placed on his mosquito net," Tonk said.

Barry followed on, "It's a bastard of an act. Apparently, it's one of his own men, from six platoon."

"Jeez, I know this sort of thing happens in the American army quite a bit – they've even got a name for it – but in the Australian army it's virtually unheard of," I said. "That'll put a damper on things at the end of the battalion's tour. What a bugger!"

"'Yeah, not only that, a lot of fellows will have to stay behind for the court martial and they won't be looking forward to that."

"The whole Company is shattered Stan, absolutely shattered, morale today is at rock bottom," Barry said

"I can well imagine. Look, I won't hold you up, I'll briefly fill you in on what us ex-9RAR blokes have been doing over at D & E Platoon. They're a bloody wary lot. We're all getting along fine though. The last week has been a real melting pot for the platoon but everybody's working well together and we've had tremendous success against the nogs already.

"Anyway, Allan, Barry, it's damn good to see you both, please give my regards to all the blokes down in four platoon and if I don't get a chance to see you again before the battalion sails, I'll look you both up when I get home in six months."

"That'll be great Stan, and you take care mate," said Tonk. "Likewise," said Barry.

Next day, the 24th of November, the Platoon was placed on ready reaction. Sgt. Jeffrey organized distribution of all the ammunition and rations we required. We remained in camp that day, but the following afternoon we were given the job of finding an enemy cache. A woman from Hoa Long said she could lead us to it. After beating around the bush for hours, nothing was found and we returned to Nui Dat at 2200 hrs. The following day we left at 0630 hrs to try and find this supposed cache. The woman led us on a wild goose chase until 1200hrs. When we realized she had no idea where the cache was Lt. Henderson gave it away and we returned to Nui Dat.

After lunch, I took the opportunity to go around to B Coy, to say goodbye to my mates who sailed for home in four days time.

The following day we were engaged in various work details around the company. Some tents needed more sandbagging and a general tidy up of the lines was the order of the day. Later, Lt. Henderson told us that Brigadier Black Jack Weir would be across to say a few words to us at about 1130 hrs. When the time came for the Brigadier's visit, Sgt. Jeffrey formed us up in ranks and, as the Brigadier approached, he yelled, "Platoon Attenshun!"

We all came to attention. He turned, saluted Lt. Henderson and said, "Your Platoon Sir."

Lt. Henderson returned the salute, "Thank you Sergeant." He turned to the Brigadier, saluted and said, "Good morning Sir." Brigadier Weir returned the salute and the compliment and told Sgt. Jeffrey to stand us at ease.

"Look men," he said, "I've come across to tell you blokes what a good job you did up north the other day. Things have been fairly quiet for a few weeks and I've been under a bit of pressure from the GOC down in Saigon to come up with something. Down there, they've mistakenly thought we've not been working hard enough of late to bring the fight to the enemy. Well, let me say this, your efforts the other day has put them right. Just when the going was getting tough, you men pulled a rabbit out of the hat for me. And a good rabbit it was. There's every reason to believe that this ambush is the most significant ambush result in the army's history here in South Vietnam. Not significant in terms of the number killed but significant in terms of who was killed. There is no doubt you have struck a severe blow to the enemy, not only here in Phuoc Tuy, but this whole part of South Vietnam. It's going to set the enemy back quite severely. A job well done men, and I thank you for it. Keep up the good work. Lt. Henderson, all yours."

With the formalities over, Sgt. Jeffrey turned around to face us and said, "Now listen in you grubby lot. We're going out bush tomorrow for the day. It's not intended we'll be out overnight but take some rations just in case."

"Any idea where we're going Sergeant" asked Blue Costello.

"Yeah, up north, to check out a bombed bunker system."

"Sounds like it'll be a lot of fun, who knows what we'll find, especially if it was occupied by the enemy when bombed. Was it just bombed recently Sarge, do you know?" asked Dave Smith. "

"Yeah, I think only yesterday. Look that's all I know, just make sure you're ready first thing tomorrow. Oh! One other thing. Lt. Henderson made recommendations to the brigadier about some of you getting a mention in despatches for that ambush. Unfortunately, it's not going to happen. The brigadier told him. No! Those buggers got the money. They're not getting medals or mentions as well!"

We left at 0700hrs aboard a troop of APCs and got to the bomb damage area at 1200hrs. There were still a lot of bunkers intact so we started removing bangalore torpedoes, mortars, grenades, anti-tank grenades and a lot of other odds and ends. Phosphorous bombs had been dropped on the system.

On exploding, a white phosphorous bomb distributes particles of un-solidified phosphorous over a wide area. It has literally rained phosphorous. Anybody caught up in it would've had a terrible time. It sticks to the skin and burns through to the bone. Furthermore, phosphorous smoke is toxic and affects internal organs. The fumes cause severe eye irritation as well.

Once we'd completed the work, the engineers with us destroyed the rest of the system. We boarded the carriers and got back to Nui Dat at 1830hrs. The next two days we remained in the lines doing odd repair jobs such as putting the weapon pits into good order.

Bluey McCabe and Barry Wakefield (rear)

Ken Earney and Barry Giles

The Author Stan Sutherland, with a captured Viet Cong flag

Phil Grenfell with a tiny monkey

John Cowan, BillGodde and Blue Costello sitting) with Frank Flockhartand Peter Eastham (behind)

Sgt. Rick Jeffrey

Allan "Doc" Kilpatrick, Platoon Medic and Signalman,
PteEcclestone

Joe Atkinson (right)

Dave Smith   *Lt. Peter Cosgrove*

"The Boss" Lt. Peter Cosgrove, who later rose to Chief of theAustralian defense Force

That morning, I was told, one section, together with three section, were going to the Long Green, as protection for the land clearing team. I can't say I was happy to be going. The Long Green, which is to the east of Dat Do, is a god-forsaken hole. In parts, it's sandy and hot. You can be in areas where there's next to no shade. The water in your bottles gets hot and there are a lot of scorpions and red drop ants that jump down onto you from their nests in the lower branches of trees. The red ants cause as much bother to us as the VC.

We boarded a TCV at 0800 hrs and arrived at location at 0900hrs. Both sections deployed around the perimeter because, basically, perimeter defence was going to be our task. Later I caught up with Des Weller and said, "Well Des, what a shit hole this is mate. I hope we're not going to be here too long!"

"Yeah, you're right Stan. It's always so bloody hot down in this part of the province."

"Well, we're stuck here for the time being anyway. Look, you can't see a bloody thing. The engineers have bulldozed up the sand to raise the perimeter more than two metres. No bugger can see in to take a pot shot at us, but we can't see out either. We can only look at each other's ugly face."

"Wait till Lt. Cosgrove and Bluey Bert's mob get here tomorrow, they're in for a shock as well," said Des.

Next day, 3rd December, our new Platoon Commander, Lt. Peter Cosgrove, and the other section turned up to what was now aptly nicknamed, "Sandy Hollow." Our role here was limited to two sections around the perimeter and the other doing daily patrol work, but we rotate tasks. After a few days we got used to lolling around under our hootchies, which we've put up to protect us from the sun. Everybody was lying around reading books, and once they've read a book, they swap it for another from amongst the diggers in the platoon. Others are just playing cards and making use of the time for a spell.

Bluey Bert had a miniature chess set in his kick and he challenged me to a few games. After he'd beaten me soundly for three games I said, "I'm buggered if I know Blue, I've got more bloody brains than you, so how come you keep beating me?"

"Well, you've gotta be a military genius mate, that's where I come in."

"Oh, bullshit Blue! Here, pack it up and piss off and leave me in peace."

Bluey Bert has been promoted to Lance Corporal a few days ago and is therefore, an acting, section commander. He was in my section when we were with 9RAR and I have enough experience and anecdotal evidence to have some concerns about his ability to lead a section. My concerns were reinforced next day. Blue took a patrol out and he reported in by radio to the effect they'd found some graves and that they looked somewhat suspicious. The loc. stats Blue sent in by radio left a lot to be desired. He knew where he was on the ground but, as for us back at base, we'd no idea where he was.

When he came back, I got a map out of my pocket and ran through some basic map reading exercises with him to bring him up to speed.

"You're the only military genius in history Blue that isn't able to read a map," I said

"Aah shit, I'm just a bit rusty that's all."

"We can't afford to have section commanders who can't read a map. You have a good opportunity here to refresh yourself on the subject. You've got a map, compass and protractor, make use of them, otherwise, if you get the blokes lost they'll give you a hiding and put you in hospital, and not only that, Lt. Cosgrove will find someone else to lead your section. He probably will somewhere up the track anyway. Piss off now Blue."

"Before I go Stan, speaking of hospitals, did I ever tell you about the time I was in hospital when I was with 7RAR?"

"No! You didn't! I hope this is not one of your bullshit stories."

"No! This is fair dinkum mate. Actually, I was in an American hospital. When I started to feel better I knocked off an American captain's uniform, put it on and walked straight out of the hospital and went into town. I was walking down the street and all the Yanks were throwing salutes at me and I was really enjoying myself, throwing back John Wayne style salutes. After a while I went into a bar but, once I opened my North Queensland mouth, that was it – my cover was blown. I took off down the street and dodged down a few alleys, but eventually the MPs caught up with me. An American MP gave me a couple of whacks on the head with his baton. If it hadn't been for an Aussie MP that was with the Yank, I would've had the crap belted out of me. The bastard thought he was playing baseball and my head was the ball. And me! A sick man and all, just up from my hospital bed. The shit hit the fan though. I ended up getting fourteen days field punishment."

"Serves you bloody right Blue. You're lucky you didn't do time on the hill. You might be able to play chess, but you're a dickhead all the same."

Bluey Bert was one of those blokes who spoke a lot of crap. You never really knew when he was bullshitting and when he wasn't. Mostly he was bullshitting, nevertheless he was good at it. He can put it over the diggers and they actually think he's a good soldier. In his kick he has a grease gun and an American Colt 45 and he flashes them around from time to time. Where he got them from, god only knows. He may well be a good soldier in a tight pinch, he's certainly mad enough. Furthermore, he's impulsive and never considers the consequences of his actions.

One day, a couple of months ago when we were both in 9 RAR, we were out in the jungle and Bluey was out on sentry. When his time was up I went out to do a shift. I was sitting there and I could smell fresh shit from somewhere close. I looked around and couldn't see anything. The reason I couldn't see it was because I was looking out and around a couple of metres. It didn't dawn on me to look right under my feet. I eventually looked down and there my rifle butt was, right in the middle of a big fresh crap. I went back into the platoon base and told another bloke to go out in front on sentry and I threw my rifle to Bluey and told him to clean the shit off of it.

The following day Des Weller took his section out to have a look at the graves Blue reported in on yesterday. After digging them up, they all proved to be graves. It is known the VC use graves as a subterfuge to store equipment and ammunition. Word was getting around amongst the diggers that, when Bluey's section found the graves and they started digging, they helped loosen up the ground by throwing grenades into the hole. Bluey Lewis was there and he told me they threw in quite a few.

We left the land clearing team on 11th December at 0900 hrs. By then we'd all had enough of the heat and sand and were glad to get out of the place. When I got back to Nui Dat, I had to report to 8th Field Hospital. They kept me waiting for four hours and I didn't get back to my tent until 1645hrs. I was annoyed because we were going bush again tomorrow and I've got to get myself organized and make sure the platoon is organized to go as well because Sergeant Rick Jeffrey is posted to other duties for a few days.

We left Nui Dat at 0700 hrs on APCs, heading north to Fire Support Base Barbara. It's our job to set up the perimeter defences, such as putting out rolls of concertina barbed wire around the perimeter, three coils high, and also dig weapon pits. We also have to build the command post. The diggers worked hard all day but in the late afternoon it started to rain and we went to sleep that night wet and tired. The following day the platoon went out on a patrol to check out a particular area. We had to wade through a swamp up to our necks. The swamp was infested with leeches and, due to us being in the swamp for more than an hour, we had a big job removing them all. It was a case of stripping right off and going to it.

For the whole day we didn't see any signs of VC activity and we came back to Barbara in the afternoon pretty well worn out.

On the 14th, December we worked the whole day on our own personal fighting pits. This involves a lot of work. First, digging your pit longer than your body length. The pit is dug about two feet deep at least. A sheet of galvanized iron is placed over the top and the dirt you've dug out is put into sandbags, which are then placed on top of the iron. Your pit is home-sweet-home when you've finished. However, once finished, you hope the enemy gives you a bit of a going over to make all the work worthwhile.

The next day we started to put an apron on the perimeter wire and we had the job completed by 1230hrs. We heard that a driver of an APC was killed when his carrier hit a mine, flipping the carrier over. It was estimated the mine contained about 23kgs of explosive. Two engineers were also wounded. They were on their way back to Nui Dat after having destroyed an enemy bunker system. The group included a section of APCs, some infantry and engineers.

There was also a large mine incident today about a kilometre up the road from FSB Barbara, which resulted in the deaths of thirteen ARVN. They were travelling on a truck when it went over a mine in the road. We went to check it out and saw that the blast from the mine created a massive hole in the road. In the bottom of the hole was an ARVN boot with the foot still in it.

On 16th December my section stayed back at Barbara while the rest of the platoon went on patrol. Later that evening, the whole platoon went on APCs to put in an ambush. Near the ambush site, the tracks lowered the rear ramp to just above ground level and we jumped out while the tracks were still moving forward. This gives any enemy who may have heard us the impression that the tracks are moving on as normal and unaware that troops have disgorged. The ambush was not triggered. The tracks picked us up the following morning and took us back to Barbara.

Lt. Cosgrove was not with us for most of this operation and the OC, Major George Pratt, an Infantry officer, wants to come out on a patrol with us. Seeing Lt. Cosgrove is not around, he feels he should come out with the troops under his command. He used the excuse of saying that the sections out on patrol yesterday must have missed something, and that we're all going back to the area – including him – to check it out again.

He called an O group meeting for 0830 hrs. When the time came, at the meeting were Major Pratt, Cpl Des Weller, Lance Cpl. Bluey Bert and myself. Major Pratt opens the map and says, "Well boys, here's where were going. We'll be leaving in exactly two hours at 1030 hrs. We're going to have a good look around and come straight back." He'd picked up a stick a couple of minutes earlier and then he pointed to the place on the map where we were to go. "Now boys," he continued, "we better work out a strategy in case we come in contact with the enemy"

"Strategy sir! There's only one strategy!" piped up Bluey Bert.

"And what strategy is that Lance Corporal Bert."

"We fuckin' well charge sir!"

"Now boys, let's not be too hasty, let's not be too hasty on this mission."

Des and I were trying to suppress broad grins on our faces. Major Pratt hadn't the slightest idea Bluey was taking the piss out of him. The timing of the verbal exchange was absolutely perfect, the execution brilliant. Bluey raised his voice a few decibels and by the time he got to the word *charge*, it was loud. It was the best bit of theatre I'd come across for a long time. I left the meeting quite convinced Major Pratt was worried and not too sure about his forthcoming D & E Platoon patrol.

The patrol went off on time. We let Major Pratt think he was in charge. All our suggestions and recommendations of where to go, what to do, when to stop for a smoke, when to stop for a brew and when to have lunch were all readily accepted by the Major.

After looking around for a couple of hours, the only thing we found was a good spot to have lunch. The trees were tall and there was plenty of shade. After sentries were posted, I said to Ecclestone, who was carrying the radio, "Eccles, you and Doc Kilpatrick stick with the Major and keep him company, I'm going over to sit with my back against that tree over there. It looks a good spot to have lunch, it's nice and shady."

"OK Stan, off you go mate we'll be right," Eccles replied.

I dropped my pack and sat with my back against the tree. I'd just started to open a can of ham slices and I happened to look to the ground on my right side looking for leeches coming my way . . . but I soon lost interest in the leeches. I could see a skeletal hand poking out of the ground only six inches away from my backside. I looked out in front of me and saw a skeletal foot poking out of the ground just in front of my foot as well.

The nearest digger to me was Dave Smith.

"Shit Smithy! I'm sitting on some poor bugger's grave mate. I'm gonna move – it looks as though he's only down six inches."

"Yeah, it's disrespectful to sit on a grave, that's poor form mate. Someone has been here before though, there's ration cans strewn everywhere."

I looked around a bit more and, sure enough, there were empty ration cans all over the place. "There must have been a contact here once upon a time, and, who ever it was, stopped long enough to bury that bloke and have a meal," said Dave.

"Well, they didn't work too hard on this nog's grave, I reckon he's only down six inches at best – look, he's sticking out everywhere. I'm damned if I saw his bones when I first sat down. I was right on top of him."

After lunch we only had a small distance to travel to the place Major Pratt was interested in. We got there within half an hour and had a bit of a look around. The only things we found were blind artillery shells. The fact they were still there further evidenced no VC had been around for a long time. We took note of the position of the shells, knowing that it would be good value to come back with a Mini Team from the Engineers and blow them up. To leave them lying around for collection by the VC is to invite their sappers to convert them into mines for use against us, as in the case of the trooper killed a couple of days ago and also the truck on Route 2 which killed thirteen ARVN. Those mines may well have been Australian ordnance collected by the VC.

We didn't find anything else of any interest and I said to Major Pratt, "We haven't come across anything sir, no tracks, nothing to suggest enemy activity in this area."

"No Cpl. Sutherland. We might as well go back to Barbara."

"May I suggest sir, that we go back on a couple of different legs with different bearings?"

"Why's that Corporal?"

"Well sir, if we go back the way we came it will serve no purpose. We've already checked that out. But if we go back say, twelve hundred metres on a bearing of 1600 mills for the first leg and then on 2400 mills that'll get us back to Barbara and we'll cover more area. We'll need to clear it with the CP first though."

I felt a little strange giving Major Pratt advice.

"It's a good idea Corporal, but to tell you the truth I'm not used to carrying a pack all day and I'm rather buggered. Let's get back the quickest way. Furthermore, it's going to pour rain soon too."

"That's the way we came sir and, as for a wet arse, us infantry get that every day."

"Well that might be so, but I for one don't like getting a wet arse if I don't have to and now I'm OC Headquarter Company you can stick the Infantry."

"Yes sir," I replied

Sure enough, the next day, 18th December, we went back with a Mini Team from the Engineers to blow the shells. On our way, we came across an elk that had been killed by mortar fire the day before. You have to feel sorry for the wildlife in this country. Artillery and mortar come down on them from harassment and interdiction – these missions are fired daily to somewhere in the province. A few of the men removed the antlers and took them back to Barbara.

After we got back it was my section's turn to go on an ambush with the tracks. It's a different sort of ambush to what us infantry are used to. We boarded the tracks late afternoon and headed off. Positioning into the ambush has to be done after the curfew for the villagers so they don't see us. The drivers have a few tricks up their sleeves to confuse anybody who can hear the motors of the APCs. Once at the spot for the ambush, the APCs generally go into a fishtail position. Claymore mines are put out to cover the rear and flanks. More claymores are directed towards the primary ambush area. The crews of the APCs have filled a few, five gallon plastic water drums with petrol and have poured a packet of soap powder into each them. The drums are placed in front of the claymores. If the claymores are detonated, the petrol and soap powder goes forth like a giant flamethrower and any VC caught in such a fireball of ball bearings and flame have no hope. The soap powder sticks on them and they run around in the dark like mobile flares, making it easy for the crews of the APCs to pick them off.

If an ambush is being put in on a track, the vehicles are positioned further back from the track than what an infantry section or platoon would be. The bulk and outline of the APCs necessitates this and they need to push back into the scrub a bit. Once the ambush has been set up, the troopers make themselves comfortable. They're able to carry all the luxuries of army life. They sleep dry inside the vehicle and, generally speaking, do it easy by comparison. The infantry doss down as best they can within the fishtail. On this particular ambush, during the set up, I noticed one fellow was like a fish out of water, not really knowing the job at hand. When it was all set up and we had time for a chat with the Armoured Corps fellows, I said to their section leader, "That bloke over there, is he one of yours? Where did he come from?"

He replied, "I don't really know, he latched on to us back at Barbara. Apparently his name is Perkins or something like that, but I'm buggered if I know where he came from, he seemed to just appear."

"Shit! He makes a bloody racket, clanging mess tins and the like," I said.

"You can say that again, he was with us on an ambush last night and he was doing that much banging around all night I had to threaten to kick his arse.

"At least you infantry blokes know more about being quiet than anyone, but, even you fellows getting on top of the APC with your rifle to do picket sometimes make a noise, but we know you blokes are conscious of it and doing the best you can. As you know, we put on London runners, which makes it easier to move around the car quietly. But this bloke, he's something else. When we get back to the Dat from this operation we'll have something to say to the boss about it and he won't be with us long, that's if he's one of ours."

"He must be some sort of pogo, a bottle-wash perhaps," I remarked.

"Yeah, I think you're right. I'm not sure that he's even Armoured Corp. God only knows where he come from."

Nothing came along during the night, so in the morning we pulled up stumps and returned to Barbara. A little after we got back the whole platoon left to patrol an area of jungle in which 9RAR had found and destroyed a bunker system less than two months ago. According to the SAS, the enemy has rebuilt the system. The area in which we were looking was dense jungle, slowing us down considerably. Unless you have a pretty accurate fix on the position, it takes a lot of time beating around the bush looking. We couldn't find the system in the time allocated us and we just made it back to Barbara before it got dark.

Over the next two days FSB Barbara was dismantled. I don't know the overall success of the operation. There was a lot of effort put in with a lot of troops involved, armour, infantry, artillery, engineers, and so on. D & E Platoon worked hard for little success I thought. Once Barbara was dismantled all the Vietnamese scavengers from the village just up the road descended on us like a plague of locusts.

On the 23rd December we picked up a Platoon off RF from the Dhuc Tan outpost and took them for a bit of a patrol. This turned out to be a waste of time. It's best to leave the RF alone to get on with it. Whatever 'it' is.

Des Weller and his section went back to Nui Dat the same day. The rest of the Platoon arrived back at Nui Dat the next day. As soon as we got there, word around the lines was that some of the One Section chaps had made a midnight raid on the kitchen and stole Brigadier Black Jack Weir's Christmas turkey. Thinking about the blokes in one section who would do such a thing, my mind turned to Jimmy Fraser, Ken Earney, Barry Giles, Fred Woodhouse, Ian McAuley and Bill Godde. That's the complete section. All these blokes would be in on the devilment. The only exclusions were Section Commander Des Weller and his 2IC, Jimmy Muir. Jim was the type of bloke who had enough brains to think up the crime, though, and it could have well been his idea, even if he didn't participate.

Out in the bush D & E Platoon worked well together. They were very experienced and there was no nonsense. Get them back to Nui Dat and it is another matter. They get up to all sorts of mischief. They frequently target Company Sergeant Major Ken Lewis. The CSM's nerves and wits were at an end trying to keep ahead of them. I always looked upon Ken Lewis as a good bloke. He didn't seem to me as to go too far out of his way to make life hard on us. Maybe he thought it best to be friendly with D & E Platoon and then they might go easy on him. Nevertheless, D & E Platoon was capable of war on anybody in HQ Company. Furthermore, they left no evidence. There were no repercussions from the stolen turkey to my knowledge.

Some of the blokes had discovered a way of pinching beer from the storeroom of the Sergeants' Mess. The storeroom, which has a louvred window, is at the back of the building and the diggers found that by removing the louvres they could slip their hands in, open a carton and remove the cans one by one. When they had all the cans out they then flattened the carton and brought it out through the window to refill it. There was one occasion they did this they were unable to close the window after the louvres were put back. You needed to be on the inside to close it.

Anyway, Jimmy Fraser and Blue Costello were making their way back to the lines with their ill-gotten goods and they were half way across the road between the lines and the Sergeants' Mess when they were sprung by a provost. Peter Eastham, twenty metres away at the edge of the lines, saw the predicament they were in and he quickly went to his tent and put on the officer's jacket he'd pinched from the officers' lines when he worked there as a batman. He came up to the provost and said, "'What's the problem here Corporal?"

"I've just caught these two men stealing beer from the Sergeants' Mess sir," the provost replied

"I see. What I'd like you to do then Corporal is take this beer back to the Sergeants' Mess and then come back here and we'll see about getting some men to frogmarch these two criminals to the lock-up."

As soon as the provost had turned the corner of the Sergeants' Mess, the three of them took off and, when the provost came back a minute or so later, he stood in the middle of the road looking in every direction, wondering where everybody had gone.

At the end of the day I went to the ablution block, lowered the canvas shower which was tied to a rope on a pulley, poured in my bucket of water, pulled up the shower by the rope and hooked the rope onto a nail on the wall. I turned the shower flower to get wet and then turned it off. I lathered up all over using lots of soap and then turned the shower flower back on to wash it off. The canvas shower held enough water to do this at least twice. Once I'd showered and washed off what I thought was a good suntan, but instead was red dirt, I put on some clean greens and adjourned to the boozer with all the others for some Christmas cheer.

Christmas Day . . . and CSM Lewis woke me up holding a cup of coffee in his hand. "Here you are Corporal, Merry Christmas," he said

"Merry Christmas to you too CSM," I replied, swinging my legs around and sitting on the edge of my bed with my feet on the floor. I took a sip of the coffee and said, "Laced with rum too, CSM, things are sure on the improve – do you reckon you can arrange this daily?"

"Our hearts are just not big enough Corporal," he remarked as he left the tent.

"Thank you for the coffee sir, but you be nice to those larrikins up the end of the lines, won't you," I called out after him.

"'It hurts . . . it bloody hurts," he called back.

Lt. Cosgrove came over about mid-morning to have a yarn and wish everybody Merry Christmas.

26th December. We're going out on another operation tomorrow. Sergeant Jeffrey has been assigned other tasks and won't be coming with us and I spent the day organizing rations, ammunition and attending to other administrative details that normally Rick would be doing. All this was completed by about 1600 hrs and a little while later half a dozen diggers are sitting around in my tent just having a yarn and a smoke. I pulled the mess tins out holding the stinking money and gave it a good shake. I said to Bill Godde, "Here Bill, have a whiff of this, is the stink gone enough to spend it yet?"

Bill took the mess tin and had a smell. "Phew! Christ almighty! You can't spend this! It stinks!"

"No, take the notes out of the tin Bill and give 'em a shake. The stink might have gone from the money into the foot powder."

Bill took out a 1000 piastre note and gave it a shake to get the foot powder off and then had another smell.

"Oh no! It's still bad! The notes are smooth from the powder. People will think they're forgeries. They feel like forgeries."

"Don't worry, when the stinks gone, we'll give 'em a good wipe with a damp cloth. That'll get the powder off and we're as good as home on the pigs back," I said.

"It'll take a while though, how long have they been in there?" Bill asked.

"Over a month."

"A month!" Christ! They must have ponged when you first put 'em in."

"Yeah, they stank enough to make you spew."

Bill McAuley cut in and said, "There's two hundred cans of beer in those mess tins Stan, you'll just have to stick with it mate."

"Don't worry Bill, I'm stickin', I'm stickin'. We had to kill some bugger for this thirty bucks so he didn't give it up easy.

"Anyhow," I continued, "seeing there's a lot of you here, I've got something else to show you. Remember that ambush up near the illegal village about five weeks ago, well this is what I scored." I pulled from my trunk the oiled cloth package and unwrapped it to show the diggers the Tokarev pistol. Everybody was sitting around on the beds and I handed it to the closest man, being Joe Atkinson.

"This is a ripper Stan, jeez! It's in good condition," Joe said.

The pistol was passed from one to another all the way around the tent, each fellow taking off the magazine, cocking it and looking in and then putting the magazine back on and then passing it on. The pistol got handed to Tom who was sitting on the bed at the end of the line. Suddenly there was a hell of a bang and a hole in the floorboards appeared where there wasn't one before.

"Christ Tom! You stupid bastard! What in hell do you think you're doing?" I said, grabbing the pistol from him.

Tom was too dumbstruck to say anything.

The Officers' Mess was directly opposite my tent, just across the other side of the road, about twenty-five metres away. The next thing we see Major Pratt coming our way. We'd all gathered outside ready to take off if necessary. "He's seen us – nobody run or we're buggered," said Fred Woodhouse.

"We'll just bullshit our way out," added Greg Kennett.

Major Pratt came up to the tent and said, "Did any of you blokes hear a shot fired?"

"A shot! When sir?" asked Dubbo.

"Why! Just now! Only a minute ago!"

"Where did it come from sir?" feigned Dubbo.

"From over here! You fellows must have heard it!"

Everybody in the group spoke up claiming they didn't hear a shot. "It might have come from the Vietnamese compound just down there, sir. They fire a shot sometimes," I lied, pointing to where all the Vietnamese interpreters and the like are billeted.

"Well, if you blokes don't know anything about it, then it must have been them. Shooting in the camp's dangerous. I'll make further enquiries and get a stop put to it. It was quite loud though, I can't understand how you fellas didn't hear it, when I did from across the road."

"We were all inside the tent listening to a tape recorder," commented Dubbo again.

Smoke from the shot was still billowing out from every flap in the tent. When the pistol was fired, all the spunk oil I'd poured down the barrel when I stowed it went up in one great cloud of smoke. Major Pratt turned to walk away. He turned around, looked at the smoke coming out from every flap in the tent and said, "Take my advice men, cut down on the smokes. It's bad for you."

Once Major Pratt was gone we all burst out laughing. "There you are Tom, we saved you from fourteen days loss of pay. You would have copped fourteen days field punishment for sure. You owe us all a couple of beers," said Woody

"You did well fellas, I'll settle up with you at the boozer tonight," said Tom.

Tom is one of those blokes we never take out into the bush. He's just not cut out for the infantry. He's also married with a young child. For these reasons we leave him on permanent rear detail in Nui Dat. Even then, we still couldn't save him because, unfortunately, on New Year's Eve he got more than his fair share of alcohol and, without authorization, he got hold of an army vehicle and, whilst joy driving, turned it upside down, killing himself. Bill Godde was called to identify his body.

27th December. We left Nui Dat at 0630 hrs to rendezvous with elements of 8RAR to put in a sweep west into a suspected enemy bunker system. The bunkers were abandoned and nothing was gained. We spent the night harboured up a little north of the Bhin Bha rubber plantation. The night was unusually cold.

28th December. Today we patrolled west of the Bhin Bha rubber looking for a likely place in which to put in an ambush. 5RAR are deployed around the village of Bhin Bha and they've been in contact with the enemy. I understand one VC has been killed and one Australian wounded.

29th December. An agent has reported the location of a VC camp said to contain about one hundred of them from D445 VC Regt. We were reacted to go and have a search for the camp. The jungle is as thick as it gets which leads us to conclude the agent is probably on the level. When they put their finger on the map, however, they only have to be out a few hundred metres and all is lost.

30th December. In the morning, at the edge of a banana plantation, we came across some freshly-cut tobacco placed out to dry in the sun. On closer examination of the area we found a well-used track leading into the jungle. Lt Cosgrove organized the platoon to check out the track and we followed it down for thirty metres or so into the jungle and there we came across a small bunker system of just three bunkers. Still cooking on a fire was a small billy, in which were eight frankfurts, similar to those found in American rations. (American rations are freely available and can be purchased at any Vietnamese village market). Whilst the contents of the billy seemed to be American frankfurts, they looked a little pale by comparison and didn't have the normal frankfurt skin on them. I thought perhaps they were some sort of Vietnamese sausages. Alongside the fire was a large heap of banana skins, enough to almost fill a forty four gallon drum.

I'm standing by the fire alongside Lt. Cosgrove, and we're both looking at the billy and its contents, which are still cooking. Lt. Cosgrove says to me, "It's obvious the poor buggers are living off bananas and not much else. By the number of sausages in the billy, it looks as though there was three of them ready to enjoy their lunch of sausages and bananas, and, on hearing the APCs coming along, decided to abandon their meal and take off. It would have been a hard decision to leave their meal though, as scant as it is. You'd think at least one of them would have grabbed the billy on the way out. It looks as though it's cooked to me."

"Not only have we made them miss their lunch, boss, we've deprived them of their tobacco as well. They're probably from the Bhin Giau guerrilla unit." Bhin Giau, only a kilometre away, is a very strict Catholic village with two churches, one at each end of the village. The village is very anti-communist. It's unlikely they'd be welcome in the village and they have to do it hard, eating bananas on the outskirts.

1st January. The dry season is in full swing now and the heat of the day is getting far more severe. We need all the water bottles we can realistically carry. The Engineers – sometimes called ginger beers – have been working flat out clearing Route 2 of land mines. Unfortunately, it's common knowledge that a lot of the mines now getting laid by the enemy come from blind artillery shells and mines from our own mine fields.

Today, a total of four ambushes were put in on the road in the space of a mile. The ambushes are set up in the hope that VC mine-laying parties will venture into them. We had no success, however. The next day we received a re-supply and we then went to the vicinity of the illegal village where we killed six VC six weeks earlier. We approached the area from a different direction, which made us unsure of the exact location. At 1900 hrs we went to within three hundred metres of the village and put in an ambush, but we weren't as lucky as last time.

3rd January. This morning we pulled up the ambush and left the area of the illegal village by APC and went to an area where we found some enemy bunkers a couple of days ago. The tracks dropped us off four hundred metres from the bunkers. Lt. Cosgrove wanted the platoon to sneak in the back way and, by the time we got there, we had marched about a thousand metres. If any enemy were in the camp they may have heard the tracks but would not be expecting us to be positioned behind them. The second stage of the exercise is for the centurion tanks to make a sweep first thing in the morning with us lying in wait, hoping some VC will be driven into our ambush. It's extremely disappointing when we go to a lot of effort for no result because our work satisfaction is directly related to the demise of our enemy. After the tanks had made their sweep the tracks came along to pick us up. We have an excellent rapport with the Armoured Corps blokes and, when we work together for lengths of time as we often do, we get to know one another quite well.

The tracks took us to Ngai Giau, the District Capital and District Headquarters for the ARVN. The Australian Army Engineers built a school there. They also erected a large tower to support a water tank. A windmill was erected to pump water from a well into the tank on the tower. This civic construction project has enabled the villagers to get water by simply turning on a tap at the bottom of the tower.

We elected Peter Couchman to cook the evening meal from rations supplied by all of us. This was a first and last attempt at communal cooking in the field. It was dreadful and we gave it to the kids from the village and they had it polished off in no time. We also gave them a tin of jam, which they liked that much they fought over it.

5th January. We went back to the illegal village to search it. The houses are spaced out from one another and each house has a sizeable garden in which peanuts, coffee, fruit and tobacco are growing, amongst other things. All the inhabitants are women and kids with only a few older men getting about. We detained one man who had a discrepancy with his ID card. His wife started to bow and scrape, holding the palms of her hands together, as if in prayer. Bowing, crying and wailing, she offered us fruit so we wouldn't take him away.

Late in the afternoon we went some distance from the village to set up an ambush but, while we were setting it up, Blue Costello, sitting on sentry duty, spotted some kids who'd no doubt been instructed to follow us and see what we were doing and where we were harbouring up for the night.

I went across to Lt. Cosgrove who by now had been informed of the kids by Cpl Des Weller. Lt. Cosgrove saw me coming and he shook his head in a manner that suggested our ambush has been compromised. We talked about if for a minute and Lt. Cosgrove said, "Well Stan, it'll be pitch dark in a few minutes. We won't move from here and we'll go ahead with the ambush just in case someone is coming into the village and hasn't heard that we're here. It's a shame though."

"It is boss, but no doubt they remember the last time we were here and killed eight of them, although we got only six bodies. (The other two died of wounds, according to reports). They won't want the same thing to happen again if it simply means having kids keep tabs on us."

The next morning we went back into the village to the place where we dumped the six dead. On a closer look, it seems to be the village square. The villagers had dug graves, six in a single row, side by side. The graves are located at the edge of the square no more than thirty yards from where we dumped them.

Vietnamese regulations provide for villagers to hold only a certain amount of rice. Anything in excess is against the law. We found one woman with barrels of rice. It was duly confiscated. The woman hopped on her bicycle to pedal down to Ngai Giau to plead her case to the District Chief and, no doubt, tell him what a pack of bastards the *uc dai loi* are.

Vietnamese villages are not conducive to accommodating APCs driving all over the place. The drivers don't care where they go and invariably bowl over gardens, fruit tree, coffee trees, tobacco plants and anything else that's in their way. This village copped quite a hammering from a whole troop of nine carriers. I was convinced at the outset it's a communist village but, if I'm wrong, they certainly are now, I thought to myself, surveying the damaged gardens as we headed off aboard the tracks for Ngai Giau.

7th January. We boarded centurion tanks for the return trip to Nui Dat. There's no comfortable place to sit on a tank. I perched myself on the turret, which is more than hard on the backside. The tankies are all fitted out with sunglasses, or goggles, whichever they prefer. A centurion tank belting down a dirt road at about forty kilometres an hour is a sight to see and even more so when there are three sections of them (two to a section) The tank in front chews up and spits out behind it everything from buffalo shit – which there's plenty of – to dirt, gravel, rocks, the lot. For the infantry, sitting on the tank behind, it is rough . . . we have nothing to protect our eyes with. The tanks hurl along about fifty metres apart, insufficient for us to avoid the crap. This adds another paragraph to the uncomfortable life of an infantryman. By the time we got back to Nui Dat we all had sore backsides and were covered in muck. Riding on the tanks is as hairy as any ride you'll get at Luna Park. Still, it's much better than walking.

At about 1945 hrs, a few of the fellows came into my tent and ten minutes later we were joined by a couple more. Six of us were sitting around smoking and carrying on a bit when Dubbo came in and said, "Hey Stan, I've just walked past the pogos' lines and there's a few of them in there tuned into a PC 25 set. I've come up with a bit of an idea for payback for the short rations in the hot boxes they gave us a couple of weeks back." The last time we went to the range I taped the M60s firing as well as SLRs and M16s. "We can get our radio set and tune in to them and pretend we're an Australian platoon stuck out in the jungle under heavy attack."

"Jeez Dubbo! I'm buggered if I know what made you think of that but it sounds like fun. Hey! McAuley, go and get Ecclestone and tell him we want him here with his radio set pronto."

Ian went off and so did Dubbo to get his tape recorder. They were back in a couple of minutes with Ecclestone.

"Now fellas, a couple of you keep an eye on the cooks' and bottlewashers' tent while we get things sorted out here, but first we'll turn our lights off. When it's all over they'll look across here for sure, but there'll be no lights on, and they'll think we're all at the movies or the boozer."

Pte. Ecclestone soon had the radio tuned into the cooks who were talking to god-only-knows who. Seeing it was Dubbo's idea, he was given the handset to do the talking and when he cut in on them, the exchange went something like this:

"Can anybody read over, I say again, can anybody read, over. If anyone can hear please come in over."

After a couple of attempts the radio crackled, and we heard, "We can read you, please identify by call sign over."

"This is Ratshit two, I say again this is Ratshit two and we're in big trouble. We need help over."

"Ratshit two, we hear you loud and clear, this is Base one. What's the problem, over."

At this point, Dubbo turned the tape recorder from pause to play and held the radio handset up to the speakers of the tape recorder. The machine guns and rifles were very impressive. At the same time Dubbo spoke into the handset for added affect. The expected reply came back.

"Ratshit two, this is base one, we couldn't make you out over."

"Base one this is Ratshit two, we're under heavy attack and badly outnumbered, you're the only radio contact we've been able to make. Stand by, don't go off the air, the enemy are attacking again over."

Dubbo gave the guns and rifles from the tape another go into the handset for about fifteen seconds

Our lookout, Doc Kilpatrick said, "Another six pogos just went into their tent. They're excited as all hell over there."

All of us were pissing ourselves laughing.

"Base one this is Ratshit two, can you help. We're a platoon caught out here in the jungle on our own. Sunray and Sunray minor are both wounded and a corporal's in charge, over."

Another solid burst of fire from the tape went into the handset of the radio.

"Ratshit two, we'll help, what do you want us to do over?"

"Base one we need artillery support, I say again, we need artillery support, can you contact the Artillery for us, over?"

More small arms fire from the tape went into the handset.

"Ratshit two this is base one, we can send a runner with a message to HQ Battery. It's only a hundred metres away. You blokes hang on out there, over."

"Base one this is Ratshit two, are you able to take down a message in writing for grid reference purposes over?"

"Ratshit two, this is Base one, affirmative over"

Base one this is Ratshit two. Write down three rounds to be fired for effect, I say again, three rounds to be fired for effect on the cook's tent, HQ Company, 1 ATF. I say again, on the cook's tent, HQ Company, 1 ATF over."

"What! What's that?" Then there was complete silence.

By this time we had all cracked up laughing our heads off. We couldn't have gone on even if we'd wanted too. Even Dubbo was at his end.

All the cooks and bottlewashers were outside their tent looking in every direction for any tell tale sign of who'd stooged them. They looked our way for quite a while but all our lights being off had them baffled.

Everyone congratulated Dubbo for a great job of entertainment. None of us could recall when we had such a good laugh and so much fun.

Naturally, the cooks and bottlewashers kept their mouths shut. D & E Platoon is the troublemaker of HQ Company. They would've guessed that it was us but they didn't want to embarrass themselves by going fishing for information to find out for sure. We talked and laughed about it amongst ourselves for weeks.

7th January. The platoon remained in Nui Dat today and Lt. Cosgrove gave us the day off to attend to personal things. I went down to Pearsons Pogo Palace for a haircut after which I went back to the lines to answer some letters from family and friends from 9RAR wishing me a Merry Christmas.

The diggers were all just resting up. I washed some clothes made filthy from the last operation. I had to change the water three times before they were anywhere near clean

Sergeant Jeffrey was looking to have a bit of a yarn. "I had a bugger of a night in the Sergeants' Mess last night Stan," he said. "You know, I'm the only combatant sergeant out of the whole lot of them and every now and then the pricks try to stick it up me but I give them back better than what they dish out. The bastards can be aggravating though."

"Sounds as though you're the only lion in amongst the sheep Rick."

"Yeah that's a good way of putting it. I'm a lot younger than them all as well, which shits them off no end."

"You should get the OK from Cosgrove and Pratt to visit the diggers in the ORs canteen for an hour or so every now and then. A beer with the rest of the warriors instead of with the pogos always tastes a lot better you know."

"I did that once Stan, Pratt told me and Russ Henderson we could spend two hours in the ORs canteen with the diggers one night. I ended up spending four and Pratt comes in and tells me he wants to see me in his office right now. The diggers knew I was in trouble and when Pratt was hauling me over the coals in his office and making some threats I invited him to look out the window. He did, to find the building completely surrounded by D & E Platoon all with their weapons. Peter Eastham was standing there with the M60. It scared the tripe out of poor old George and he let me off. He's hated D & E ever since you know."

8th January. D & E Platoon arrived down at the Badcoe club in Vung Tau on TCVs for two days leave on R & C. It's been quite some time since we've had any leave and all the troops are looking forward to it. Once everybody had jumped from the trucks, Lt. Cosgrove lined us all up for a pep talk and warned, "Now boys, you're down here for two days. Go into town, enjoy yourselves but above all behave yourselves. If any of you land up in the slot you'll have me to deal with as well. Don't get drunk more than necessary. Don't fight or abuse the Yanks. Don't fight the pogos, don't wreck the bars, keep out of the way of the White Mice (South Vietnamese Police) and observe the curfew. If you're in town make sure you allow enough time to get back to 1ALSG before they close the gates. I don't want to be spending the next two days getting you lot out of trouble. Now, don't say I didn't warn you. Clear off, have a good time and stay out of bloody trouble."

I spent the whole of next day from 0900hrs to 2100hrs sitting in a bar drinking American Budweiser beer. I didn't let them take the cans away and by the end of the day I had 33 cans lined up on the table. For such a good customer, the Mama San gave me a bowl of rice for lunch and another one in the evening. Near the end of the day Bluey Lewis walked in and I said, "Hey, Bluey come and have a look at this mate, thirty-three cans and I can walk straight as a die. As a matter of fact, I'm just as sober as what I was when I walked in here this morning.'

"Yeah, this American piss is like having sex on the beach," said Bluey, ordering a can.

"What do you mean by sex on the beach, Blue?"

"It's fuckin' near water mate," he said with a big smile on his face. I thought that was quite funny. I hadn't heard the expression before.

"You're not wrong there Blue, but I've had enough, it's almost 2130 and time to get back to the Badcoe Club to beat the curfew. I don't want to spend the night in the lock up."

We found a Lambretta as soon as we walked out from the bar. We told him to take us to the *uc dai loi* camp. On the way out Bluey rolled a couple of five cent notes around some other paper he had to make it look as though it was a big wad. When the driver pulled up at the gate, Bluey handed him the wad and we took off making it through the gate before he could unwrap it to find he'd been ripped off.

Earlier in the evening Jim Fraser, Ken Earney and Blue Costello were having their own fun. They gave a Lambretta driver a hard time, repeatedly calling him a VC. The driver, at the end of his tether, took hold of the chain which he uses to secure his vehicle with and swung it around his head in a threatening manner as if to lash out at them. This was too much for Jim, Bluey and Ken, so the three of them set about wrecking his Lambreatta. Jim picked up a rock and smashed his headlights and Bluey and Ken picked up the Lambretta and turned it over. Ken burnt his hands when he inadvertently got hold of the exhaust pipe when turning it over. Vietnamese civilians came to support the driver and they were picking up rocks and throwing them at the three troublemakers. A few minutes later, the White Mice came speeding around the corner. One jumped from his vehicle and ran towards them drawing his pistol at the same time. When he got to them he fired a shot in the air and placed the muzzle of his pistol against Jim's temple. This action had a very calming effect on the three of them. Shortly after, the Aussie MPs arrived and took charge of proceedings.

Earney asked one of the MPs if he could have a look at his burnt hands under the headlights of the MPs vehicle. The MP said, "OK, but don't forget you're under arrest."

"I won't, but thanks, I'll just have a quick look at my hands, they're bloody sore and I'll only be a few seconds."

Ken walked over to the vehicle, which still had its lights on, parked at the side of the road. He was looking at his hands and he heard a Lambretta coming along. As soon as it got near him, he made a bolt for it, jumping aboard and scaring half to death the Vietnamese woman who'd hired the vehicle. Ken commandeered the vehicle, taking no notice of the woman who was swearing and cursing at him in Vietnamese. He pulled a five dollar note from his pocket and waved it under the nose of the driver and told him to step on it.

Naturally, he got away.

Jim Muir thought he would assist with a gaol break and, getting hold of Lt. Cosgrove's battle jacket, he and Earney presented themselves at the cells, Jim claiming to be the officer in charge of the unit to which Jim Fraser and Blue Costello belonged. He was discussing the gravity of the misdemeanours with the cell keeper and requested that the three miscreants be placed into his charge. Whilst in the middle of his negotiations, the real Lt. Cosgrove turned up and he took one look at Jim in his officer's jacket and said, "I think you better get yourself back to camp Jim."

Meanwhile, in the cells, Bluey was pretending to be asleep. He'd made up his mind that when a provost came to wake him up he would lash out and hang one on him. Unfortunately it was Lt. Cosgrove that came to him, giving him a shake and saying, "Are you all right Blue?" Bluey, thinking it was a provost, got the boss in a headlock and Earney's yelling, "Bluey it's the boss! It's the boss! It's the lieuey Blue!"

Lt. Cosgrove got them out of the lockup. If he came down with 28 men, he wanted to go back to Nui Dat with the same number.

Back at 1ALSG the troops were all quite subdued. Lack of sleep, too much beer or whatever other poisons they drank, plus frolicking with the bar girls of Vunga's had taken its toll. Unlike the pogos down at 1ALSG who had the good life and had learned how to pace themselves, the infantry units always went on a spree and, generally, those who overdid it and gave the MPs a hard time saw the inside of the slammer.

Lt. Cosgrove was pleased to be able to deflect any problems even though he had to visit the cells. It would be just too much to ask for a quiet, incident free two days. The only way you can have peace and tranquillity as the Platoon Commander or even for myself as acting Platoon Sergeant is to take them out into the bush on operations. Out there, they're at their absolute best. Back at Nui Dat, they're a nightmare for those in charge. CSM Lewis will vouch for that and, for even all his trouble with them, he still likes most of the blokes in D & E, and most like him, as far as I could gather, everyone has a strange way of showing it.

There are some that disagree with me though. From time to time, the CSM, on wandering around the lines checking things out has been heard to say, "I'll kill em, I'll kill the buggers." There was never any doubt he was referring to – D & E Platoon.

After breakfast everybody packed up, weapons were handed back and all boarded the trucks in the convoy to go back to Nui Dat. We arrived at 1100 hrs but everybody was too under the weather to do anything.

12th January. Sergeant Jeffrey called the Platoon out on muster so that Lt Cosgrove could give them an idea of what they're likely to be doing in the next few days. Lt. Cosgrove came across and said, "Today, Sergeant Jeffrey will be organizing rations for three days for each man. We'll be going bush in a few days and I want you all squared away and organized. We may not get much warning. Tomorrow, however, we're going to the range to fire off our old ammo and zero in our weapons."

"Is that it sir?" I asked.

"Yes, that's it, I may have more tomorrow."

The following day we went to the range for what the diggers call a 'yippee' shoot. The shoot was to test fire and zero in our weapons. As it happened, one of my section's machine guns broke down and when we got back to the lines the gunner went to the armourer and had it replaced with a new gun.

14th January. Lt. Cosgrove informed us that we've been placed on a fifteen-minute standby ready-reaction force, known as Hawk Force. Furthermore, we must be ready to be choppered to anywhere in the province as, in effect, we're a fully mobile infantry platoon.

15th January. The platoon was reacted for a two-day operation. We'd mustered, all kitted out, waiting for Lt. Cosgrove to come and brief us. He was over a minute later and said, "Well men, we're climbing to the top of the Warburton Mountains today, coming back tomorrow. The trucks will be here any minute. We're going down through Baria and then up towards Bien Hoa for five or six kilometres, dismounting at a small hamlet, the name of which just escapes me for a minute. Here are the trucks now. Are we all here Stan?"

"Yeah, all except Ecclestone sir, he's making sure he's got a fresh battery. Here he comes now."

An hour later we dismounted at a small hamlet. We were about two kilometres from the foot of the Warburtons. The Warburtons remind me of the Dandenong Ranges 20 miles east of Melbourne. They look similar in height and size. We sorted ourselves with Bluey Bert's section taking the lead. My section is to bring up the rear.

Lt. Cosgrove and Sergeant Jeffrey were waiting for Bluey's section to pass them before Platoon Headquarters entered the line in single file.

I went up to Lt. Cosgrove and before I could say anything he said, "Look at those civvies Stan, they're pretending to be working but they're keeping an eye on us at the same time.

They'll be counting us, observing our weapons and seeing where we're headed."

"Yeah I'd noticed it too boss, as soon as we got off the trucks. That bloke over in the doorway of that thatched hut over there, he's had a real good look."

"They'll keep an eye on us as far as possible to see which way we're headed and, no doubt, they'll let their own know up top by radio that we're on our way," Cosgrove said. "We'll make good time and surprise them all the same. Right Stan, I'm away." He joined in the file. Before Sgt. Jeffrey entered the file he said to me, "Have your tail end charlie keep a good lookout behind him, Stan. We don't want any villagers following us up with a rake over their shoulder pretending they're going into the fields."

The first two kilometres were relatively easy going over flat ground, mostly rice fields. Being the middle of the dry season, the fields were now bone dry. After half a kilometre the rice paddies gave way to low scrub as we passed through a defoliated area. The area defoliated extends to Baria, in the southeast, as well as Dat Do and Long Dien in the south. The idea of the defoliant is to cut off places like Baria, Dat Do and Long Dien from the Warburtons, preventing the enemy coming and going under cover of jungle.

After clearing the low scrub, we picked up a well-worn and quite wide track headed directly towards the Warburtons. Lt. Cosgrove had us follow this, as a subterfuge, until we were near the base of the Warburtons, then we diverged for about half an hour through the light jungle at the base of the mountains. We stopped for fifteen minutes for a very quick lunch and a breather. The day is very hot and we've had little shade up until now. After something to eat and a brew, we started to climb. The first part of the climb was not too bad, but the climb got steeper the further up we went. Everybody is doing it hard and the gunners are swapping over from time to time with their number two. The gunners have their work cut out carrying twenty-three kilos of gun and ammunition plus their pack and working their way up steep inclines through jungle. At times we're pulling up the bloke behind us using toggle ropes to help along the way. Sergeant Jeffrey stops from time to time and checks on everybody as they pass, asking them if they're OK. Their shirts were wet, which is always a good sign.

We stopped on the climb up for one five-minute breather. Lt. Cosgrove is anxious to get us to the top, find an ambush site and be under good cover before the enemy has a chance to act on the information we expect them to have by now. We got to the top at 1500 hrs and there we had another spell until the tail-end charlie, this time Ken Earney, reached the top.

After a ten-minute spell we headed along a saddle and travelled about four hundred metres, coming across a fairly well used track. The primary growth is quite thick and the secondary growth, also thick, affords us plenty of cover. We investigated the track to find a good stretch suitable for an ambush. The part of the track Lt. Cosgrove picked for the ambush runs east and west. He gave his instructions for the ambush to Sergeant Jeffrey who then passed them on to the three Section Commanders.

We set up the ambush with a machine gun and claymores covering the east and another machine and claymores on the track covering the west. A distance of about thirty metres of track separates the two guns. Once the rest of the men were positioned for our ambush, using a clock face as a reference, there is a machine gun at three o'clock, a machine gun at nine o'clock, a machine gun at twelve o'clock and another at six o'clock. Two machine guns are carried in three section and the two gun groups in the section swap over from time to time, taking turns to assume the role of the principal gun group. The remainder of the men are spread out to fill in the circle. The killing grounds are the two sections of track extending from the guns at three o'clock and nine o'clock. Claymore mines have been put out along the track's edge, eight to a single bank in front of each of the guns covering the track. Other claymores, not as many, have been put out in front of the other two machine guns on the flanks. Once the ambush is established, Lt. Cosgrove orders no cooking, not even for a brew. We ate cold rations and, as everyone was worn out from the climb up, those not on picket were quite happy to call it a day.

At daybreak Lt. Cosgrove had everyone – except the gun groups covering the track – withdraw to a position fifty metres south of the track. A few minutes before 0900 hrs Sergeant Jeffrey came across to me and said, "The boss wants you to relieve Des Weller and his gun group at 0900 hrs Stan. Let your blokes know."

At 0900 hrs I took Jimmy Floyd and his number two on the gun out to relieve Des Weller's gun group, namely Bill Godde and Blue Costello. I placed myself to the right of Floyd and naturally his number two was on his left. We were in a good spot with a clear view up the track. Our only cover was that provided by the leafy undergrowth, however it concealed us well. It was very quiet and the sun shone through the canopy in shafts of light that highlighted the various greens of different species of vegetation. Rain forest type jungle is cool and quite comfortable compared with other areas of the province.

After a few minutes we got a strange feeling. Everything seemed to go quiet and we lay down on our stomachs keeping a good lookout up the track to our front. Then we saw the first VC approaching along the track. Proceeding very cautiously, looking to his right and left, he is cautiously approaching our position. He's carrying an RPG2 (a rocket propelled grenade) and moving in a manner which leads us to believe he knows we're around somewhere close. Floydy picked up the clacker to fire the claymores.

I whispered in his ear, "Not yet Floydy, let him come right in, there'll be more behind him." Floydy nodded in acknowledgement. We soon saw another VC behind the first and then another behind the second. We never took our eyes off the first as he approached to within ten metres of us, then he stopped. Something obviously concerned him. He half turned as if to communicate his concerns to the man behind him. I thought to myself, any second now and we're going to unleash a wave of incredible violence into this peaceful and leafy section of forest.

Floydy got the same vibe as me. He pressed the clacker to fire the claymores and I fired my rifle up the track, using up the whole magazine of rounds in one good burst, spraying the rounds up the track as if I was watering the garden. As quick as he could, Floydy opened up with the M60. I fired off another magazine and, quickly changing the magazine, fired several more controlled bursts and stopped. I hit Floydy on the shoulder to get his attention and motioned with my hands to cease firing. It took quite a few seconds for the dust and smoke to clear. Up until then, we couldn't see a thing. The claymores had shredded all the leaves off the trees and scrub in front of us up to a height of three metres.

We could hear Lt. Cosgrove yelling orders to the platoon. Seconds later, the platoon was sweeping across our front towards the ambush site. I could see Lt. Cosgrove in the middle of the line and Greg Kennett and Demo sweeping across on my right. Demo was firing bursts of three to four rounds from his machine gun. He saw the body on the ground out in front of me and put a short burst into it from thirty metres to make sure. The body jerked from the impact and puffs of smoke arose, which I thought must be from the tracers.

Lt. Cosgrove had the men sweep through thirty metres beyond the ambush site to secure the position. The three VC, by the way they were armed and their cautious approach, had all the hallmarks of a scouting party. There is always the danger of a larger and well-armed force coming behind them. For all we know, they could have been a scouting party for a hundred or more. Then we'd be in for it. Lt. Cosgrove didn't waste any time. He gave orders for the dismantlement of the claymores covering the west and east. He then came across to where I was and said, "Stan, once we've attended to the bafflefield clearance, we're out of here. You never know, there may be a large force behind these fellows, and if they come armed with RPGs firing them into these trees, it'll make things awkward for us. Furthermore, we're out of radio contact from here so we're not going to hang around."

"Yes Sir," I replied. "To me they're a scouting party and by the way they were coming along the track, they definitely knew we were around here somewhere. The villagers below let them know we were coming that's for sure."

Sergeant Jeffrey was making sure everybody had the business at hand under control as well.

I went to the body closest to me. Dubbo was also there by this time and was looking down at the body, which was lying face down. I said, "Dubbo help me turn this bloke over will you?" Dubbo got hold of his feet and I got hold of his torso and we turned the body over. I hadn't noticed that the claymores had taken the top of his scull completely off, just like a knife capping a rock melon. When he was rolled over his brains fell onto the ground only an inch in front of my right boot. The pink cavity of his head wasn't a pretty sight, one I'll never forget. He was carrying two grenades for his RPG. The other two dead VC behind him were each carrying AK 47s.

The claymores had literally shredded their clothes. They would have known nothing about it. I remember thinking again, nobody knows you're dead, except us. Not your comrades, your family, nobody, only us, but we respect you as soldiers doing your duty just as we are. We left the bodies where they had fallen. No doubt their mates would be along shortly to take care of them.

Lt. Cosgrove ordered the platoon down the mountain, returning the same way we came up. At the bottom, we made our way back to the same spot the TCVs dropped us off. On passing the houses in the hamlet, the diggers were unable to curb their enthusiasm and couldn't refrain from displaying the captured weapons to the villagers. They held them above their heads for all to see.

The villagers would have heard the shooting a couple of hours earlier and were counting us again. They were now fully aware that their VC mates came off second best.

The diggers filled the boozer that evening, telling war stories to the pogos. The pogos love to hear a good war story. Furthermore, the blokes are good at it, garnishing their stories well. The pogos sit around hanging off every word, their eyes and mouths wide open as the men embellish the story. D & E Platoon celebrated quite freely, happy with the day's success.

17th January. CSM Lewis almost had a coronary. To his chagrin the area around the boozer was littered with stray beer cans. He chased me down and said, "Corporal Sutherland, do you know anything about the litter around the ORs' canteen?"

"Me sir, no sir! Why would I know?"

"I thought you might have been there last night."

"Well I was sir, but I'm not a pisspot like most of them. I went to bed long before the boozer closed."

"By the number of cans strewn all over the place it looks as though the boozer stayed open all night," the CSM remarked.

"Well sir, D & E Platoon had a big day yesterday, they'd be pretty tired I guess. I certainly was, so it was probably the cooks and bottlewashers. D & E wouldn't make a mess. They're too responsible."

"Bullshit they wouldn't, and they're not responsible. You couldn't put 'em in charge of a public toilet, none of them, I know what I'm going to do. I'm closing the boozer for twenty-four hours. That's what I'm doing, closing the boozer. You can spread the word."

I thought, a fat lot of good that's going to do. There are boozers all over the place. D & E went all over 1ATF to all sorts of units drinking in their boozers. They even go as far as the American Artillery base, a good kilometre away. Headquarter Battery is the closest though. They can look forward to a lot of visitors tonight, me included.

Ten minutes later Sergeant Jeffrey came across to me and said, "I've a few things to attend to Stan so can you, sometime later this morning, draw rations for the troops and get them re-supplied with fresh ammunition?"

"Yes, I'll look after that Sergeant."

"That trip up to the top of the Warbies the other day is probably my last operation. I might be involved in some small daily tasks if they crop up. But by in large I'm getting ready to go home Stan so you'll be doing a lot of my work from here on."

"Shit Rick! The diggers will miss you mate."

"Only for a couple of days Stan . . . out of sight out of mind, you know how it is."

"Yeah, we've all gotta go home, thank Christ. We get used to people coming and going. That's how it is in this man's army. Any word on who will be coming to replace you?"

"Not as yet. It's still early days. I'll still be around but it's just that I won't be going bush as much. You'll be doing most of what I do."

"You're going to be a tough act to follow Rick – I only hope I'm up to it."

"I'm sure you will Stan. Anyway, Cosgrove wouldn't ask you to do the job if he didn't think you're up to it."

After evening mess we all hot-the-trot down to Headquarter Battery's boozer. As expected, they made us welcome. They also liked to hear good war stories from the infantry. At 2315 the boozer closed and, somewhat inebriated, we left. There were about twelve of us. On the way back to our lines, Bluey

Costello said, "I suppose most of you feel suitably punished by the CSM for throwing empties about the place."

Ron Mitcherson, walking alongside Bluey, replied, "The CSM's bloody tough alright Blue, we've learnt our lesson. Tomorrow, I'm going to say to him: Please, sir, don't close the boozer again. Do whatever you like to us CSM but don't close the boozer."

"You sound like Brer Rabbit Ron," remarked Ken Earney.

"Yeah, that's the idea Ken. Good old Brer Rabbit and please don't throw me into the brambles Brer Fox, tar and feather me, but don't throw me into the brambles." Everybody laughed.

18th January. The Platoon remained on Hawk Force but we were not reacted. Most of the fellows put extra water bottles on their webbing. The dry season is in full swing and it's all thirsty work now. We break into a sweat as soon as we swing our legs out of bed in the mornings. I pulled my mess tins with the money in them out of my trunk and gave them a good shake again and put them back.

19th January. At 0900hrs the platoon was reacted by chopper to a feature, which rises steeply from the flat landscape around it. The feature is called Nui Nghe. Our task is to locate three mortar base sites the enemy used to lob mortars into Nui Dat the night before. It was hard going climbing, the vegetation was very thick and the day hot. When we got to the top Lt. Cosgrove had us have a good look around but we found nothing to suggest the mortars were fired from up here. We came down and headed south to some other suspected sites. We camped out overnight and continued the search the following morning.

During the course of the day we located the mortar positions. It appears the VC inserted the mortars by ox cart. Lt. Cosgrove made us thoroughly search the surrounding area looking for a permanent cache but we didn't find anything and, when we'd all gathered, he said, "All right fellas, that's enough for the day. We've found what we were looking for, have something to eat and a brew and then we're going back to Nui Dat." We returned to Nui Dat by chopper that afternoon.

For the next few days we remained at Nui Dat doing odds and ends. The only exciting activity was going to the range on 22nd January for M72 rocket firing practice. We fired at empty forty-four gallon drums at the end of the range. There was a mixture of good hits, near misses and a few wide shots. My rocket failed to fire so I missed out.

23rd January. Today we were placed on two weeks ready reaction in order to assist counter any VC initiative they might launch for the Tet period (New Year). If they try anything like they did in 1968, we'd be ready.

24th January. Lt. Cosgrove, myself and half the platoon went to the Long Hais as support troops for an American self-propelled, 175mm gun. This gun has an accurate range of thirty kilometres. From its position at the road's edge, firing into the Long Hais, a distance of two kilometres is firing at point blank range. The barrel of the gun is set to only a few degrees to fire into the caves halfway up the feature.

Lt. Cosgrove and I were watching the firing with interest and I said to him, "You know boss, they should do to the Long Hais what the Poms and Australians did at the Battle of Messines, in the First World War."

"What happened there?" he asked.

"Well, I have an interest in it because two of my mother's brothers were wounded there on the same day. They were both in the thirty-seventh battalion. One brother, my uncle George, died of his wounds and the other, uncle Willie, survived to return home. Another brother, my uncle Les, was in the First Light Horse Regiment in the Middle East at the time. The three of them signed on within weeks of one another in 1916. Uncle Les was also wounded, but more than a year later than George and Willie. Les was wounded in November 1917, but remained on duty. My grandfather, the silly bugger, put his age down and also signed on. He was of the view that if his three boys went then he'd go also. When the army found out he had three sons already on active service overseas they threw him out. Just as well too I suppose.

"My mother was the youngest of ten. The three eldest boys signed on for the First World War. When the Second World War started, the three younger brothers signed on and unfortunately one was killed in New Guinea. My grandfather, on my father's side, was at Gallipoli and, after the evacuation, went on to France. He was wounded in France somewhere along the line and subsequently repatriated back home."

"Well," said the lieutenant, "what does your mother think about you being here?"

"She's never said anything sir, but I guess she'll be glad to see me home."

"Your mother must have got an unwelcome surprise when you volunteered to come back here a second time."

"I suppose so. You know, I didn't really think about it."

"Yes, we're like that when we're young. We tend to only think about ourselves and what we're doing. We don't give enough thought to how our decisions might affect others."

"It's not only me sir, I've two brothers in the services as well. Both of them are in the navy. Douglas, he's in the Fleet Air Arm and Lance, well, he did a trip to Vietnam on the *Hobart* a couple of years ago. The Hobart, a destroyer went up and down the coast shelling hell out of the place.

"Anyway, I've got off the track sir. Messines.

"Using former English coal miners and Australian gold miners, they tunnelled for almost two years, driving a system of something like twenty tunnels under the mountain. When they dug the tunnels to where they wanted, they stacked tons of explosive at the end of each tunnel. They used about 600 tons in all, if my memory serves me correct. They blew the lot to start the Battle of Messines. They reckon something like ten thousand Germans were killed in that first big bang. They say the bang was heard across the channel as far as Dublin.

"So, I was thinking, they should do that here sir, to the Long Hais. A lot of Australians have already lost their lives in these hills and I daresay more will. Six hundred tons of explosives dumped into those caves and blown would be cheap by comparison. We could level the place and turn it into rice paddies for the villagers."

"It's a damn good idea Stan, but these days nobody thinks on such a big scale as those First World War soldiers."

"Just as well boss, the war would be over in a week. What would you and I do then?"

"I don't know, stay in the army I suppose, but life won't be as exciting."

At 1700hrs we returned to Nui Dat having spent a rather easy day watching the 175.mm.

25th January. An agent reported that a small party of VC from D445 Regiment were in the vicinity of grid square 4070. The platoon was reacted to go and have a look around. After searching the area for a few hours we could find no evidence of them having been there. However, we did find a well used ox cart track and Lt. Cosgrove decided to put in an ambush on the track. The ambush was just a hundred metres from the village of Ap Suoi Nghe.

This village, built by the Australian Army Engineers, is now home to people relocated there so they wouldn't be subject to control by the VC. The houses are of weatherboard construction, concrete floor and galvanized iron roof. The engineers also built their rice paddies for them. All the same, it's a godforsaken hole, no shade in the village at all. There's dozens of musky dirty kids though, all seasoned cigarette smokers. A lot of them have sores on their legs, which should be attended to.

We crept into our position after dark and set up the ambush. Unfortunately, no VC left or entered the village along the track we were on.

In the morning, the villagers came along, driving their ox carts in convoy fashion to go into the forest to cut timber. We were still on the ground well concealed watching them approach. The first cart got to fifteen metres from our position and the oxen balked. The boy driving them was only about twelve. He gave the two oxen a whack with his whip but the oxen were fidgety and shaking their heads. The kid, completely unaware of us in the scrub nearby, gave them a few more whacks with the whip. Unlike the driver, the oxen had smelt us stinking foreigners and they weren't going anywhere. With this, the kid stands up from his seat and gives each oxen one great whack with his whip. The oxen take off, bolting through the scrub opposite our side of the road.

These carts are not well sprung. The boy driving the cart thought he'd better sit down to avoid falling out. The cart went over a log, the kid's bum left the seat by at least three feet. The oxen weren't stopping for anybody and the last we saw of the cart and its driver was when it vanished into the bush a hundred metres away. Lt. Cosgrove also saw this and he said to me, "We'd better reveal ourselves before some poor kid gets killed."

The villagers in the ox cart convoy got a shock when we all stood from our concealed positions only metres away. They soon got over it and started to bot cigarettes or anything else that was going. We moved out a few minutes later and went on quite a long march, taking several hours to get into a jungle area. After crossing a creek, we were climbing a medium sized hill. The jungle was thick but good progress was being made. The platoon stopped and a signal was passed down the line to the effect that Lt. Cosgrove wanted me up front. I made my way up to him.

"Stan, have a look at this will you, you've been around a long time in the bush – have you ever seen anything like this before?" He pointed a few metres in front of him at a two-foot high barricade made out of small branches, twigs, grass, bark and other vegetation. The barricade stretched off to our right and left into the distance both ways, suggesting it circled the hill.

"As a matter of fact I have sir," I said. "The VC make this as a form of trap to catch Mouse Deer."

"Mouse Deer! What are they? How do they do that?"

"A Mouse Deer is about the same size as a hare, but unlike a hare, it has cloven feet like a deer. It's sort of fawn in colour with a few white spots on it. I've actually seen one here in Vietnam. The Mouse Deer come from the top of the hill down to the creek we just crossed to get a drink. They run into this barricade and follow it along looking for a way through. They find a gap purposely made, but it's snared. The VC, if successful, have nice fresh meat to dine on."

"We don't get nice fresh meat to dine on sir," remarked Doc Kilpatrick, the platoon medic who was standing alongside Lt. Cosgrove.

We stood examining the barricade for a minute and then I said, "If we follow it along a bit sir we'll find an opening." We moved about ten yards and we found a gap. I poked around with my bayonet and up sprung the snare. "That's interesting Stan, now that I've seen one, I'll know what it is next time around. I'm an expert too now."

We covered a fair distance for the day but, apart from the animal barricade, there was nothing else of significance in our day. The tracks picked us up later in the day and we returned to Nui Dat.

27th January. Nothing much happening. CSM Lewis has a purge going on in the lines. We're expecting our new Company Commander, Major Phil Bool, to arrive today or tomorrow. This evening, we had a practice "Stand To" which means everybody is standing-to in their designated weapon pits. There's no movement around the camp. The Medical Officer mustn't have been informed though. He comes walking nonchalantly up the road and gets to just opposite the Sergeants' Mess and Garry Hutton, in a pit off to his right, yells out, "Halt who goes there? Stop! Or I'll shoot."

"It's me, Starlight! Don't shoot! Don't shoot!"

Darrell McKinley in the same pit as Garry said loud enough for the MO to hear, "Shoot him Garry! Shoot him!"

"For Christ's sake, nobody shoot! It's me, Starlight!"

"Come into the light and be identified!" yells out Graham Hawkins (Hawkeye) from the next pit. The Medical Officer walks under a roadside light and stands there a moment looking towards where the voices have come from. "Starlight may proceed," Hawkeye concedes.

"You bastards!" replies the Medical Officer as he realises he's been had. We all had big grins on our faces. The MO nearly shit himself.

28th January. Last night 6RAR spotted a large body of VC in the rubber east of Binh Ba. They called in artillery and the VC broke into small groups and dispersed. One of these groups ran into an ambush set by 6RAR. D & E Platoon has been reacted to sweep through the area. Our sweep turned up nothing and we harboured up for the night. The next day we boarded the tracks and went south. There is a whole troop of tanks out and, supported by a section of tanks, we did a sweep in the vicinity of Nui Dat 2 (a hill feature). The sweep had negative results though, and we returned to Nui Dat at 1815 hrs.

29th January. About ten of the blokes from D & E platoon went down to the American artillery base for a few drinks in their boozer. Everything was fine until Darkie Dickson started playing around with their pet canary. He kept putting it in his mouth and closing his mouth and then taking it out again. The Yanks thought this was good fun and they were laughing at

Darkie until about the fourth time. Darkie put the bird in his mouth and he left it there for a couple of seconds and then took it out minus its head, which he spat on the floor. This made the Yanks mad and a fight started, but the diggers gave the Yanks a pasting. When it was all over they returned to lines.

30th January. Two battalions of enemy were seen in the area around the village of Duc My, which is a village to the north of Nui Dat on the western side of Route 2. The ready reaction force was reacted and we did a sweep in the area. Intelligence received information that the enemy had cached supplies of mortars and ammunition near Duc My. The sweep proved negative, but our Platoon came across a blood trail, which we followed for a distance until Lt. Cosgrove decided to let it go. We returned to Nui Dat aboard the tracks the same day.

After we'd cleaned up I went to the boozer for a beer with Ken Earney. Ken's one of those blokes who likes to organize the boys a bit and he's generally in the thick of any shit D & E Platoon are up to. The both of us were sitting having a quiet beer when along came five more of the fellows, Peter Eastham, Ron Mitcherson, Laurie Round, Bill Gorman and Allan Purches. Ken loves a bit of an audience and it's not long before he's spinning a few yarns.

He says, "Did I ever tell you blokes what I did to Lt. Russ Henderson a couple of months back?"

Ron Mitcherson said, "I've just started on my happy pills and I'm not sure I should be sitting here drinking and listening to your bullshit Earney."

Allan Purches added, "And that goes for me too Ken, just keep to the facts mate, no gilding the lily."

Ken pulled up his chair and made himself more comfortable. "We were out in the bush. I don't really know where, but it was rubber and jungle. It mighta been up Bihn Ba Way. Anyway, Henderson took a small group of us out on a recce. We'd gone probably about seven hundred metres away from the rest of the platoon and he says to me, 'Earney, shoot up there and have a look and report back to me.'

"Now, I didn't like the look of what he was asking me to do. It looked bloody dicey to me so, thinking about it, I up with my rifle and fire a shot. By this time Henderson had turned his back to me. He got a helluva fright, and turning around, he says, 'Christ Earney! What in the hell do you think you're doing?' 'Obeying your orders sir,' I reply. 'Orders! What bloody orders?' he says.

"You told me to shoot up there, take a look and report back. Well I did sir, and I can tell you the ground drops away fifty metres and you can see bugger all from then on.'

"Well, Henderson was dumbfounded, he didn't know what to say. All he could do was shake his head. When we got back to the rest of the platoon an hour later, Rick Jeffrey saw us coming in and he says to the boss, 'What was that shooting about boss?' Henderson replies. 'I dunno! Ask fucking Earney.'

We all laughed and Earney went on, "After that, whenever Henderson wanted me to go anywhere he was always quite specific as to what he wanted and from then on he always said 'Earney I want you to walk up there and . . . so on.'

Bill Gorman said, "Now Earney, it's a bloody good story but I think you're bullshitting us."

"No Bill, it's fair dinkum mate."

We all passed a few comments and Peter Eastham said, "Well one thing's for sure Ken, you're not one to let the facts bugger up a good story."

31st January. D & E Platoon have been invited back down to the American artillery boozer to bury the hatchet from the fight a couple of days earlier and to have a few friendly drinks. As they entered the boozer they noticed that no Americans were there, so they sat down and ordered some beers. Gradually, a few Yanks started coming in and taking seats at the tables, but they were not ordering any drinks. After a while, quite a few had entered the boozer and Jimmy Fraser noticed the doors were being guarded. Jim, seeing this, got the vibes that something was amiss and he decided to make himself scarce and managed to get out just in time thinking 'If only I can make it to the rubber trees before I'm set upon, I'll be right.'

Meanwhile, back in the boozer, all the exits were now blocked by big Afro-Americans and the diggers knew they were in for trouble. One big Yank stood up and said, "I'm speaking on behalf of the Americans – who's your spokesperson?"

Frank Malisani stood up with his shirt undone, as was his normal way of wearing it, and said, "I'm speaking on behalf of the Aussies." No sooner had the words left his mouth and a sock on the jaw knocked him down and out. Then it was on. There were about twenty-five Yanks pitched against ten Aussies. Darkie Dickson is a very capable fighter and his straight right jabs were as quick as a flash and he had this Yank's head going backwards and forwards as though his head was attached to Darkie's fist with a strong rubber band . . . crack, crack, crack, and the Yank went down on his knees and started crawling for the door. Every digger had more than two against him.

Frank Malisani came to, but was knocked out again before he could do much damage.

Bill Gorman was in the thick of it and there was blood streaming from his face. Bill is a little over six feet tall and two Yanks were trying to pull him to the floor while a third was lining up to sink the slipper in. Bill, seeing his predicament, spun around with all his strength, knocking the two Yanks to the floor instead. As one of them got to his knees, Bill socked him as hard as he could in the back of the head and the Yank's face hit the floorboards like a wet mop. The other two were still trying to pull him down but Bill knew once he was on the floor he was buggered and he kept throwing punches on his feet. Eventually all the diggers were knocked out and carried to the door and thrown out. There were just two many Yanks for the ten Aussies to handle.

Ken Earney and Jimmy Floyd, both only small blokes, were reluctant to step up to big heavyweight so they sat at their table and didn't move. When all the other Aussies had been thrown out a big Yank came up to their table and asked, "Are you two with them?"

Ken Earney said, "Never seen them before!"

The Yank said, "Aussies aren't welcome here tonight – you can either walk out or be carried out." Floydy and Earney thought it better to walk out.

Darkie Dickson wasn't finished with the fight yet. He got his rifle and went back and put three bullet holes through their boozer. When he got back to the lines the MPs were waiting for him. They bagged him up and I didn't see Darkie at all after that. It's the hill down at Vungas for him.

Bill Gorman said after the fight, "You know, if we only had two to one to beat, we'd have done 'em, but three to one was just too many, the bastards had us fucked, but what a bloody ambush they sucked us into. Fancy them inviting us down for a drink. What a bunch of pricks. I'm not going back there to patronize their boozer, they can stick it."

The Tet period is now over and D & E Platoon have been taken off the ready reaction force. The platoon remained in Nui Dat for four days.

On the 3rd, February I went down to Vung Tau. My job was to collect two men from Headquarter Company who have been in detention for the last twenty-eight days. The detention centre at Vung Tau is known as "The Hill."

I asked one of them his name.

"John D'Aloisio, Corporal," he replied.

I asked what he'd been doing time for.

"I was a bit stiff. I was working at the Officers' Mess and it was pouring with rain and I was busting for a pee. I didn't want to get soaking wet going to the lines and I thought to myself, I'll just have a pee off the veranda. I'm halfway through and Pratt, the OC, catches me. I fronted up on a charge and ended up with twenty-eight days hard labour, and loss of pay into the boot."

"What did they have you doing?" I asked.

"Filling sand bags from dawn till dark every day. We were allowed only three cigarettes a day, that's if you had them, and then we had to ask permission to smoke them. We also had to call the NCOs in charge, sir. Like, excuse me sir, permission to have a smoke sir, or, permission to have a pee sir."

"Sounds as though it was pretty tough," I said

"Yes it was. I'm bloody glad to be out. It was an expensive pee, that's for sure." The hard work did him good though. He looked like a body builder.

4th. February 1970. The platoon left Nui Dat with six days of rations. We're going to be patrolling and ambushing around Duc My. At 1300 hrs, the platoon commenced putting in an ambush. At last light for the day, Lt. Cosgrove and three section moved to within two hundred metres of Duc My and there we set up another ambush. Before dawn, we pulled up stumps and returned to the rest of the platoon. We re-established our day ambush and remained there all day. At 1700 hrs, Lt Cosgrove and my section left the position to put in another ambush at the edge of the rubber. The ambush had negative results.

The next day, the platoon moved south, crossing a large swamp, which was heavy going. After clearing the swamp we came across a good flowing creek where we stopped for a rest. I took out a small reconnaissance patrol. The forward scout heard Vietnamese voices coming from upstream. We quietly made our way forward towards the voices until we were only a few metres away. I peered through some scrub to see a civilian tending his fish trap in the creek. He was talking to his two children who were with him. Being unnoticed, I observed him for a while and, instead of jumping out and scaring him half to death, I decided to remain concealed. His fish trap was made of bamboo and was large enough to go from bank to bank of the creek. It was designed to funnel the fish coming down the creek into a bamboo barrel-shaped chute in the centre of the trap. The chute, about five feet long, fed into a holding cage from which the fish could not escape. It looked a very effective set up. We watched him for a few minutes and then quietly withdrew. When we rejoined the platoon we went north looking for a spot to put in an ambush for the night.

8th February. Lt. Cosgrove had us pull out of the ambush position before first light and we went into a good patch of bamboo where we could remain concealed for the day. Towards evening, we moved to a position in the rubber to put in another ambush. At 1830 hrs. two VC were seen but, unfortunately, the distance was too far to engage them. Lt. Cosgrove ordered my section to go to where they were seen but they'd moved on.

9th February. Today we marched six thousand metres. At the end of the trek the diggers were hot and tired. We searched the village of Duc My. A woman VCI on the black list was detained and handed over to the RF. During the course of the day, choppers dropped in a re-supply and we then moved to the eastern side of Route 2 to put in an ambush. When we were setting it up a digger in Des Weller's section shot himself through the foot. He was subsequently dusted off and the set up of the ambush continued.

Lt. Cosgrove is annoyed, the ambush has now been compromised and there is talk amongst the diggers that he did it on purpose. Whether he did or not, I don't know. The incident was in another section and at least sixty metres from me. If he did it on purpose, it was a stupid act. He could have maimed his foot to a dreadful extent for life. On the other hand, to accommodate the notion it was an accident is a bit much to ask as well. The diggers, who talk and whinge amongst themselves, always have a good feel for what's going on. To wound yourself in the field on purpose is an act the diggers will never forgive. They view it as cowardly and a let down to the team.

Lt. Cosgrove knows there are enemy in the area because, only the night before, VC had moved in close to a platoon of 6RAR. They cut their claymore leads and deloused their trip flares before putting in an assault on the platoon. Lt. Cosgrove, conscious of the welfare of his own platoon, had every right to be annoyed.

We remained in the rubber overnight and all the next day until evening. We then moved to put in an ambush on a track junction at the edge of the rubber. The ambush was not triggered and we remained motionless in the rubber so as not to be seen. In the evening, we moved again to put in another ambush but the French plantation owner saw us. It's difficult to tell where his sympathies lie. It is well known he has entertained VC in his house in the past and it's difficult to understand how he can remain in his situation in this environment unless he's of use to the VC. If he falls out with them, they'll simply kill him. We remained in the area for a few more days, either patrolling by day, or lying low and concealed in day, and then moving in the evenings to ambush tracks etc.

The only enemy activity was on the night of the 13th February, when an estimated platoon of VC entered the village of Binh Ba and had a shoot out with the Vietnamese Regional Forces.

15th February. We were picked up by TCVs and driven back to Nui Dat. A few nice cold beers cheered the men up. After mess I went to the boozer and Greg Kennett was in there all fired up and quite agitated. I asked, "What's the matter with you tonight Greg?"

"Ah shit! You know that pogo prick, the one you picked up from the hill recently, what's his name?" He asked.

"D'Aloisio, John D'Aloisi I think."

"Yeah that's him. He was in here ten minutes ago mouthing off about D & E Platoon and I told him if he didn't shut his mouth, then I'd shut it for him with a bunch of fives. You know what the prick said then? He says to me 'You couldn't beat a bloody egg.'

"Well Stan, that was like a red flag to a bull and I'm into him."

"Did you manage to land a couple Greg? He looks a strong muscle bound looking prick, he looks as though he can handle himself pretty well."

"He can and he did." Greg waited for a few seconds and then, as an afterthought, added, "But I was better."

16th February. We were placed back on ready reaction today and to celebrate the OC put on a BBQ. It was a great turn. The steaks were good and there was enough beer to go around.

17th February. CSM Lewis was onto me all day to supply work parties all over the place. The diggers seemed to know what was going on and made themselves scarce. I couldn't find enough blokes to fill the work parties, which aggravated the CSM even more. I couldn't understand why he was in such a bad mood. When the day was done and the diggers filtered back into the lines from their hiding places to go to the boozer, I went over to Peter Eastham and said, "Where in the hell have you blokes been hiding? I've had a prick of a day. Lewis has been on my back all day and I've been the only sucker around."

"Yeah, sorry about that Stan, but the boys sent the CSM a package with a live snake in it. We knew the shit would hit the fan so we hid out for the day. We were hiding in that room, you know, the one down behind the TV room."

"Bloody hell, no wonder he's got shit on the liver," I said

The next two days were quiet for most of us.

19th February. Des Weller's section was deployed to the Long Hais today in the wake of a contact, which resulted in two Australians killed in action and about 28 wounded. We heard one mortar track (armoured personnel carrier from which mortars are fired) was completely destroyed and a centurion tank damaged. There were two other APCs damaged by RPGs as well.

20th February. I left Nui Dat with the convoy to Vung Tau. I'm spending five days at the R & C Centre in Vung Tau. The centre, which provides motel style accommodation, is a former French hotel but has now been taken over by the Australians. It provides meals and has a nice bar set up on the top of the building. For the next five days, I'll just take it easy, relaxing over nice cold beer.

On the last day at Vungas, I picked up a suit for Brian Grace, which he'd ordered from an Indian tailor and I spent the rest of the day in a place called Queens Bar. The following day I went on the convoy back to Nui Dat, arriving there at 1630 hrs.

27th February. Lt. Cosgrove informed us we're on ready reaction until 3rd March. He also told us that 8RAR are having a lot of trouble in the Long Hais.

28th February. We learned today that 1 Platoon, A Company 8RAR, lost nine men killed and fourteen wounded taking out a bunker system. Nobody likes to hear this sort of news and we all know, but for the grace of god, go we.

Later in the day we went to the range to practise firing M72 rockets and grenades from our rifles. The following day we returned to the range and gave all the machine guns in the platoon a good test fire.

2nd March. The platoon worked on different projects in the morning and then went to Luscombe Field in the afternoon for a show put on by some Australian entertainers. When we got back, Lt. Cosgrove met us and said loudly so that we all could hear, "Corporal Sutherland, make sure these blokes are all organized. We're going out on a five-day ambush type operation up north first thing in the morning."

The men trickled away to get themselves ready. I didn't have to say a thing. A little while later Rick Jeffrey came across to tell us he's going home on the 18th of March and that he's starting on his happy pills tomorrow. Rick will be missed by the men – he's a good Sergeant with the ability to relate to the men and to keep good control and discipline. He's also very good for morale amongst the troops.

D & E Platoon's (kill) scoreboard

Joe Atkinson, Peter Couchman and Stan Sutherland on Long SonIsland, April 1970

Ken Earney

Colin Moyle on Long Son Island

Jim Floyd

Bob Pollard   *Graham "Hawkeye" Hawkins*

Pte. Ecclestone (signalman)

Colin Moyle having a shave

GregKennett

John O'Malley

Ian McAuley

Jim Fraser

The following morning Lt. Cosgrove and I were waiting all kitted out for the operation and standing outside a tent that he has taken over to use as an office for himself. The tent is about ten metres from my tent and on the main track to the orderly room from D & E platoon lines. The tent has a door made of plywood and is fitted with a fly wire screen. Lt. Cosgrove is telling me how good it is as an office and how pleased he is to have it.

Jimmy Fraser walked over to us, and said, "Sir, Des Weller has just told me I'm not going out on this operation – is that right?"

"Yes Jim, that's right," Cosgrove replied.

"Why fuckin' not sir? I want to go."

"Well, you can't Jim. Your dentures are broken. You've got no bloody teeth."

"What's that got to do with it sir?"

"Everything Jim. I'm not having people out in the bush with no teeth."

"So that's it, is it sir?"

"Yes Jim! That's it!"

Jim's response was to clench his fist and let go with a forceful right jab which went straight through the plywood door on Cosgrove's office, putting a big hole in it.

"For Christ's sake, settle down Jim, that sort of behaviour will only get you into trouble."

"Ah fuck it. If I can't go bush, then fuck it," were Jim's last words as he stormed off towards his tent.

The diggers much preferred to go bush and be with their mates even though the work was hard. Remaining back in the lines has no joy all for good infantry soldiers. Even nightly access to a cold beer at the boozer doesn't measure up to being with your mates. Lt. Cosgrove was aware of this and didn't make an issue out of Jim's frustration. He just looked at his smashed in office door and said, " I had the office looking good for five minutes there you know."

I said, "I can get the boys to hunt down another door if you like sir, they'll pinch it for you one dark night and put it on. They're good at that sort of stuff. If they can pinch the Brigadier's Christmas turkey and beer from the Sergeants' Mess, amongst other things, a door won't be a problem."

"When you say 'they', Stan, who do you actually mean?" Cosgrove asked.

"The whole platoon sir," I replied

"I was afraid you'd say that."

"Some of them got good at it from working in the officers' lines as batmen. They didn't like the job and wanted to be put back into D & E Platoon to be with their mates. They organised themselves to pinch items like ballpoint pens or writing kits, even a jacket here and there, you know, just small bits and pieces. One bloke used to even swap officers' boots around. He'd pick two officers who both wore size nine for example and just change one boot over, a left for a left. The officers would get up the next morning and put their boots on and wonder why one boot was suddenly uncomfortable. In the end the officers jacked up and told the OC that they didn't care where he got their batmen from as long as they're not those thieving bastards from D & E Platoon."

"No, don't worry about the door Stan, I'll see about getting this one fixed when we get back. Don't tell me any more, I won't be able to take it."

The choppers came to pick us up. We flew into the LZ and quickly filtered into the jungle at the edge. We travelled about a thousand metres through the jungle and came across a well-used track. The prospects for a successful ambush are good and Lt. Cosgrove has us tasking on it for the night. There is a river nearby and we'll be keeping somewhere near it to refill our water bottles.

We remained in the ambush all the next day and night. We were sure we'd be successful as it is such a good track and we only have to stay here long enough. Unfortunately, on the morning of the 5th, the task force requested Lt. Cosgrove to move the platoon about two thousand metres south west to try to locate a cache a Hoy Chanh said was in the area. (A Hoy Chanh is a VC who comes over to our side). Being in such a good ambush set up, the boss didn't want to pack up but he had no alternative and we left at 1400 hrs.

Searching for caches in the past have been exercises in wild goose chasing more often than not. We felt this would be another one. The going proved very tough. We're in an area where there's a lot of red ants nests in the lower branches of the trees. They're particularly fond of a tree that has a shiny green leaf. When we pass underneath, the ants jump or drop down on us, getting down our collars and under our shirts, biting the hell out of us. They've got a particularly mean bite and, with dozens of them biting you at once, it's guaranteed to make you move and swear as well. We're very used to these ants jumping on us from above and we can shed our packs and have our shirts off in a flash. It's very rarely you can go into the scrub and not be set upon by the red ants. The chomper ants that appear at night, as bad as they are, are more preferable to the red ants of a day.

We came upon a small river, filling our water bottles as we crossed. The rear of the lead section was about thirty metres in front of me, going up a slope on the other side of the river. The jungle was quite thick and we were flat out keeping the man in front of us in sight. I'd just got out of the river and was about ten metres up the slope. Suddenly, the troops up in front were yelling, "Shit! Look out," and they were jumping out of the way. They made a noise pushing the scrub aside in order to get out of the way. I didn't see the problem but I heard a big splash in the river upstream. Warren Handley who saw it swore black and blue it was a crocodile. Whatever it was, it made a big splash when it jumped into the river. I can swear to that.

"I didn't know there were any crocodiles in Vietnam," said Bluey Lantry who had crossed and was now standing on the bank alongside me. Bill Gorman was in the middle of the river standing there with water up to his waist. "I didn't either and look at all the swamps and rivers we've been in up to our necks. Can't be too many though. I've been more concerned about bloody water snakes. You know, those big ones, anacondas I think."

"Wrong continent Bill. They're in South America," I said.

Before Bill could say any more, Lt. Cosgrove had moved up to investigate the hold up and said, "C'mon you blokes, get a move on, we've got work to do."

"Bill's just standing in the river discussing crocodiles and anacondas sir. He's pretty game considering a crocodile just jumped in upstream ten metres or so causing the hold up," I replied.

Bill woke up to his predicament and said, "Shit! I forgot about that. The damn thing will have me, let's get out of here!"

Bluey Lantry, with a big grin on his face said, "It's good to see that he can move his arse when he has to Stan, don't you reckon – look at him go."

John Martin and John O'Malley were the next to cross and, excited by Bill's rapid exit from the river, wasted no time in doing so. John Martin tripped and went totally under water, coming up spluttering. The diggers coming across behind them had got the word and they crossed the river quite rapidly.

We moved on for another hour until it was time to harbour up putting in an ambush on a track.

The following day I remained with my section in the ambush position and Lt. Cosgrove took the other two sections on a reconnaissance patrol. One of the advantages of having two machines guns in my section is that, when the platoon is split – which it is from time to time, Lt. Cosgrove having one half, and getting me to take the other half – both parts of the platoon have two machine guns. A comforting situation, due to the firepower we can deliver. It's always good to have a back up gun as well.

The next day we picked up and went south travelling through a large swamp. After we'd patrolled a thousand metres, we stopped and Lt. Cosgrove sent out two reconnaissance patrols for a look around the area. When they returned, we moved on another four hundred metres to a night position.

8th March. We were extracted today. Our relief was in the area only an hour when they killed a VC. We were informed they had a *hoy chanh* with them who led them straight to an enemy camp.

9th March. The men engaged themselves doing a few odd jobs around the lines until mid afternoon. At 1500hrs, three section, plus Platoon headquarters, were airlifted to Long Son Island. The rest of the platoon is following tomorrow.

Once the remainder of the platoon joined us we spent some time doing some routine patrolling. There's no stream on the island from which to fill our bottles. Water is going to be a problem. The only water we know of is a well the villages use and which is a couple of kilometres north west of Long Son village, the only village on the island. Each morning, young girls leave the village with two four-gallon kerosene tins attached to a pole they carry across their shoulder. They return carrying eight gallons of water. On top of the water they place a few green leaves which serve to stabilize the water and prevent it from splashing out.

There is a lot of weight in eight gallons of water and the little girls are perspiring on their way back to their homes with the water. In my view, it's not a good thing for young girls to be carrying this type of weight. In Vietnam, you see a lot of elderly people stooped right over. I think it's from all the hard work, like carrying eight gallons of water for kilometres when they were young.

11th March. Lt. Cosgrove had us checking out a few areas but mainly we were employed as a blocking force while the RF did a sweep. It was only a small operation and we weren't involved long. Water was supposed to be flown in today but none arrived. All the men are almost out of water.

With no water available to us, Lt. Cosgrove had us move to an area where there was a modest amount of shade under some bamboo. I was completely out of water and suffering a little as a result. I asked Lt. Cosgrove for permission to take a small party out looking for water, to which he gave the OK. After an hour of searching, the closest thing we came to water was a buffalo wallowing hole. The water was green with slime and flavoured by buffalo manure. We were that thirsty we filled our bottles and put in some sterilization tablets. When we rejoined the remainder of the platoon we ran the water through our canvas filtering bags. I resorted to drinking it only to vomit it up almost immediately. I couldn't understand why I was so damn thirsty as I have a high tolerance to the heat. We all spent a dry throat night and it was the thirstiest occasion I experienced in Vietnam.

12th March. The Forward Observation came to the island today by Sioux helicopter, commonly referred to as a "possum." The Sioux has a bubble in the front of it which houses the pilot and passenger. The aircraft and pilot was made available to Lt. Cosgrove.

Calling me over, he said, "Stan I want you to go up in the chopper and have a good look around. See if you can spot from the air a good-looking track for us to ambush tonight. Go up now. We only have the chopper for a certain period."

I hopped into the chopper and sat in the right hand seat alongside the pilot. He asked me to put the earphones on and, when I had them on, he said, "When you wish to speak to me, press that little red button there and talk into the microphone." I had a couple of practice goes and then he took the aircraft into the air to a height of 120 feet, according to his altimeter. We were skimming over mostly prickly bamboo and we got a good view of everything down below. What I'm looking for is a well-used footpad under the bamboo.

After a few minutes in the air the pilot came in over the intercom and said, "I think I saw something just back there. I'm going back and we'll take a second look." The pilot turned the craft around and went back a distance. "Can you see that down there?" he asked.

Pressing my red button, I said "No! All I can see is bamboo from here."

"I'll go down a little lower and turn the chopper around a few degrees and you'll be able to see what I'm looking at. It's a bunker."

With that, he lowered the chopper to about fifteen metres above the bamboo.

"There! Can you see those bunkers?" I could.

Before either of us could make further comment, a VC dressed in green emerged from under the bamboo and lined us up with his AK47.

"Shit! Look out!" said the pilot.

At this point I'm looking straight at the VC, who has us right in his sights – I'm sure he's going to bring us down. How can he possibly miss? I'm thinking, at the very least, he'll get the pilot, but what's the difference. If he gets the pilot, the aircraft will fall out of the air, then I'm done for too. It's a moment frozen in time. The VC gives us two good bursts, emptying his magazine from what is virtually point blank range.

Next thing over the intercom, I hear from the pilot, "Fuck! I'm outa here." And spinning the aircraft around with nose down and tail up, he was off. He'd had enough, there was to be no more looking around for tracks for him.

On the way back I could see his hand on the stick shaking all over the place. The craft seemed to wobble from side to side like a drunken bee flying back to its hive. He came back in over the intercom and said, "Fuck! That was close. That's the closest thing I've ever come up against."

"Yeah," I said. "How he missed I'll never know. We must have been within sixty feet of him. I was sure he had us buggered."

The pilot didn't don't know if he'd hit the chopper – "I hope to hell he hasn't. I'll have a look as soon as we land," he said.

A few seconds later, we were back at the platoon. The pilot, with too much adrenalin coursing through his veins, brought the chopper down too fast. When we hit the ground the chopper bounced three metres back into the air, jarring all the bones in my body. When we came back to the ground again we bounced once more but this time not so hard. The craft finally settled on the third go and I hopped out, ducking my head as I ran under the rotor blades to the side.

Lt. Cosgrove had heard the shooting and came up to me to ask what had happened. "Some little noggy bugger thought he was going to be awarded Hero of the People for bringing down a chopper. To tell you the truth, for a moment there, I thought he was too," I replied

"Did you see anything? How'd it come about?"

"Yeah, we saw some bunkers. I didn't see them at first. I was on the wrong side of the chopper and the pilot lowered so I'd be able to get a better look. That's when this little prick comes out from under the bamboo. I think he got a surprise to see us hovering only sixty to eighty feet above him. He lined us up almost at point blank range and gives us a couple of serves with his AK47. But don't ask me how he missed – I can't believe it. The size of a chopper makes a pretty good target."

"He must have got such a surprise at his golden opportunity that he forgot to take aim."

"Either that sir, or we were fortunate enough to draw the worst shot in the National Liberation Front. Jeez, we were lucky though."

I told him I didn't have a clue where we were at the time. "Once we got shot at, the pilot nearly shit himself and he just took off."

Lt. Cosgrove said, "When I heard the shooting, I took a compass bearing. We'll quickly pick up from here and go and have a look around. Are you alright though?"

"Yeah boss! Don't worry about me – I'm alright."

A few minutes later the platoon was all set to go. We did a sweep through what we thought was the area but we didn't find the bunkers.

The next day was Friday the thirteenth. I thought to myself, I'm glad today wasn't yesterday, no point in tempting fate. Three section went into the village of Long Son to protect the army engineers who have some villagers labouring digging a trench in which to lay pipes for a village water supply. Apparently the Aussies are providing everything apart from labour. The village has to supply workers each day to dig the trench. Our job is to protect the workers and army engineers. Thank god it's an easy job. I feel absolutely miserable today and it seems as though the sun and heat has got through to me.

14th March. Lt. Cosgrove shifted the platoon closer to the village. Later in the day he ordered a half platoon ambush. My section and a couple from another section are going. The remainder of the platoon is to remain where they are and set up an ambush there. At 2000 hrs, a trip flare was tripped at the base ambush and one of the claymores was fired. The next day, rumours were flying around the village to the effect the *uc dai loi* killed two VC.

Long Son is an interesting village. At the eastern end of the village live the Cao Dai. This is a religious sect, distinguishable by their long hair, which they don't cut. It seems to me the Cao Dai have all bases covered. The religion was founded in Vietnam in the 1920s. The main tenets of the religion have been extracted from Buddhism, Hinduism, Islam, Christianity and Judaism. They've taken a little bit from everywhere.

15th March. The new OC, Major Phil Bool, an Artillery Officer, paid us a visit today. A patrol was organized and the OC wanted to come along. In the middle of the island is a small mountainous range. It's quite steep, though. The patrol is to go to the top of this range. The OC, who is not used to this type of work, had the stuffing knocked out of him. When we got back to platoon base he was happy to have done it and left the island satisfied with his effort.

Lance Corporal Bluey Bert had his section, which is number two section on the Engineer protection detail. At the end of the day Bluey returned to the platoon almost dragging his rifle and his eyes were rolling around in their sockets. One or two others looked under the weather as well. Apparently they got involved with the locals drinking rice whisky, which is a strict 'no no'.

Lt. Cosgrove sacked Bluey as Section Commander and sent him back to Nui Dat on the next chopper leaving the island.

As I said earlier, Bluey is not one to consider the consequences of his actions. We never saw or heard of him again.

The next day it was three section's turn to look after the engineers. I was glad to be able to sit in the shade. I'm not feeling well either. About mid-morning, a backhoe is flown in. If we had to wait for the villagers to dig the distance of trench required we'd be here for months. The villagers are delighted. They've never seen anything like it before. They are also glad to be relieved from their pick and shovel work. Doc. Kilpatrick even had a go with the backhoe while the engineers stopped for a break. He did a good job too.

17th March. Nothing of interest happened today. It is damn hot and boring as well.

18th March. The engineers wanted to go out and inspect the well, over which they're going to erect a platform to place a water tank on. The village chief has told the engineers that the VC will shoot holes in the tank if they don't put a tap at ground level for the VC to use.

My section is the protection party. When the engineers had inspected the well, I sent some of the men back with them. The remainder of us stayed behind. We wanted to observe a pagoda which it has been made known to us that some villagers meet there with the VC at times.

20th March. The RF conducted an operation today in which they killed one VC. It turns out the dead VC was carrying a Thompson Sub Machine Gun. They also shot a large Asian python. Fourteen men stood shoulder to shoulder to gauge its length. The snake is as thick as the top of a grown man's thigh. The head is half again the size of a human's. I've never seen anything like it before.

The task Force brigadier flew in today and made a few decisions. He's going to send a section of APCs together with D Company, 6RAR, to the island for a week.

21st March. Today we banned the villagers from the western end of the island. Lt. Cosgrove asked me to take my section to the western end to find a track and ambush it for the night. We left early in the morning to be in a concealed position for the day. At 0900 hrs, some civilians came along despite the ban. I threatened them with a few strokes of my index finger across my throat. They readily understood this universal sign and went back the way they came. Nobody came into the ambush and we headed back the following day. We were hot and bothered when we passed a paddock of nice, ripe watermelon. I told the men to grab a couple of melons each, and we'll go into the shade to eat them. We had a very enjoyable half hour eating the melons in the shade. When I told everyone to saddle up, we struggled a bit as we'd taken our webbing belts off to relax. Having full bellies of melon, we couldn't get them on again without letting them out a notch or two.

22nd March. D Company, 6RAR arrived on the island. A section of 81mm mortars has also arrived to give them support. The mortars are located in our platoon base camp. D & E Platoon is providing four men along with Corporal Des Weller to stay with the RF on hill 84, which they use as an observation post. It will be Des's job to ensure the RF don't fire their weapons indiscriminately, as they're often prone to doing.

I have a splitting headache today. Once the heat of the day reaches its zenith I seem to go down, feeling extremely miserable. There is definitely something wrong with me but it keeps coming and going. I'm extremely grateful to the fact that I've not had to do a lot of physical work over the last couple of days.

The mortars set up their base plates and started firing late that afternoon and well into the night. My splitting headache is being sorely aggravated. There's nothing I can do but suffer it out. Listening to the Corporal in charge yelling orders with respect to bearings and the charge level to fire the mortars is punishing me severely. When he yells 'number seven charge', I say to myself, oh NO! Then, BANG, as the mortar is fired. The next mortar is maybe fired on a number two charge and I say to myself. "That's better, stick on number two." The mortar still goes off with a loud *bang* but nowhere near as bad as number seven. My head feels it's going to split right open if this keeps up much longer.

25th March. The rest of the platoon joined us today for a platoon re-supply. In all probability cold cans of soft drink, one for each man will come with the re-supply. I'm running a temperature of sorts and I'm really looking forward to a cool drink. Whilst I feel a little better I'm devoid of energy.

26th March. I woke this morning feeling very ill and vomited for the first time since I started feeling unwell seventeen days ago. Knowing I'm unable to carry out my duties as Acting Platoon Sergeant or anything else for that matter, I didn't want to compromise the platoon at a later stage in a more important situation than what we're in today. I went up to Lt. Cosgrove and said, "I'm sorry boss, but I'm as crook as a dog. I've been unwell since coming to the island but I was hopeful of shaking it off. Every day I've got worse though. I can't do my job in this condition and I thought I'd better come forward and tell you."

"You look terrible Stan, just hang on I'll get the medic to take your temperature."

He yelled out to Doc Kilpatrick, "Hey Doc, bring your medical kit over here will you. We've got a patient."

My temperature measured 104. "That's high Stan, no wonder you feel crook," said Lt. Cosgrove. "We'd better get him off to hospital Doc. I'll get on the radio and call in the med evac."

It didn't seem long before the chopper arrived to take me to hospital. I was helped aboard by a couple of diggers and then the chopper lifted into the air and we were away. As the chopper climbed and the cool air was streaming through the aircraft from the rotor blades, I started to feel a lot better straight away.

The chopper landed on the helipad at the hospital in Vung Tau. Hospital staff were waiting and helped me off the chopper and into the hospital where I was seen by a doctor straight away.

Lying on the examination table he poked and prodded around my lower torso. After a bit of prodding, he said, "You've a swollen spleen, what you've got is malaria."

The next thing I know I'm in bed in a ward with a fan blowing on me to bring my body temperature down. At regular intervals a male nurse comes along and gives me tablets to take. The following day I'm well enough to have a meal. The male nurse brings a meal of roast beef and vegetables. I thoroughly enjoyed it and when he came back to gather up my plate I said to him, "Thanks mate, that was really bloody nice."

He didn't say anything but just gave me a strange look as if to say, "How can frozen peas, powdered potatoes and frozen carrots be nice?"

He walked towards the door with my plate in his hand, then looked back at me and shook his head. I think, 'These pogos don't know shit from clay. If he'd been out in the bush eating combat rations for the last eighteen days he'd then think it a nice meal too.'

After a few days in hospital I started to feel a lot better. Some strength was returning and I was able to do some reading. The doctor tells me I'll be right to join my mates in three or four days. I tried to walk to the hospital mess for the midday meal. I had to walk about thirty metres but I only got halfway there and a spell of dizziness came over me and I turned around and went back to my bed. Later in the day a group of entertainers from Perth came and put on a show, which I enjoyed immensely.

29th March. A quiet day spent in hospital.

30th March. The doctor came around and checked me over. He said, "You can return to your unit in the morning."

"That's good," I replied.

31st March. It's good to be back on my feet again. I left hospital and went to the Badcoe club for a few beers. In the afternoon I returned to Nui Dat and rejoined Headquarter Company.

1st April. Spent the day cleaning the dirt and leaves from my tent. The platoon will be back from Long Son Island on the 4th and I'm really looking forward to seeing them again.

2nd April. I spent the day painting my steel trunk. I'm going to send all unnecessary gear home well in advance so that it will be there when I arrive home.

3rd April. Today I did a few odd jobs in preparation for the platoon's return from Long Son tomorrow. I took my trunk to the Q Store and had it dispatched to Australia.

4th April. The platoon returned, arriving just after lunch. They're all pleased to get off Long Son for a bit of a break. Furthermore, they're all looking forward to going to Vung Tau tomorrow to cause a bit of mischief.

5th April. The convoy with all the diggers on board arrived at the Peter Badcoe club, Vung Tau, at 0900. Lt. Cosgrove lined them up again and said, "Now boys, you know what I said last time, I'm not going to repeat myself, clear off and have a good time. Costello, Earney and Fraser – be careful. I'm on to you three."

Notwithstanding the boss's address, three of our fellows were in the slot before nightfall, two of them being Ken Earney and Bluey Costello. They refused to leave the Grand Hotel at curfew and when the MPs came to take them away Bluey and Ken resisted once they got onto the street. An Aussie MP had Ken in a headlock and the Yank MP had drawn his baton to give him a good whack as soon as he could get a clear shot at him. Bluey had his hands full struggling with three other MPs. Ken got a mouthful of the arm of the MP that had him in a headlock and bit as hard as he could. The MP let out a hell of a scream, letting go the headlock. Ken came up spitting flesh out of his mouth and he later said he was only spitting to get rid of the bad taste of the MP.

6th April. Vung Tau has changed very much for the worse now that the Yanks are pulling out of the province. The gangs of cowboys are getting a lot more noticeable and significantly braver. I was mobbed today with them all pushing and pulling. When I managed to shove them away and tell them to piss off, I was minus my army issue mickey mouse watch. I resolved to give the next kid who touches me a smack in the ear and act as if I'm stark raving mad. That'll sort them out, I thought. An hour later, another gang of cowboys was sizing me up. The first one made a move closer to talk to me to get my attention and distract me from the others moving in. When he got close I pointed over his head and said, "Hey, look!"

He turned around to see what I was pointing at.

I gave him a fair kick up the arse that lifted him off the ground a couple of feet and sent him sprawling in to some poor Vietnamese vendor's stall, knocking merchandise everywhere. The vendor didn't see me kick the kid's bum and thought the kid was deliberately causing confusion so his mates could steal from his stall. The vendor gave the kid a smack under the ear at the same time as shouting something at him in Vietnamese, which I couldn't understand. He grabbed a lump of wood like a club from under his counter and waved it above his head and chased the kid down the street a few metres. I smiled and thought to myself, that'll teach 'em. We can't let the buggers get on top of us now that there's less American servicemen in town.

The going price for ten dollars MPC in Vungas is now 2100 piastre, evidencing a drying up of MPC now that a lot of Americans have gone. This is a considerable rise in value for our MPC.

The next day we returned to Nui Dat and spent the rest of day recovering from our sojourn down to Vungas.

8th April. The platoon relieving D & E on Long Son Island was contacted by VC firing rocket propelled grenades and small arms fire at them. We didn't hear if there were any casualties though.

Des Weller arrived back from R & R leave today and was admitted to hospital straight away, suffering from malaria.

9th April. We were airlifted back to Long Son Island, arriving there at 1000 hrs. After Lt. Cosgrove had arranged establishment of the platoon base and the diggers were all settled into their positions, he called me over and said, "Stan, I want you to take ten men and look around for a good spot near the well being developed and ambush it for the night. Leave at last light but give yourself enough time to get there so you can see what you're doing."

We left base camp and made our way to the area of the well. After looking around a bit I decided to put in an ambush at the junction of two tracks. The ambush was set up in lineal fashion using eight claymores. Machine guns were placed at each end of the line, which gave us protection all round if needs be. The junction of the two tracks presented an ideal position on which to ambush. We were well concealed and had good vision. Unfortunately, no VC came along and the diggers were disappointed.

The following morning we retrieved the claymores, packed up the ambush and returned to platoon base and spent the rest of the day there. The platoon is tied down a bit because of the job of protecting the engineers.

11th April. Today we detained some villagers we caught entering an area forbidden to them. The villagers were escorted back to town and handed to the RF for questioning, after which we returned to the platoon base to spend the night

12th April. It's Three Section's turn to take it easy in platoon base today. The only excitement we had was when a group of kids came along to trade watermelons. We traded cans of rations in exchange for the melons. The kids are familiar with what's in the cans and drive a hard bargain.

13th April. At 0530 hrs, the whole platoon moved out and we went to an area we know the VC use to build their bunker systems. It's probably the same place the pilot of the chopper and I were shot at a couple of weeks ago. We were patrolling through an area that was almost totally prickly bamboo. At 1100 hrs, we surprised a man moving deeper into the area. He had no ID card and was carrying two bread rolls and three pints of water plus a small quantity of tobacco which the boss and I were convinced were supplies for his VC mates. Lt. Cosgrove said to me, "I bet these items are for the bloke who shot at you in the chopper Stan."

"Could very well be boss, I think we should confiscate it all and the bugger out there somewhere can go hungry and thirsty and run out of tobacco."

The VC supply man is middle aged and Lt. Cosgrove and I both came to the conclusion that he most likely had a son with the VC and was taking the items to him. "He has a dejected look on his face boss, maybe he thinks we're going to shoot him. What are we going to do with him now he's our prisoner of war?"

"We'll take him with us and move to a position suitable for a platoon harbour and we'll sort out what's what with him there."

Platoon headquarters was in its normal position, being the centre of the harbour. Lt. Cosgrove and I were the only two in Platoon Headquarters. The signalman, Ecclestone, normally a part of platoon headquarters, had left his radio with Lt. Cosgrove and, together with the medic, had strolled away to talk to some mates. Lt. Cosgrove and I were both squatting like locals facing one another a metre apart. The prisoner was with us and he was squatting at right angles to us but facing us. Lt. Cosgrove was carrying his M79 Grenade launcher and he had this crocked over his arm with the barrel facing the prisoner. We were discussing what to do with the prisoner who, by this time, had taken quite an interest in the boss's M79 and had moved himself into a position so he could look down the barrel. He closed his left eye and looked down the barrel with his right. His eye was only a centimetre from the muzzle of the weapon.

We looked at one another and then we both looked at the prisoner again who was still gazing down the barrel. Lt. Cosgrove said to the prisoner, "You can't do that mate, besides it's a bad habit," knowing all the time that the prisoner couldn't understand a word of it.

The prisoner was still peering down the barrel when the boss shifted the weapon and faced it in the other direction.

"Do you have a cigarette Stan?" Cosgrove asked.

"Yes boss, do you want one?" I replied.

"Not for me, for our prisoner here." He looks worried." I handed a cigarette to Lt. Cosgrove who handed it to the prisoner.

I struck a match and beckoned to the prisoner to light up. He lent forward with the cigarette in his mouth and lit up. At this point he smiled for the first time, perhaps thinking we weren't going to shoot him after all.

We ended up taking him to the local RF for them to question. Once we'd got rid of our prisoner, we harboured up. In the evening Lt. Cosgrove came over to me and said, "Tomorrow Stan, in the morning, I want you to take a fighting patrol to the western end of the island and for you to stay out most of the day having a look around.

"Righto sir, I'll let the blokes I'm taking know."

"Take a sig as well."

"Yes sir."

The following morning the men readied themselves for the patrol. Coming with me on the patrol was my section less the rear detail and L/Cpl. Jim Muir's section. Leaving the platoon position we had a distance of about one hundred and fifty metres to clear the village precincts. The area of the village in which the platoon base camp was situated was on the western side of Long Son village, in what is predominately orchard and small rice paddies.

Generally speaking, there's good visibility and we're not expecting any trouble in the village itself. Leading out is Laurie Round, forward scout, followed by L/Cpl. Jim Muir and then Pte. Bob Geaghan carrying an M60 and his number two, then myself as patrol leader and Bluey Costello carrying another M60 and his number two, Fred Woodhouse, then two more riflemen and the medic. We passed the last house on the right hand side of the track and then passed through an embankment; the village is now behind us. The track goes straight ahead for the next fifty metres. The right hand side is open ground, which leads down to a small inlet serving as a harbour for sampans. The left hand side of the track is sparsely treed with fruit and banana trees. Laurie Round is a little more than half way across this section of clear ground. I'm conscious of four or five kids talking to us and trying to bott cigarettes as we're going along. The kids are on our right hand side and just behind me.

Suddenly, there's a massive explosion and a cloud of black smoke rises into the air. I know by the colour of the smoke that it is a mine but what sort I can't tell. Slightly in front of me and off to the left is a large tree and I can hear shrapnel smacking into the branches and other shrapnel whizzing past my ears. The tree is directly on Jim Muir's left side. The troops are immediately responding, having been well trained from countless contact drills. Within next to no time, Bob and Bluey have their machine guns positioned and are firing to our front supported by the riflemen. I've already perceived the danger zones to be directly ahead and off to about ten o'clock on our forward left. This area is slightly uphill from our position, affording any enemy a reasonable position from which to lay down fire upon us. This is where our fire is directed. After a few seconds of rapid and intense fire I give the order to cease fire and, further orders, once carried out, better secured the position. We can now assess the number of casualties and attend to the wounded.

It's apparent the worst wounded is Laurie Round and next worst Bob Geaghan and then, to a lesser degree, Jim Muir. These are our only three casualties, thank goodness. Bob Geaghan, despite a broken leg and other wounds, was still able to move forward and operate his machine gun in the initial return fire period. Jim, on the ground a few paces in front of Bob, had expended hot shell casings from Bob's machine gun go down his shirt collar. The platoon medic, who'd only been in country for four days, went to work on Laurie and Bob and I'm attending to a wound on Jim's face. The shape of Jim's face wound looks like a spoon has hit him. I have my thumb pressing on Jim's face wound to stop it bleeding and I can hear Lt. Cosgrove, who's come running forward from platoon base with a small band of diggers to give support. He's promptly taken charge and has set about organizing the medical evacuation.

Ken Earney, who came up with Lt. Cosgrove, went to Bob Geaghan and took the rubber band off Bob's boot to loosen his trousers from his leg wound. As soon as the band was removed a reservoir of blood held in by the band came out from the bottom of the trouser leg and, Bob seeing this, got another fright. He thought he was going to lose his leg.

It wasn't long before the med evac chopper came in and we loaded the wounded on board. When the chopper had safely cleared the area, Lt. Cosgrove and I went forward to investigate the source of the blast. Having gone a small distance further along the track we got to a small plank used as a bridge over a ditch. That's where we found the blast area. Two electrical wires led down to the inlet and we followed them down to the water's edge.

I recalled immediately the events following the blast. I said, "Damn it boss, I saw a sampan here with three men on it dressed as fishermen, and there were a couple of kids around down here with them as well as the ones hanging around us. As soon as the mine went up, the kids took off and the three men motored their sampan up that channel there. They turned left out of my view where you can see the channel sweeping into the mangroves on the left hand side and by the time I realized it was them, it was too bloody late. They were almost around the bend. I can see it clearly in my mind's eye. My immediate concern was to return fire in the direction of the blast and that bit of high ground up there. I wish to hell I could turn the clock back, I'd give them a serve."

"Everybody did well Stan, we've got three wounded. They've targeted the patrol with a directional mine and if they'd been more experienced and patient we would've ended up with a few of ours killed for sure."

"You're right – they exploded the mine too early. I'm sure what saved the day for us was the kids hanging around our heels. After the blast I looked back to see where the troops were placed and I saw the kids scampering like buggery over that embankment back there. The VC are probably from the village themselves and didn't want to get the kids caught up in it. I'm sure this was the factor in making them detonate the mine too early."

"As bad as it is Stan, with three wounded, we can consider ourselves lucky. If they'd bowled more of us over, they might have even moved in for the kill. We'll never know. One thing is for sure though, by our quick response they got a bloody good lesson on how well trained we are. Anyway, we'll get everybody back to platoon base, I've only left a few blokes there. We'll take stock of things back there.

"Tomorrow, though, I want you to take out another patrol but add two more men. We don't want the enemy to think they can impact on us. We'll go about business as usual."

Later in the day, well after dark, the medic who'd attended the wounded giving them morphine injections and applying field dressings, took a turn for the worse. It seemed his nerves got the better of him. He hadn't the time to acclimatize and get a feel for things. Lt. Cosgrove felt the need to have him evacuated to hospital as well.

We picked a landing area adjacent to our harbour position, which was suitable for the chopper to come in on. We marked the boundary of the landing zone with burning hexamine tablets, which we use to cook our rations. Lt Cosgrove told the pilot by radio what to look for and the chopper came straight in. The medic was put on board and they were up and away inside ten seconds. I don't think we saw him again either, but for a young bloke only in the country a few days, he did a damn good job.

Evacuation of the wounded from Long Son Island after the ambush of April 14th, 1970. Wounded were Laurie Round, Bob Geaghan and Jim Muir

The following morning I took twelve men out to where we were supposed to go yesterday. This time we were careful to avoid areas that lent themselves to ambush. The diggers were alert after yesterday's experience. Lt. Cosgrove also sent a patrol into Long Son village so that the villagers could see for themselves it was business as usual. When we got to our destination we had a good look around but didn't find anything of significance. A Canberra bomber was making bombing runs, dropping five hundred pound bombs onto an abandoned bunker system nearby. We had a grandstand view.

One of the bombs failed to go off. Some time later, the boss came in over the radio. "Sunray minor, this is Sunray come in, over."

"Sunray this is sunray minor, I read you, over" I replied.

"Sunray minor this is Sunray, did you see the bombing raid, over."

"Roger Sunray."

"Sunray minor, one of the bombs was a blind. Please locate and report back to base, over."

"Sunray, roger, out."

I told the blokes we had a job to do in locating the unexploded bomb. "What if it goes off when we just get there corporal?" asked Pte. Couchman.

"Well, we're fucked! What do you think?"

I took a compass bearing to the bombsite and we headed off. The compass bearing was hardly necessary as smoke from the area was billowing into the sky from the raid. When we got there the whole area was burning from the bombs and I said to the forward scout, "This is a bit risky, let's find the bloody thing and get out of here".

"Why don't we tell 'em we looked but couldn't find it Corporal?" We don't want to hang around here."

"No! The VC will find it and god only knows what their sappers will do with it, a five hundred pound bomb can really do our blokes some damage."

I split the men into two groups and we started searching in a coordinated manner. After twenty minutes we saw where it had ploughed into the earth. We could only see the slightest bit of the tail fin, the bomb having penetrated right into the ground. I took a note of the position knowing we'd have to lead the engineers back tomorrow for them to blow it up. We wasted no time in getting out of the place though.

16th April. We received news that we'd be leaving the island on the eighteenth. Also, we heard the wounded men were going to be OK. Laurie Round is still on the very seriously ill list and Jim and Bob are very satisfactory. We were all pleased to hear this

17th April. Lt. Cosgrove shifted the platoon closer to the well. This will enable the infantry platoon relieving us to keep a good eye out in the area.

18th April. The platoon returned to Nui Dat, arriving in the late afternoon. I had three beers at the boozer and they put me in a very merry state of mind.

19th April. There's nothing much going on today. The task force is moving forward tomorrow and the men are preparing to go bush again. Des Weller returned from hospital. I spotted him walking by my tent and called out to him, "Hey Des, how'd you get on in hospital mate?"

"G'day Stan, yeah alright. The Brigadier gave me the shits though."

"Why? What happened?"

"He made a visit to the hospital and when he got to my bed he asked, 'And what's the matter with you soldier?'

"Malaria sir" I replied.

"Malaria eh. Not taking your pills."

"I've been taking my pills sir."

"Then Stan, do you know what the bugger said? He says to me 'You're lying soldier, you couldn't have been taking your pills.' And I say to him, quite forceful like, 'Sir, I *have* been taking my pills.'

"With that, he just walked off. Fuck him, I say."

"I was taking my pills too Des," I said, "every day without fail, morning and night, and I still got malaria. Just because you're taking your pills doesn't mean it's a hundred per cent effective."

"You're right Stan. Jeez! The bloody brigadier made me mad though. His attitude was shithouse."

"Don't worry Des, everything's fine mate. Welcome back."

"Thanks Stan. I'd better go and get myself sorted for tomorrow. I'll see ya later."

20th April. The platoon left early this morning by convoy. The lead track hit a mine and one man was killed and another eight wounded. The APC was flipped onto its back and one poor bloke, his legs badly damaged and pinned under the APC, had his legs amputated on the spot.

That evening I had a yarn with Lt. Cosgrove.

"Well Stan, you're getting short!" he said.

"Yes boss! Only a couple of weeks to go."

"What are you going to do? Are you signing on again?" he asked.

"No. I don't think so. I only signed on to do my bit in Vietnam and after two tours there's not much more to do."

"Yes! Enough is enough I suppose. The army will miss you though. If you do want to stay on I can get you onto a sergeants' course."

"Thanks sir, but don't worry. I'll take my discharge and throw in my lot with the outside world. At the moment I feel I've done everything in the army. I know I haven't, but I feel as though I have. Anyway, after all this time in Vietnam, I feel my luck is running out. The VC got two chances at me in the last few weeks. I don't want to push my luck too far."

"Well, it's been bloody good working with you Stan."

"Thank you sir."

22nd April. I'm now at Nui Dat. I start my happy pills tomorrow to kill any malaria bugs I have in my system. Now that I'm short it's best to keep away from the Orderly Room as much as possible. If you poke your nose around there you're bound to get a job.

23rdApril. I took the first of my happy pills today. They've knocked me around a bit. I don't even feel like a beer. Apart from that, it's been a most uneventful day.

24th April. Went to the PX store today to buy a few things. They let in only twenty diggers at a time, and I had to wait three hours in the queue before I could go in. When I got back to my tent I pulled the money out from the mess tins and gave them a good shake to get rid of most of the foot powder and I got hold of a damp cloth and gave the three notes a good wipe. The smell was no longer detectable without having a close smell of the notes.

"Right Doc," I said. "Take these to the boozer and shout the boys a piss up. I'll be there shortly. I've sold my pistol for $60 and the transaction takes place in five minutes so I've got to hang around here until then."

25th April. The Company held a Dawn Service today in commemoration of Anzac Day.

26th April. Nothing of interest to report today.

27th April. A small group of us went down to Vung Tau to see the three who were wounded a couple of weeks ago. They're in good spirits and don't expect to be in hospital much longer. It's tremendous to see them getting better and we talked about the day we copped the mine, thinking ourselves lucky. Unlucky we got hit, but lucky to get out of it as good as we did.

28th April. Today I did a few small jobs that have to be done before I leave. Later in the day I went down to the Regimental Aid Post for my medical examination.

29th April. This morning I went to the Q store and handed in my weapon, bayonet, machete, magazines, compass etc.

My ammunition, grenades and smoke flares were distributed amongst the men.

After the evening meal at the mess, I went to the boozer for a few beers. The diggers presented me with a plaque and a farewell speech. I returned a speech in kind. Phil Grenfell the postie came up to me and wished me well and bought me a beer. Phil is a good bloke, well liked by D & E Platoon. He hands out our mail to us and we all look forward to seeing him come to our lines with a bundle of letters to hand out.

30th April. This morning, the Orderly Room runner woke me at 0500hrs. He shook me by the shoulder and said, "Wake up Stan. You're wanted over at the Q Store."

"What! Now?" I asked.

"Yes mate! Now"

"Who wants me do you know?"

"Dunno mate!"

"I suppose I'd better go then. Jeez, it's bloody early – it must be important."

I quickly got dressed and made my way to the Q store, going inside I found Lt. Cosgrove there to meet me. He'd erected a small table on which was laid a white tablecloth and on the table was a bottle of champagne and two champagne glasses.

"I thought I'd like to have a quiet drink before you go home Stan, just you and me," he said.

"That's very kind of you sir. I really appreciate this, thank you."

"Not at all. I'm here to thank you."

For the next hour we drank the champagne and talked about life in general. It was the most rewarding hour in the two tours of Vietnam, and an hour I'll never forget.

At 0600 hrs, we shook hands and said our goodbyes.

At 1000hrs, I flew out of Nui Dat to Saigon to catch my Qantas flight home.

"Goodbye Vietnam."

◁ COVER: The photograph shows Stan Sutherland when he was a machine gunner in the 1st Australian Reinforcement Unit on his first tour of Vietnam. It was taken in April 1968 during a routine patrol around the village of Xa Hoi My in the south of Phuoc Tuy Province.

© Published by Stan Sutherland
46 High Street, Yackandandah 3749

ISBN: 978-0-646-47181-5

PRINTED AND HAND-BOUND BY MURRAY TUCKER
HILLTOP PARK, TRARALGON 3844

FIRST EDITION MARCH 2007
36 COPIES ONLY

Epilogue

Like tens of thousands of other diggers who served in Vietnam, I took my discharge from the Army on my return home. After a few weeks considering what I should do with my life, I bought myself a small suburban sandwich bar business in the Melbourne suburb of North Richmond. Alas! the change from active army life to making sandwiches was all too much for me and after three months I decided to sell the business. I then reapplied to join the National Bank of Australasia. Fortunately, they gladly took me back after an absence of 3½ years. I spent the next 26 years with the bank, rising to a position of District Commercial Manager. I enjoyed working with the bank as my position enabled me to mix and communicate at a business level with a lot of people in all walks of life. Following my bank career, I had a property maintenance and accommodation business in the Victorian high country above the snow line. My eldest son and his wife now own and run this business.

I married in 1971 and my wife and I had three children, two boys and a girl. They have now grown to be good citizens, pursuing their own destinies.

Over the years I have kept in close touch with most of my ex army mates and this has been a cornerstone of my life.

As a volunteer to Vietnam, I'm extremely blessed in that I can look back at this time of my life with lots of fond memories, surrounded by good mates. I know of no other career in which the bonds of friendship are so strong.

All in all, life has been good to me, and my retirement afforded me the opportunity to write "*In This Man's Army*". I hope you've enjoyed reading it as much as I have in writing it.

<u>Stan Sutherland</u>